THE PRACTITIOI

Marilyn Cochran-Smith a

A Critical Inquiry Framework for K–12 Teachers:
Lessons and Resources from the U.N.
Rights of the Child
JOBETH ALLEN & LOIS ALEXANDER, EDS.

Democratic Education in Practice:
Inside the Mission Hill School
MATTHEW KNOESTER

Action Research in Special Education: An Inquiry
Approach for Effective Teaching and Learning
SUSAN M. BRUCE & GERALD J. PINE

Inviting Families into the Classroom:
Learning from a Life in Teaching
LYNNE YERMANOCK STRIEB

Jenny's Story: Taking the Long View of the Child
—Prospect's Philosophy in Action
PATRICIA F. CARINI & MARGARET HIMLEY, WITH
CAROL CHRISTINE, CECILIA ESPINOSA, & JULIA FOURNIER

Acting Out! Combating Homophobia
Through Teacher Activism
MOLLIE V. BLACKBURN, CAROLINE T. CLARK,
LAUREN M. KENNEY, & JILL M. SMITH, EDS.

Puzzling Moments, Teachable Moments: Practicing
Teacher Research in Urban Classrooms
CYNTHIA BALLENGER

Inquiry as Stance:
Practitioner Research for the Next Generation
MARILYN COCHRAN-SMITH & SUSAN L. LYTLE

Building Racial and Cultural Competence in the
Classroom: Strategies from Urban Educators
KAREN MANHEIM TEEL & JENNIFER OBIDAH, EDS.

Re-Reading Families: The Literate Lives of Urban
Children, Four Years Later
CATHERINE COMPTON-LILLY

"What About Rose?" Using Teacher Research to
Reverse School Failure
SMOKEY WILSON

Immigrant Students and Literacy:
Reading, Writing, and Remembering
GERALD CAMPANO

Going Public with Our Teaching:
An Anthology of Practice
THOMAS HATCH, DILRUBA AHMED, ANN LIEBERMAN,
DEBORAH FAIGENBAUM, MELISSA EILER WHITE,
& DÉSIRÉE H. POINTER MACE, EDS.

Teaching as Inquiry: Asking Hard Questions to
Improve Practice and Student Achievement
ALEXANDRA WEINBAUM, DAVID ALLEN, TINA BLYTHE, KATHERINE
SIMON, STEVE SEIDEL, & CATHERINE RUBIN

"Is This English?" Race, Language, and
Culture in the Classroom
BOB FECHO

Teacher Research for Better Schools
MARIAN M. MOHR, COURTNEY ROGERS, BETSY SANFORD,
MARY ANN NOCERINO, MARION S. MACLEAN, & SHEILA
CLAWSON

Imagination and Literacy:
A Teacher's Search for the Heart of Learning
KAREN GALLAS

Regarding Children's Words:
Teacher Research on Language and Literacy
BROOKLINE TEACHER RESEARCHER SEMINAR

Rural Voices: Place-Conscious Education and the
Teaching of Writing
ROBERT E. BROOKE, EDITOR

Teaching Through the Storm: A Journal of Hope
KAREN HALE HANKINS

Reading Families:
The Literate Lives of Urban Children
CATHERINE COMPTON-LILLY

Narrative Inquiry in Practice:
Advancing the Knowledge of Teaching
NONA LYONS & VICKI KUBLER LABOSKEY, EDS.

Writing to Make a Difference:
Classroom Projects for Community Change
CHRIS BENSON & SCOTT CHRISTIAN, WITH
DIXIE GOSWAMI & WALTER H. GOOCH, EDS.

Starting Strong: A Different Look at
Children, Schools, and Standards
PATRICIA F. CARINI

(continued)

PRACTITIONER INQUIRY SERIES, *continued*

Because of the Kids: Facing Racial and
Cultural Differences in Schools
  JENNIFER E. OBIDAH & KAREN MANHEIM TEEL

Ethical Issues in Practitioner Research
  JANE ZENI, ED.

Action, Talk, and Text:
Learning and Teaching Through Inquiry
  GORDON WELLS, ED.

Teaching Mathematics to the New Standards:
Relearning the Dance
  RUTH M. HEATON

Teacher Narrative as Critical Inquiry:
Rewriting the Script
  JOY S. RITCHIE & DAVID E. WILSON

From Another Angle:
Children's Strengths and School Standards
  MARGARET HIMLEY WITH PATRICIA F. CARINI, EDS.

Inside City Schools: Investigating
Literacy in the Multicultural Classroom
  SARAH WARSHAUER FREEDMAN,
  ELIZABETH RADIN SIMONS, JULIE SHALHOPE KALNIN, ALEX
  CASARENO, & THE M-CLASS TEAMS

Class Actions: Teaching for Social Justice in
Elementary and Middle School
  JOBETH ALLEN, ED.

Teacher/Mentor:
A Dialogue for Collaborative Learning
  PEG GRAHAM, SALLY HUDSON-ROSS,
  CHANDRA ADKINS, PATTI MCWHORTER, &
  JENNIFER MCDUFFIE STEWART, EDS.

Teaching Other People's Children: Literacy and
Learning in a Bilingual Classroom
  CYNTHIA BALLENGER

Teaching, Multimedia, and Mathematics:
Investigations of Real Practice
  MAGDALENE LAMPERT & DEBORAH LOEWENBERG BALL

John Dewey and the Challenge of
Classroom Practice
  STEPHEN M. FISHMAN & LUCILLE MCCARTHY

"Sometimes I Can Be Anything": Power, Gender, and
Identity in a Primary Classroom
  KAREN GALLAS

Learning in Small Moments:
Life in an Urban Classroom
  DANIEL R. MEIER

A Critical Inquiry Framework for K–12 Teachers

Lessons and Resources from the U.N. Rights of the Child

Edited by

JoBeth Allen
Lois Alexander

Teachers College, Columbia University
New York and London

NATIONAL WRITING PROJECT
National Writing Project
Berkeley, California

Published simultaneously by Teachers College Press, 1234 Amsterdam Avenue, New York, NY 10027 and National Writing Project, 2105 Bancroft Way, Berkeley, CA 94720-1042

The National Writing Project (NWP) is a nationwide network of educators working together to improve the teaching of writing in the nation's schools and in other settings. NWP provides high-quality professional development programs to teachers in a variety of disciplines and at all levels, from early childhood through university. Through its network of nearly 200 university-based sites, NWP develops the leadership, programs and research needed for teachers to help students become successful writers and learners.

Library of Congress Cataloging-in-Publication Data can be obtained at www. loc.gov

ISBN 978-0-8077-5394-1 (paperback)
ISBN 978-0-8077-5395-8 (hardcover)

Printed on acid-free paper
Manufactured in the United States of America

20   19   18   17   16   15   14   13   8   7   6   5   4   3   2   1

Contents

1. A Critical Inquiry Framework for K–12 Teachers:
    Lessons and Resources from the Rights of the Child   1
    JoBeth Allen

2. Poverty, Power, and Action: A Primary Grades Study
    of the Right to Health and Well-Being   20
    Andrea Neher and Stephanie Smith

3. It's Not Easy Being Flat: A 3rd-Grade Study
    of the Rights of Students with Disabilities   35
    Tonia Paramore

4. Latinos for Involvement in Family Education:
    Parents Promoting Educational Goals That Respect
    Their Values and Culture   54
    Stephen Lush and Lindsey Lush

5. Protection from Deportation and Family Separation:
    Middle School Students Explore Their Rights as
    Recent Immigrants   72
    Kelli Bivins

6. "I Need a New Way of Lyfe":
    High School English Students Inquire into the Right to an
    Adequate Standard of Living   90
    Lois Alexander

7. Becoming Thrice-Born: 10th-Grade History Students
   Inquire into the Rights to Culture, Identity, and
   Freedom of Thought   109
        Paige Cole

8. PeaceJam:
   High School Student Activists Work for Human Rights   127
        Lindy Crace

9. Literature as a Springboard for Critical Inquiry:
   An Annotated Bibliography   150
        Jaye Thiel, Jen McCreight, and Dawan Coombs

References   173

About the Editors and Contributors   179

Index   183

A Critical Inquiry Framework
for K–12 Teachers

A Critical Inquiry Framework for K-12 Teachers

Lessons and Resources from the Rights of the Child

JoBeth Allen

Article 2 of the United Nations Convention on the Rights of the Child "applies to all children, whatever their race, religion or abilities; whatever they think or say whatever type of family they come from. It doesn't matter where children live, what language they speak, what their parents do, whether they are boys or girls, what their culture is, whether they have a disability or whether they are rich or poor. No child should be treated unfairly on any basis."

Flat Stanley (Brown, 1964) is a ubiquitous storybook character who is often "mailed" around the country to have adventures. The Flat Stanley Project (http://www.flatstanley.com/about.php) invites teachers to host Flat Stanley and to encourage their students to write Flat Stanley journals of his adventures. Students in 3rd-grade teacher Tonia Paramore's classrooms had read the book and participated in the project for several years. But the year her class studied the UN Rights of the Child, Flat Stanley took on a very different role, that of a child with a disability who had rights.

CHRISTA: Everyone laughed at him and made fun of him.
DANIEL: You know, one of our rights is to be treated
  kindly, and Stanley didn't have that right.
MAX: Yeah, he was different on the outside so people picked on him.
OSCAR: It wasn't his fault. God made us that way.
Ms. PARAMORE: What way?
OSCAR: We're all different.

KELLIE: But we all have feelings.
CHRISTA: We all have hearts.
MS. PARAMORE: Why do you think people were mean to Stanley?
YELITZA: Maybe they didn't have any reason. Sometimes people
    are bullies because something is wrong at home.
KELLIE: Stanley had a couple of disabilities. He was laughed at
    like some kids laugh at other kids with disabilities.

From this conversation, Tonia developed Critical Literacy Invitations (Van Sluys, 2005) as her students deepened their study of the Rights of the Child (Chapter 3, this volume). They engaged in social criticism, guided by their teacher who, like the other teachers in this book, sees it as her responsibility to prepare students to be active citizens who shape and participate in a democracy by developing students' abilities to critique social institutions and policies and to speak freely with evidence and insight in order to bring about a more just society.

The authors of *A Critical Inquiry Framework for K–12 Teachers*, elementary through high school teachers, believe in these rights and responsibilities. We formed a study group to discuss, implement, and critique critical pedagogy that honors student voices and engages students in critical inquiry into social issues relevant to their lives such as race, social class, language, and other aspects of citizenship in a democracy still under construction. Because we teach in schools where the majority of students are affected by poverty, we were particularly interested in critical inquiry into the complex relationships between literacy learning and social class.

Many educators who are drawn to critical pedagogy share a commitment to Freirian problem-posing, or critical inquiry. Much has been written about adopting a critical stance as a theoretical backbone, critical literacy as a specific application of critical stance, and posing critical questions to guide inquiry; we address each of these briefly in this chapter. There are outstanding published examples of critical pedagogy, e.g., in the journal *Rethinking Schools*, some of which we review in this chapter. What we felt a need for—and we suspect some other critical educators may seek—is a *critical content framework*, concrete subject matter in a cohesive structure that can serve as a basis for critical inquiry across disciplinary areas.

A CRITICAL CONTENT FRAMEWORK

Some teachers develop a commitment to critical pedagogy in their teacher education programs, from involvement in social action outside of schools, or from interacting with or reading the works of other critical educators (Ritchie, 2010). However, many of us struggle to teach in ways consistent with our beliefs. Where do we start? Seasoned critical educators help students examine their worlds critically, question textbooks and media, and inquire into power relations from their earliest years in school (Cowhey, 2006; Vasquez, 2008) through high school (Christensen, 2000; Morrell, 2004) and college (Shor, 2009). There is a sense from reading some accounts of teaching for social justice that content frequently presents itself organically, that teachers will become adept at recognizing injustice and will be able to design inquiries around texts or events, and that students will raise critical questions and the curriculum will evolve with great passion and participation from students.

We believe all these things happen—just not all the time, just not quite so obviously, and just not in ways we can always tie into our increasingly mandated curriculum.

The purpose of this book is to demonstrate that a critical content framework such as the UN Rights of the Child is an invaluable resource for critical K–12 educators that does not replace an organic, response-to-injustice stance but complements it. We argue for both a critical content framework and the development of a pervasive classroom culture of critical inquiry. In our own classrooms, we were better able to develop our critical consciousness as well as critical curriculum repertoire by using the UN Rights of the Child to frame inquiries. We feel this framework may be useful to other teachers, especially those who have not engaged in critical inquiry previously. Further, as teachers and students develop a culture of critical inquiry, they may decide to connect issues that arise more organically from critical reading of texts and local events with specific Rights of the Child to provide a more global context.

Why did we adopt the Rights of the Child (ROC) as our framework? As we read and discussed examples of critical pedagogy, especially related to issues of inequities based on social class, we looked for ways we could make critical inquiry central to our teaching. We explored "broad themes" (Wade, 2007) and "enduring understandings" (Wiggins & McTighe, 2005); however, we wanted an explicit focus on issues of power and social justice and a framework that could guide us across content areas, grade levels, and state standards. In the UN Convention on the Rights of the Child (http://www.unicef.org/crc/), we found a critical content framework that met our criteria, one with a fascinating history of addressing human rights globally.

After the atrocities of World War II, as part of the creation of the United Nations, an international committee with members from various political, cultural, and religious backgrounds chaired by Eleanor Roosevelt wrote the Universal Declaration of Human Rights (UDHR) to affirm that all human beings should be treated equally and with respect. The United Nations adopted the UDHR in 1948, and promoted its dissemination and discussion in schools. (The contents thereof can be found at http://www.un.org/en/documents/udhr/history.shtml)

However, many people saw the need for a specific treaty to protect the rights of children who in some societies were viewed as the property of their parents or government institutions (e.g., the military). Drawing on the UDHR and related human rights treaties (e.g., the International Covenant on Economic, Social and Cultural

Rights), a UN committee proposed the Convention on the Rights of the Child in conjunction with the 1979 UN International Year of the Child. For the next 10 years, "governments, non-governmental organizations, human rights advocates, lawyers, health specialists, social workers, educators, child development experts and religious leaders from all over the world" created a universal set of standards "that takes into account the importance of tradition and cultural values for the protection and harmonious development of the child" (http://www.unicef.org/crc/index_30229.html).

The Articles of the Convention on the Rights of the Child provide positive statements of what a just society ensures for its children. The Articles directly address issues that critical educators often use as the basis for inquiry such as the right of the child to his or her views (Article 13) and the right to learn about and practice their own culture, language, and religion (Article 30). The UN General Assembly unanimously adopted the Convention on the Rights of the Child on November 20, 1989, and it became legally binding in September 1990. All countries have now ratified it except for Somalia and the United States (http://www.unicef.org/crc/index_30197.html).

Critical inquiry into the Rights of the Child (ROC) operated at two levels for us. First, the teachers in this book are all teacher consultants with the Red Clay Writing Project. We formed a study group that explored the ROC and became allies with our students in advocating for students' own rights to free speech and to social criticism. One would think these would be inalienable rights, but there are countless examples to the contrary (Apple, 2009). Second, our students studied the rights of children as set forth in the Articles of the Rights of the Child as integral parts of the language arts and social studies curriculum standards. In this book we 1) demonstrate the applicability for critical educators of a critical content framework; 2) offer invitations to seven classroom inquiries based on pertinent Articles in the Right of the Child (see Table 1.1 at the end of the chapter); 3) detail adaptable processes for engaging students and families in critical inquiry; and 4) provide an extensive annotated bibliography of children's literature that can support critical inquiry.

In this chapter, we'll explain what "critical inquiry" came to mean for us and for our students in terms of critical stance, critical literacy, and critical questioning. We'll share the influence of critical researchers and educators who focused us on literacy and social class, and the story of how Rebeccah Williams Wall and her students led us to the UN Convention on the Rights of the Child. Finally, in the spirit of examining multiple perspectives, we address some of the controversy surrounding the Rights of the Child.

CRITICAL INQUIRY

The critical teacher does the same as the progressive teacher—but more.
The [critical] teacher uses the food drive as the basis for a discussion
about poverty and hunger. How much poverty and hunger is there in

our neighborhood? Our country? Our world? . . . What is the role of the
government in making sure people have enough to eat? (Bob Peterson,
5th-grade teacher, 2007)

Peterson and his colleagues who write for *Rethinking Schools* adopt a "question-ing/problem-posing approach" (p. 30) to education, as advocated by Paulo Freire (1970). This approach, also known as critical inquiry, includes taking a critical stance, engaging in critical literacy, and asking critical questions.

Critical Stance

In his fourth letter to teachers as cultural workers, "On the Indispensable Qualities of Progressive Teachers for their Better Performance," Freire (1998) explored the creative tensions, or dialectics, involved in being a progressive/critical educator. Such teachers must demonstrate both humility and self-confidence. As they take risks, they acknowledge fear and show courage, because "there may be fear without courage . . . [but] there may never be courage without fear" (p. 41). Critical educators also experience a constant tension between patience, which by itself could lead to resignation and immobility, and impatience that could "lead the educator to blind activism, to action for its own sake" (Freire, 1998, p. 44).

We have experienced each of these tensions as striving critical educators, but perhaps no dialectic is as troubling as the tension between taking an open, inquiring stance and bringing a critical perspective to bear on social issue. We constantly wrestle with following our students' leads and leading our students' critique. Freire recognized that critical teachers investigate and question, along with their students, but they are also decisive because "indecision is perceived by learners as either moral weakness or professional incompetence" (Freire, 1998, p. 43). As bell hooks noted,

> When we try to change the classroom so that there is a sense of mutual responsibility
> for learning, students get scared that you are now not the captain working with them,
> but that you are after all just another crew member—and not a reliable one at that.
> (hooks, 1994, p.144)

As you read these chapters, you'll have to decide where you would have been more or less decisive, where you might have steered the ship in a different direction—or not at all.

Freire (1998) believed that decisiveness and confidence come from "political clarity, and ethical integrity" (p. 43). Many of us throughout the Rights of the Child project turned to Paulo Freire to sharpen our political clarity, and to test our ethical integrity. In our relationships with students, Freire urged us to testify to "our constant commitment to justice, liberty, and individual rights, of our dedication to defending the weakest when they are subjected to the exploitation of the strongest" (p. 56). We struggled to address the dialectic tensions through dialogue, to make clear to our students that through dialogue and learning another person or group's perspective, "changing one's position is legitimate" (Freire, 1998, p. 56).

One aspect of our stance as critical educators is our use of language, especially the language of schooling. Educational language constantly needs to be interrogated and "refocused" on terms that do not denigrate students or their families or absolve schools from their responsibility to teach (Fennimore, 2000). We agree with Fennimore's admonition that "talk matters," and with her we continue (not always successfully) to ask these critical questions: "How might a balance be achieved between an honest acknowledgment of children's problems and a determined vision of their present and future possibilities" so that teachers can be "*advocates* who use their knowledge and experience to build political support for improved child and family policies" (Fennimore, p. 7)? How do we talk about poverty, disability, immigration issues, and other social conditions and constructions as advocates? Our hearts were willing, but at times our vocabularies were weak as we tried to eliminate deficit language and thinking during the years we met as a study group.

In all honesty, some of this language restructuring occurred during the writing and rewriting of this book. Fennimore (2000) offered guidelines that we found most helpful in restructuring our language.

> Is the information couched in terms of respect for children and responsibility to do all that is possible for them, or is it couched in terms of a sense of hopelessness and a lack of professional accountability? *How* are challenges or deficiencies explained and described, *why* are some children rather than others consistently engulfed in an impersonal cloud of negativity (such as children who are poor), and what happens when deficit-based descriptions carry unfair generalities that lead to the assumption of inferiority and school failure? (pp. 7–8)

You will note different, seemingly conflicting, terms at times. For example, we adopt the term *Latin@*. Wallerstein (2005) noted that the use of *Latin@* creates a non-sexist term, since *Latino* and *Latina* are gendered. *Latin@s* refers to "those who come from and identify themselves with the countries of what is today called Latin America" as well as to "those within the United States who are descended from the first group" (Wallerstein, p. 31). We use it where we can; however, when groups named themselves (e.g., Latinos for Involvement in Family Education), we honored that choice. With our focus on social class inequities, we struggled throughout the book to talk about the impact of poverty in ways that respect students and families, that are not overgeneralized and deterministic, and that acknowledge the strengths and agency of students and families who have been affected by poverty.

Critical Literacy

Critical literacy, which undergirds the critical inquiries in our Rights of the Child work, is a central curricular manifestation of critical pedagogy. Reading and writing must be for "something that children need and that we too need," noted Freire (1998, p. 24); literacy must be meaningful to students and serve a purpose in their lives. Maureen McLaughlin and Glenn L. DeVoogd (2004) drew on the work of Paulo Freire to define critical literacy, arguing that critical literacy

> is not a teaching method but a way of thinking and a way of being that challenges texts and life as we know it. Critical literacy focuses on issues of power and promotes reflection, transformation, and action. It encourages readers to be active participants in the reading process: to question, to dispute, and to examine power relations. (p. 150)

If that is what critical literacy does, what do critical teachers do to foster its development? Critical educator Maria Sweeney (1999) supplies teacher action verbs:

> I strive to create a classroom atmosphere and curriculum that prepares my students to build and participate in critical democracy. I help my students gain the necessary skills and knowledge to critique their world, unveil injustices and needless suffering, and work for social change. I nurture a strong sense of compassion and equity, and I urge children to get angry and do something. (p. 97)

The emphasis on doing something is echoed in "reading and writing for social action," the subtitle of Randy Bomer and Katherine Bomer's *For a Better World* (2001). They stress that social action must be grounded in students' lives. Students in Katherine's elementary classroom develop a critical discourse and social justice concepts as readers. Through independent reading, "reading clubs," and "critical conversations" of texts Katherine reads aloud, students learn how to analyze and discuss issues of fairness/justice, voice/silence, multiple perspectives, representation, gender, race, class, money, labor, language, intimate relationships and families, nature, violence and peace, and individualism/collectivism.

Critiquing the ills of society can be paralyzing and depressing if students (or adults) feel impotent. Katherine Bomer teaches students to move toward social action by creating coalitions of others interested in their inquiry topics (generated from their writing notebooks, including "think pieces" on current issues). These teams learn from texts, mentors, parents, community members, and older students in related organizations. They develop social action plans and write persuasive letters, petitions, and other texts specific to the audience and purpose of persuasion.

You will see some of these critical literacy practices throughout this book.

Critical Questions

Teachers who take a critical perspective encourage students to go beyond the words on the page (or the Internet). As students inquire into topics and read, view, or write texts, critical educators equip them to question and evaluate, pushing toward deeper levels of understanding. Students discuss power structures related to issues that directly affect them, their families, and their communities: race, social class, sexual orientation, gender, language, religion, family structures, ability, and many other cultural constructs.

Maria Sweeney challenged her 4th-grade students to confront inequities and work toward a more just and democratic society by teaching them to consider alternative viewpoints in the texts they read and wrote. She taught her students to ask questions—to engage in critical inquiry—in all kinds of texts: children's literature, events they observed, various media, and textbooks (Sweeney, 1999, p. 97):

> Is this fair?
> Is this right?
> Does this hurt anyone?
> Is this the whole story?
> Who benefits and who suffers?
> Why is it like this?
> How could it be different, more just?

Similarly, in his analysis and critique of American high school history textbooks, *Lies My Teacher Taught Me*, James Loewen (1995) also emphasized the importance of students and teachers asking critical questions of all texts:

> "[W]hose viewpoint is presented? . . . What interests, material or ideological, does the statement serve? Whose viewpoints are omitted? . . . [I]s the account believable? . . . [I]s the account backed up by other sources?
>
> [H]ow is one supposed to feel about the America that has been presented?"
>
> (p. 317)

Freire (1998) stressed, "The teacher becomes a role model setting forth the values of democracy" (p. 8). Students have many questions of their own, many of them critical. However, they may have learned that such questions are not always welcomed in schools. We as critical educators must be role models, showing students that asking critical questions is central to the values of democracy, and critical in examining the universal Rights of the Child.

Many educators who are drawn to critical pedagogy share our commitment to this questioning/problem-posing inquiry education: critical stance as a theoretical backbone, critical literacy as a specific application of critical stance, critical questions to guide inquiry. Teachers have learned from outstanding published examples of critical pedagogy, some of which we illuminate in the next section. Yet some of us are unsure of ourselves in identifying issues, others in feeling like we can (or should) lead students in the "right" critique, and still others struggle with prioritizing issues in relation to content in textbooks and state standards. In the Rights of the Child, we found a critical content framework rich with global implications and ripe for local action.

CRITICAL INQUIRY THROUGH THE RIGHTS OF THE CHILD

Our inquiry began as a study group, part of the National Writing Project's funding of local writing projects to work with teachers of students from communities affected by poverty: Project Outreach. Over half of the authors of this book teach in a county where the poverty rate was over 30% at the time we wrote, the fifth worst rate in the country for counties with populations greater than 100,000 (U.S. Census Bureau, 2010). The other authors teach in rural counties affected by poverty. The NWP grant was for 3 years; the impact on our thinking, writing, and teaching lasted far beyond the funding.

Phase 1: Studying Literacy and Social Class

For the first year, the Red Clay Project Outreach study group read a wide range of education and popular-press literature on the relation between learning and social class. Insights about the complexities of American social class differences came from Alex Kotlowitz (1992) and Jonathan Kozol (1992, 1996, 2006). We walked in the thin shoes of a minimum-wage worker with Barbara Ehrenreich (2002). Likewise, David Shipler's (2005) analysis of interviews with *The Working Poor* helped us understand the "both/and" rather than the "either/or" of social and personal responsibility.

From these sociological and journalistic views of poverty, we moved to scholars who analyzed and illuminated social class policy (Berliner, 2006) and investigated the impact of class related to language and literacy differences between home and school (Heath, 1983) and to how families view parenting and interact with schools (Lareau, 2000, 2003). We learned from bell hooks's (2000) insights from her upbringing and education in a working-class family and her insistence that "class matters" and cannot be separated from the gendered and racialized natures of poverty.

Most of us had previously read Ruby Payne's (1998) *Framework for Understanding Poverty* and/or attended school-district in-services led by her ubiquitous corporate trainers. We were troubled by gross generalizations about people affected by poverty, the lack of research, and what struck us as overt commercialization. However, it was not until we read Ng and Rury's (2006) critique and Gorski's class-based analysis (2007) that we had a deep understanding of the flaws in Payne's framework. Ng and Rury argued that, among other things, Payne stereotypes and essentializes the poor, and ignores social science research that suggests that many of the attitudes that Payne attributes to the poor are also evident to varying degrees among non-poor groups who are not as likely to suffer as a result of similar behaviors because they have more monetary resources. Gorski used a critical social theory lens to develop three main shortcomings: Payne's failure to consider class inequities, her deficit perspective, and her conservative values. Detailing how Payne ignored the responsibility of social institutions for creating economic inequities, Gorski argued,

> Payne protects our privilege and gives us permission to do the same. . . . [W]e can not secure equity and justice if we do not authentically confront inequity and injustice. . . . [A] genuine framework for understanding poverty prepares us to be change agents. . . . (p. 19)

After reading Payne's response to Gorski, his critique and rejoinder still resonated with our experiences teaching students affected by poverty.

As is evident throughout this book, Paulo Freire (1970, 1994) provided our theoretical anchor and educational/ethical compass. Gonzáles, Moll, and Amanti (2005) debunked the deficit myth and helped us focus on the funds of knowledge children bring to school from their families, including environmental knowledge, life-skills, additional languages and/or dialects, interpersonal relationship skills, and other information children learn in homes and communities. Freire and Gonzáles et al. led us to other critical educators and empowering practices that allow children to develop their own approach to dealing with social issues in their communities. We began reading the work of critical educators specific to our grade level and teaching situations. Colleagues in the National Writing Project (2006) employed critical literacy, including useful protocols for democratic discussion to promote social action. *Rethinking Schools* and collections of *Rethinking Our Classrooms* (1994, 2001) provided multiple, detailed classroom examples.

At the elementary level, Cathy Compton-Lilly (2004) detailed what happened when children examined the power relationships in their own lives and how they learned to interrogate and dispel myths related to living in poverty. Stephanie Jones (2006) helped us recognize, deconstruct, and reconstruct schooling practices. She wrote not only about but from a working-class culture that is at best marginalized and at worst maligned in schools. She recounted how her students connected—and disconnected—with children's literature and celebrated their writing about the windows of their worlds. In Vivian Vasquez's multiethnic classroom, 3- to 5-year-old students raised questions from the storybooks Vasquez read to them, things they heard about on television, or conversations at home. They tackled school (who is left out of the books in our library?), community (how do people become disadvantaged?), and global issues including saving the rain forest. Vasquez invited parental perspectives through three "open dialogue nights." For primary grades teacher Mary Cowhey (2006), the social justice curriculum generated by both her and her students *is* the curriculum, all day, every day; for example, critical questions Cowhey and her students raised about the school-sponsored food drive led to inquiry and action into local poverty and homelessness, similar to Bob Peterson and his 5th-grade students (2007).

At the secondary level, Bill Bigelow and his colleagues and contributors at the journal *Rethinking Schools* and their book *Rethinking Our Classrooms* (Au, Bigelow, & Karp, 2007) provided in-depth classroom accounts of critical pedagogy across the curriculum. Linda Christensen (2000) took us into her high school classroom with vivid examples of critical pedagogy, discussions, and writing by students examining their own lives and the social issues that impacted them most directly. Ernest Morrell (2004) taught in a summer program for urban Los Angeles youth who had not always been successful during the academic year. Yet Morrell and his colleagues engaged these students in reading critical theory; learning research techniques including interviewing, videotaping, and Internet research; and documenting issues in their community that directly affected their lives. They confidently presented to university faculty, lawmakers, and others in their community.

We were inspired. We were ready. Rebeccah led the way.

Phase 2: Focusing on the Rights of the Child

"We can make a difference if we are vigilant to create a new kind of society, more compassionate, more caring, more sharing where human rights, where children's rights, are respected and protected." (Archbishop Desmond Tutu, foreword in UNICEF, 2001)

In the midst of our discussions about critical pedagogy related to social class, Rebeccah Williams Wall, a Title 1 2nd-grade teacher in our study group, came to one of our meetings excited about an inquiry she and her students were doing on the United Nations Convention on the Rights of the Child. She recounts her class's story in this section.

My students and I began by discussing and defining "rights." It was harder than I thought to explain in 2nd-grade lingo. I needed a way to develop the abstract concepts in children's terms, so we read *Universal Declaration of Human Rights: An Adaptation for Children* by Ruth Rocha and Otavio Roth (2000). This picture book presents the essence of the UN Declaration of Human Rights on which the Rights of the Child is modeled. In simple language, with vivid illustrations by Brazilian artist Otavio Roth, the authors made each article more concrete. For example,

Rocha and Roth translated Article 1 into child-friendly language: "All people are born free. All people are born equal and so have equal rights. People can think for themselves and understand what is going on around them. Everyone should act as brothers and sisters."

We moved from these human rights to discuss the rights of children. The students generated a chart of the rights of children that they believed were most important.

All children should have the right to:

- home/shelter
- clothes
- food
- to play
- to be healthy
- to have a family
- to be safe (in body, mind, and spirit)
- to be well treated, loved, and taken care of
- to learn
- to have books
- to learn to read
- to go to school

We expanded some of the initial ideas through discussion; for example, I asked students what they meant by "safety" and we talked about safety of body, mind, and spirit. I was very excited that they came up with many ideas on their own, such as having books, learning, and the right to have a family. Next, they grouped these into broad categories; for example, the last four on the list they grouped under "the right to education."

Students then took a survey developed by the Minnesota Human Rights Resource Center, Taking Human Rights Temperature of Your Classroom (http://www.hrusa.org/thisismyhome/project/documents/HRTEMP5-10SURVEY.pdf). The survey included 10 statements to ponder, including:

1. At my school, students are safe.
2. People at school are treated the same no matter what they wear, who they hang out with, or what they like to do.
3. Students at my school do not allow mean actions or bad words in the school.

Students responded to each statement by circling a happy, neutral, or sad face. Most of my students circled happy faces. I wanted to help students think beyond our school. I prompted, "We may have things like free education, but some children don't in other parts of the world. Let's look at each of the rights on our chart and ask, 'What makes it hard to . . .' like, 'What makes it hard to learn to read, to be healthy, etc.?'" The students struggled with pushing the inquiry to this critical level. We needed another concrete example.

To help them "see" the rights of the child, we read *For Every Child: The Rights of the Child in Words and Pictures* (Castle, 2001). We read the foreword by Bishop Desmond Tutu, including the quote that opens this section. Students loved the brilliant illustration by international children's book illustrators such as Rachel Isadora, Claudio Muñoz, and Jerry Pinkney. The book includes the original ROC wording and rewording from a child's perspective of 14 of the most salient articles. For example,

> "Allow us to tell you what we are thinking or feeling" (Article 13).
> "If we are disabled . . . treasure us especially and give us . . . care" (Article 23).
> "Teach us all to read and write . . ." (Articles 28 and 29).
> "In times of war . . . shelter us and protect us from all harm" (Article 38).

Now my 2nd-graders took off, discussing text and illustrations, asking questions, and making connections to the chart of rights they had generated. They were so proud to see that they had identified several of the UN rights. They decided to focus on Article 29, Aims of Education, because it included so many rights they had identified.

Children's education should

1. Develop each child's personality, talents, and mental and physical abilities to their fullest potential;
2. Encourage children to respect human rights and fundamental freedoms;
3. Develop respect for the child's parents, his or her own cultural identity, language, and values, for the national values of the country in which the child is living, the country from which he or she may originate, and for civilizations different from his or her own;
4. Prepare the child for responsible life in a free society, in the spirit of understanding, peace, tolerance, equality of sexes, and friendship among all peoples, ethnic, national, and religious groups and persons of indigenous origin;
5. Teach how to respect the natural environment.

Rebeccah's accounting of how she engaged her students in this critical inquiry had a profound effect on us. We had found a critical content framework, a set of moral principles deep enough to engage students in studying the issues of their lives. Although Rebeccah moved and was not able to continue in the study group, the Rights of the Child provided a rich context for the rest of us to teach not only the required curriculum standards, but also the foundations of citizenship in a just and democratic society. And in a democracy, all people have a right to be heard, so in the next section, we share the opinions of some who disagree.

NOT WITHOUT CONTROVERSY

The UN Convention on the Rights of the Child continues to generate controversy and opposition in the United States. Critics say the treaty, which creates "the right of the child to freedom of thought, conscience and religion" and outlaws the "arbitrary or unlawful interference with his or her privacy," intrudes on the family and strips parents of the power to raise their children without government interference (Joseph Abrams, Fox News.com, February 25, 2009, http://www.foxnews.com/politics/2009/02/25/boxer-seeks-ratify-treaty-erode-rights/). Steven Groves, a fellow at the conservative Heritage Foundation, warned, "To the extent that an outside body, a group of unaccountable so-called experts in Switzerland have a say over how children in America should be raised, educated and disciplined—that is an erosion of American sovereignty" (Abrams, 2009).

Another group opposing ratification is Parental Rights (United Nations Convention on the Rights of the Child, 2009), which calls this "a new level of intrusion" and "silencing a parent's voice." This group cites two core principles of the Convention on the Rights of the Child, the "best interests of the child" and the child's "evolving capacities," that could result in government intrusion on decisions parents make. They argued that "all decisions affecting the child . . . are now suspect and can be overruled if they do not satisfy these two principles."

Some parents who home-school their children also actively oppose ratification. Michael Smith, president of the Home School Legal Defense Association, fears that parental rights would be threatened if countries adhered to the principles that "the best interests of the child shall be a primary consideration" and that "nations should ensure that children are capable of expressing their views freely in all matters affecting them, giving due weight to the age and maturity of the child." Smith wrote,

> This is contrary to traditional American law, which provides that absent proof of harm, courts and social workers simply do not have the authority to intervene in parent-child relationships and decision-making. . . . The international committee in Geneva, in reviewing the laws of practice of countries that have ratified the CRC, has expressed its concern that parents could home-school without the view of the child being considered; that parents could remove their children from sex-education classes without the view of the child being considered; that parents were legally permitted

to use corporal punishment; and that children didn't have access to reproductive health information without parental knowledge. (http://www.washingtontimes.com/news/2009/jan/11/un-treaty-might-weaken-families/)

These concerns are raised by parents who care deeply about the education and welfare of their children. We believe they should be part of the ongoing dialogue about the Rights of the Child. As you read the remaining chapters of the book, we encourage you to keep these concerns in mind, and to critique our teaching through this parental lens, knowing that there are many other parents who applaud critical inquiry into the rights of the child. We were fortunate to have broad parental support in each of our inquiries, as you will read.

The invitation to dialogue is one you will find in various forms throughout this book. In the next section, we explain how we invited students—and how we invite you—into critical inquiry through the Rights of the Child.

INVITATIONS TO CRITICAL INQUIRY

"Together, critically literate people can imagine and create a better world."
(Van Sluys, 2005, p. 134)

Each chapter in this book opens with an invitation. Critical invitations, as defined by Katie Van Sluys (2005), have nine interrelated properties. These properties align well with our intentions—which, of course, are not always the same as how our practice played out—in the Rights of the Child units. Critical invitations

1. occur in social learning environments
2. focus on making meaning around experience
3. welcome varied experiences, languages, and resources
4. represent our best current understandings
5. embrace opportunities to use multiple ways of knowing to construct and contest meaning
6. value alternative responses
7. promote the social aspects of learning by taking up issues in students' lives and placing inquiries within social contexts
8. encourage practices that reach across all dimensions of critical literacy
9. invite further inquiry.

Invitations for exploring *Critical Inquiry through the Rights of the Child* include the following sections, based on the format for critical invitations (Van Sluys, 2005):

1. Initiating experience: need for the inquiry.
2. Invitation to inquire: authors invite you to
   think, explore, challenge, collaborate
3. Suggested questions: connect, disconnect,
   question, adapt, expand, and act
4. Texts, tools, and resources: including which Articles
   of the Rights of the Child are addressed

We invite you to explore, connect with, critique, and challenge us as you respond to these invitations. We hope that our chapters promote learning related to your students' lives, encourage critical literacy, and invite further inquiry.

Just as some of us issued multiple invitations to our students, we offer you the opportunity to read the chapters that are of most interest to you. Readers often look first for grade level or school type (all our schools receive Title 1 funding) connections. You may also want to explore intriguing content or teaching dilemmas. Table 1.1 provides information on grade levels, school populations, and the rights being addressed.

THE CHALLENGE OF CRITICAL INQUIRY

"Students of all ages need adult coalitions to help them win language rights to free speech and to social criticism" (Shor, 2009, p. 284): We are the adults. "We are the ones we have been waiting for," to quote June Jordan (1980). Our hope is that the chapters in this book will raise questions, generate divergent perspectives, and spark your own inquiries.

> The stakes are high, for our students, our communities, and our world.
> The more we respect students independently
> of their color, sex, or social class,
> the more testimony we will give
> of respect in our daily lives, in school,
> in our relationship with colleagues,
> with doormen, with cooks, with watchmen,
> with students' mothers and fathers,
> the more we lessen the distance between what we say and what we do,
> so much more will we be contributing
> toward the strengthening of democratic experiences. . . .
>
> (Freire, 1998, p. 90)

Table 1.1. Chapters, Grade, and School Demographics, and Rights Being Addressed

Chapter	Grade(s), School Demographics	Primary Articles of UN Rights of Child Addressed
2. Poverty, Power, & Action: A Primary Grades Study of the Right to Health and Well-Being	*1st and 2nd* Latin@ (Mexican, El Salvadorian, Costa Rican) and African American. Small city urban.	Article 12: *Respect for views.* Children have the right to say what they think should happen and have their opinions taken into account. Article 17: *Access to information.* Children have the right to get information that is important to their health and well-being. Article 24: *Health.* Children have the right . . . to safe drinking water, nutritious food, a clean and safe environment. . . . Article 27: *Adequate standard of living.* Children have the right to a standard of living that is good enough to meet their physical and mental needs.
3. It's Not Easy Being Flat: A 3rd-Grade Study of the Rights of Students with Disabilities	*3rd* European American, El Salvador, Mexico, the Philippines, and West Africa. Rural.	Article 23: *Children with disabilities.* Children who have any kind of disability have the right to special care and support, as well as all the rights in the Convention.
4. Latinos for Involvement in Family Education: Parents Promoting Educational Goals That Respect Their Values and Culture	*K–5* 6% Latin@ parents in 94% European American school. Rural.	Article 29: *Goals of education.* . . . Education should aim to develop respect for the values and culture of their parents. Article 17: *Access to information.* Increase access to information . . . in languages that minority and indigenous children can understand. Children should also have access to children's books.

continued

Table 1.1. (continued)

Chapter	Grade(s), School Demographics	Primary Articles of UN Rights of Child Addressed
5. Protection from Deportation and Family Separation: Middle School Students Explore Their Rights as Recent Immigrants	*7th and 8th* Recent immigrants from Mexico, El Salvador, Guatemala, and Bolivia. Small city urban.	Article 10: *Family reunification.* Families whose members live in different countries should be allowed to move between those countries so that parents and children can stay in contact, or get back together as a family.
6. "I Need a New Way of Lyfe": High School English Students Inquire into the Right to an Adequate Standard of Living	*10th-grade literature collaborative class* African American, Mexican and Cuban American, European American. Small city urban.	Article 27: *Adequate standard of living.* Children have the right to a standard of living that is good enough to meet their physical and mental needs. Article 28: *Education.* Young people should be encouraged to reach the highest level of education of which they are capable.
7. Becoming Thrice Born: 10th-Grade History Students Inquire into the Rights to Culture, Identity, and Freedom of Thought	*10th-grade U.S. History* European American, Laos, Moldova, Turkey, South and Central America. Exurban/rural.	Article 8: *Preservation of identity.* Children have the right to an identity. . . . Article 13: *Freedom of expression.* The child has the right to express his or her views including the right to share information in any way they choose. . . . Article 14: *Freedom of thought, conscience and religion.* Children have the right to examine their beliefs . . . [with] respect for the rights and freedoms of others.

Chapter	Grade(s), School Demographics	Primary Articles of UN Rights of Child Addressed
8. PeaceJam: High School Student Activists Work for Peace and Justice	*9th–12th students in afterschool club and/or elective class* European American, African American, multiracial, Polynesian, students from India and Central and Latin America. Small city urban.	Article 2: *Non-discrimination.* Children should not be discriminated against because of their race, religion, or abilities; beliefs or self-expression; or type of family they come from. Article 19: *Protection from all forms of violence.* Young people have the right to be protected from being hurt and mistreated, physically or mentally. Article 24. *Health and health services.* Children have the right to good quality health care . . . and to safe drinking water, nutritious food, a clean and safe environment, and information to help them stay healthy. Article 28. *Education.* Young people should be encouraged to reach the highest level of education of which they are capable. Article 30. *Children of minorities/indigenous groups.* They have the right to learn about and practice their own culture, language and religion.
9. Literature as a Springboard for Critical Inquiry: An Annotated Bibliography		Article 17: *Access to information.* Children have the right to get information that is important to their health and well-being. . . . Children should also have access to children's books.

2

Poverty, Power, and Action

A Primary Grades Study of the Right to Health and Well-Being

Andrea Neher and Stephanie Smith

Invitation to Explore:
The Right to Health and Well-Being

Initiating Experience:

Reading the work of critical educators in early childhood classrooms like Mary Cowhey and Alma Flor Ada inspired us to invite our students to explore important issues including poverty, an issue that affects many of our students and our community as whole, as well as movements for social change. As middle-class European American teachers of African American and Latin@ 1st- and 2nd-grade students from poor and working-class families, we asked ourselves how to approach topics related to classism (Poverty Inquiry) and social injustices such as racism (Peace, Power, and Action Inquiry). Our chapter addresses Article 17 (Access to information) of the Convention on the Rights of the Child: Children have the right to get information that is important to their health and well-being.

Invitation to Inquire:

We invite you to explore issues of poverty, peace, power, and action with us and with the children who were in Andrea's 1st-grade and Stephanie's 2nd-grade classroom. Think with us about what you might have done differently. Raise concerns you might have about taking on such serious topics with young children, and think about what resources you might use. Join us in a 2-year journey that includes moments of jubilation and despair.

Suggested Questions as You Read:

1. How can we help students reflect on how issues of poverty and peace, power, and action have affected their lives and understanding of the world?
2. What print, digital, and human resources could we use with 1st- and 2nd-grade students in studying these topics? What resources would you use with older students?
3. How can we support groups working simultaneously on two inquiries? What strategies for inquiry, group work, and reflection should we teach?
4. How can we challenge students to imagine their own roles in working for a more just society?
5. How can we help students when their attempts to work for change fail?

Texts, Tools, and Resources:

We incorporated children's literature, film, and local human resources, including Coretta Scott King's secretary during the civil rights movement, a congressman, the mayor, and members of the Urban Food Collaborative. We addressed the Rights of the Child Articles 12, "Children have the right to say what they think should happen and have their opinions taken into account"; 17, "Children have the right to get information that is important to their health and well- being"; 24, "Children have the right . . . to safe drinking water, nutritious food, a clean and safe environment . . ."; and 27, "Children have the right to a standard of living that is good enough to meet their physical and mental needs."

Enacting critical literacies in elementary classrooms is like traveling on a rocky, winding, unpaved path. Though there are no maps, no teacher-proof curriculum guides, no scripts, there are stories and calls to action written by those who have traveled the road before (Cowhey, 2006; Van Sluys, 2005). Critically aware teachers position themselves as co-learners, as traveling companions, and sometimes as tour guides for their students. By reading "the word and the world" (Freire & Macedo, 1987), teachers and students explore their learning within larger social, political, and cultural contexts, always with an eye toward power relations.

Over the course of 2 school years, we, two primary grades teachers, invited our students to explore poverty, peace, power, and action. Beginning as a literature-centered inquiry with 1st-graders, this work evolved over the following school year into a social justice and community action project. During this critical literacy journey, we learned valuable lessons about our community, our students, and ourselves. Along the way, we encountered a few flat tires and some gridlock that made us want to turn around and go straight home. But we discovered that if we took time to enjoy the scenery, talked to some locals, and put aside our to-do lists, the most important part of the experience was the journey itself, not the destination.

The setting for this inquiry, Forest Hills Elementary School (FHES), is on the outskirts of town. Most of the students who attend FHES walk from nearby rental mobile home communities or duplexes, or ride the bus from subsidized housing areas. Of the district's 13 elementary schools, FHES had the highest percentage of children receiving free or reduced-price lunch, over 95%, and was often described by district leaders as a "majority-minority" school. The students who participated in this project were of Latin@ (Mexican, El Salvadorian, and Costa Rican) heritage and African American heritage. FHES is a wonderful and challenging place for both students and teachers, and like any school, faces obstacles that come from both inside and outside the classroom walls.

Our inquiries focused on providing students access to information that was pertinent to their lives. Article 17 of the United Nation Rights of the Child states that "children have the right to get information that is important to their health and well-being." While we weren't sure just where this inquiry would take us, we knew that providing students access to literature, movies, photographs, and other texts that address social issues was critical. We wanted to read and discuss these powerful texts, not to "frighten children or instill in them a sense of hopelessness" (Harris, 1993), but to provide students access and then a discourse with which to discuss challenging themes related to their health and well-being.

ANDREA'S FIRST STEPS

As a European American, middle-class woman who taught African American and Latin@ children from working-class backgrounds, I constantly struggle and reflect on how my race, class, and culture influence my classroom and pedagogy. For years, I infused the required curriculum with critical perspectives that focused on equity and social justice. I now understand that "it's not okay for me to assume that because I place a book in our story corner which I think foregrounds poverty, race, or gender issues that those books will necessarily make poverty, race, or gender any more visible or understandable than they were before those books existed in our classroom" (White, 2001, p. 194). Looking back, I do see those attempts as good first steps in creating critical spaces in primary classrooms that set the stage for the work that followed.

STEPHANIE'S FIRST STEPS

Like Andrea, I am a European American, middle-class woman. Unlike Andrea, my path to this project was more accidental. As an undergraduate student, I was placed in Andrea's 1st-grade classroom as an intern. I watched as Andrea engaged the students in inquiry-based learning and I listened to the dialogue that Andrea fostered with and among her students. I realized that this was the type of class-room I aspired to have: one where students of diverse backgrounds and culture interacted as a community of learners.

After I graduated, I was fortunate enough to be hired to teach 2nd grade at FHES. I had learned about the power of inquiry-based learning in college and throughout my observations, but it wasn't until I experienced it firsthand through the Peace, Power, and Action project that I became truly committed. Watching as students connect, respond, and engage in quests for relevant knowledge is a pow-erful learning experience for the students, yes, but it was especially powerful to me as their teacher. Did I do it perfectly? Absolutely, positively not!

FORGING THE CRITICAL LITERACY LANDSCAPE: ANDREA'S 1ST GRADE

For many classroom teachers, the end of standardized testing in the spring of each year signals a sigh of relief—both literal and figurative—and a time to "go back to teaching again." I had recently read *What If and Why: Literacy Invitations for Multilingual Classrooms* (Van Sluys, 2005), so I decided to combine Van Sluys's invitations for critical inquiry where students examine a concept from multiple perspectives with the Rights of the Child Article 24: Children have the right to an adequate standard of living.

I created two invitations: "Poverty" and "Peace, Power, and Action" (Figures 2.1 and 2.2). It had been an exhausting year and I wasn't sure how the invitations would work with my 1st-graders. As a group, they were the most insightful, enthusiastic, and curious kids I had ever taught. At the same time, they were

---

Figure 2.1. Peace, Power, and Action Invitation

How can we work for a better world?

You are invited to read the books in this basket to learn more about actions real people and characters have taken to make the world a better place!

As you read the books, think about these questions:

- Who took action?
- What risks did they take?
- What action did they take?
- What can you learn from each story?

Figure 2.2. Poverty Invitation

How do we see people in poverty in the books we read?

You are invited to read the books in this basket to learn more about how people in poverty are pictured in books!
As you read the books, think about these questions:

- What do people in poverty look like?
- What do they do?
- How do the other characters in the book treat them?

---

at times impulsive, selfish, and aggressive. Despite my misgivings about how invitations would work with my kids, I was ready to push my critical pedagogy. I issued the invitations.

On the first day of the project, I gathered collections of books in two separate baskets. I did not include the actual invitations in the baskets on this first day because I wanted to encourage students to look through and discuss all of the collected texts in both invitations. My goals were for the children to explore the books and get excited about the project. The books in one basket were all centered on themes of peace, power, and action, including *The Big Box* (Morrison & Morrison, 1999), *Something Beautiful* (Wyeth, 1998), *If A Bus Could Talk* (Ringgold, 1996), *Click, Clack, Moo: Cows that Type* (Cronin, 2000), and *Michael Recycle* (Bethel, 2008).The second basket contained books with characters affected by poverty such as *The Teddy Bear* (McPhail, 2002), *The Adventures of Taxi Dog* (Barracca & Barracca, 1990), *The Family Under the Bridge* (Carlson, 1989), *Beatrice's Goat* (McBrier, 2001) and *Fly Away Home* (Bunting, 2004). All of the texts included in this first round of invitations were books, although magazine or newspaper articles, photographs, and/or poems could have been included.

The children talked excitedly as they browsed. Many of the titles were familiar, especially *Something Beautiful* (Wyeth, 1998) and *The Teddy Bear* (McPhail, 2002), which we read while focusing on specific reading comprehension strategies. At the end of this first session, children signed up for which invitation they wanted to pursue. The groups were pretty even, with eight children wanting to work on "Peace, Power, Action" and six children wanting to work on "Poverty." If the groups had not been so evenly split, text-sharing would have been trickier and I would have had to gather additional materials.

Although I was intrigued by the notion of fore-fronting poverty, I worried about making it the focus of one of the invitations. I was anxious talking about poverty in my classroom, filled with students who all received a free lunch at school. bell hooks (2000) commented on this class-conscious insecurity: "It's the subject that makes us all tense, nervous, uncertain about where we stand" (p. vii). Social class inequity was the elephant in the room. I knew these inequities affected my students in a variety of ways but we didn't talk about them. I was quite comfortable talking with students about racism, sexism, and cultural discrimination, but we had never openly talked about differences afforded people from different social classes, and this was in a community with the fifth-highest poverty rate for a city its size in America. I know this class avoidance is not rare. hooks noted that "just when we should all be paying attention to class, using race and gender to understand and explain its new dimensions, society, even our government, say let's talk about race and racial injustice" (hooks, 2000, p. 7).

When I'm honest with myself, I know that my discomfort with discussions of class stems from my own elementary school years. I was forced into social class awareness, more accurately, shame, on the first day of 1st grade. My mother dropped me off in our 1974 powder blue Lincoln Continental, whose ignition required a screwdriver, amid a sea of mid-1980s Volvos and Mercedes. This was only one of the more visible signs of American class stratification. As Ada and Campoy (2004) explained, "Putting life experiences into words is the beginning of listening to those who have been ignored or unseen, and it can be the first step toward a process of liberation" (p. 3). Drawing on these experiences continues to influence my teaching.

I hoped that these invitations represented an opportunity for my students to experience that liberation themselves by describing their experiences and how they'd made sense of them. Because I didn't know how else to do it, I decided not to talk about social class and poverty before the invitations began. When I presented the poverty invitation, I grounded my description of poverty in the character of the homeless man in *The Teddy Bear* (McPhail, 2002). I reminded the kids of him and said that he could be described as someone who lived in poverty, and left it at that.

On the second day, the children began working in their invitation groups. Within each, I assigned "invitation partners" to support those students who might need help reading and reflecting. During each workshop, the invitation partners got together, reread the invitation, selected a book from the basket to read and discuss, and then wrote individual reflections. I helped structure their reflections by creating a graphic organizer that provided a place for the children to record 1) what they learned from the book, 2) what they wondered about the book, and 3) what they wanted to remember about the book. After reading *Something Beautiful* (Wyeth, 1998), Precious wrote on her reflection sheet: "I learned that you all have something beautiful in your life. Now I wonder [if] she finds something else beautiful," and on the back of her paper she drew a little girl in her classroom writing on the chalkboard, a scene from the book.

Each 60-minute workshop ended with sharing time where partners could share their thoughts with each other. In response to *The Story of Ruby Bridges* (Coles, 2004), Dacia wrote, "I learned that Ruby Bridges was brave. She was not afraid of the people who had the gun. Now I wonder why they were so mean." On the back of her reflection sheet, Dacia drew two buildings—a church and a school, both important forces in Ruby's life.

After we had been in this routine for about a week, I called the students together to discuss what they had learned so far. I wanted to take stock of their thinking and understandings. I asked, "What does it mean to be in poverty?" and "What do peace, power, and action look like?" The children recorded their responses on chart paper. Then, the two groups reconvened to share their work. As they shared, I noticed some common themes among the two invitation groups. On both charts were words and phrases such as "strong (inside and outside)," "Never give up!," and "sharing." As the children discussed the books, they realized that many of the characters who were affected by poverty embodied characteristics of peace, power, and action as well. Ruby Bridges was a terrific example of this, as were the father and son in *Fly Away Home*.

The next day, I told the class, "You have been exploring what other authors have to say about themes of poverty, and peace, power, and action. Now it's your turn to share your own ideas." I tried not to give them too much structure. I remembered that "invitations push us to set aside our need for tangible products, to trust that learners' activities are or will be purposeful, and to realize that process is as important as product, if not more so" (Van Sluys, 2005, p. 9). For those who needed help getting started, I encouraged them to think about how their own experiences had either been connected or disconnected with the texts they had explored.

This part of the process was perhaps the messiest. It was my cue to "trust that learners' activities are or will be purposeful." Most important, it was my job to support and encourage the children in whatever directions this inquiry led them. White (2001) reminded me: "When we say we want to hear from children, are we really prepared to hear about their culture?" (p. 181). I was apprehensive, not about what the children might share, but about how I would react to it. Of course, I wanted to be open and supportive, creating a safe space for my students to talk about their lives and experiences.

For the next 3 days, the children worked on their projects. All chose to write narratives, and all accompanied their writing with detailed illustrations. One student wrote,

> Lots of times my mom used to lose her money. When she went to the store, she didn't have a car. We were in poverty and we were strong on the inside and outside. We would walk to the store and help carry the bags. We had a few friends and cousins and we never gave up. We were all working hard

until my mom got her car. When we got our car we were happy. It was a white Honda. Sometimes my mom didn't like to stay there because she didn't like there cockroaches. We didn't want to stay in poverty. I liked the movie that we watched yesterday because the man (Cesar Chavez) helped the other people get out of poverty. I liked that!

I was deeply touched, even after 7 years of teaching in this school, by the personal stories the children told. As White (2001) explained, "We have to put aside blame and not get lost in pity. And we have to look at what we haven't wanted to see" (p. 196). Having access to information (Article 17) that is too often kept from children, especially about issues of poverty (Article 27), provided a powerful catalyst for their stories. As the children wrote and shared their work, I worried about them feeling embarrassed about their experiences, the way I had felt about "home" and "family," compared with classmates when I was their age. I was taken aback by how freely they wrote these stories. I respected their bravery. For my students, these stories were a source of pride about the strength and resiliency of their families.

MAPPING THE COURSE: STEPHANIE'S 2ND GRADE

One pleasant Sunday afternoon just after school had begun, Andrea invited me to meet her at a coffee shop to talk about the critical inquiries her class had done the previous year. Knowing Andrea's ability to create powerful learning opportunities, and that I was teaching most of her students in my current 2nd-grade class, I was intrigued. She shared the critical literacy invitation framework (Van Slays, 2005) and some provocative, heart-touching reflections from these 7-year-olds. Andrea asked me to consider how we might continue the work she had begun with these students, now my 2nd-graders, along with the students in her new 1st-grade class. She left it open-ended, and we talked at length about how I might weave inquiries into "Poverty," and "Peace, Power, and Action" throughout our social studies curriculum.

I was immediately on board. I wasn't sure how and I wasn't even sure what, but I knew I wanted to be a part of the experience. I went home and started making lists. What could I do to tie in with this project? How would it impact my kids? Would they still be interested in these inquiries? Who could I get from our Athens community to help me? How could I implement teaching standards during this whole project? These questions and millions more flurried through my mind. I didn't even want to go to bed; I thought I might sleep through a breakthrough idea. Over the next few weeks, I developed plans to integrate a required social studies focus on government and civic understanding with reading comprehension and writing under the overarching theme of "Peace, Power, and Action."

My first job was to provide access to meaningful texts on these issues. After perusing the school and public library, I created a browsing basket in our classroom library called Peace, Power, and Action. Because the students were familiar with this lingo from 1st grade, they immediately became fascinated with the books. Many books they recognized from the previous year, like *The Big Box* (Morrison & Morrison, 1999) and *Martin's Big Words* (Rappaport, 2002), but some titles were new like *America Is Her Name* (Rodriguez, 1998) and *Amazing Grace* (Hoffman, 1991). Students read and discussed these books with great interest during independent and buddy reading for a week before I read them aloud.

I began our study with a quick write. Students walked among three large pieces of chart paper respectively labeled with Peace, Power, and Action. I told them they could write words on the charts or draw pictures of what the word made them think or feel. It didn't take long for my bunch to begin chattering, and although my idea was for it to be a quiet write, I decided not to stop the conversations, or limit their freedom of expression around peace, power, and action. Students were making sense of these heavy words and they needed their classmates to help with some of the unpacking.

When the students came back to share, there was confusion with some of the words. For instance, "peace of pizza," "action movies," and "superpowers" were not what I was looking for, but they made sense in the children's world. It meant we had some groundwork to lay before we could explore these themes. Some students wrote about peace by referencing their church pastor or the book *We Can Get Along* (Payne, 1997). One wrote that "power is you can lrne [learn]"; another described action as "I can think about my words before I say them." I decided that the study of peace and people who demonstrated peace would be a good starting place. Over the next few weeks, I read aloud from the Peace, Power, and Action browsing basket. As we discussed each book, the students completed "We learned . . . Now we wonder . . ." reflections on a t-chart with their newly selected action partner. Over several weeks, our focus shifted from peace to power, and then how characters in the stories used peace and power to take action.

The students discussed many different portrayals of social injustice in the literature and connected the injustice in the books to their own lives through text-to-self connections. So now what? I knew there was a "danger in bringing sensitive issues from children's lives to the fore without active engagement. . . . [Therein] lies . . . the potential to accept the *status quo*" (Hart, 2006, p. 25). I wanted students to feel empowered, capable of creating change through their peaceful actions. My job as their teacher was to "provide students with a conceptual framework" (McLaren, p. 80) so they could then respond to their burning questions and feelings of injustice. The students needed to see that people are not powerless in the face of injustice. They needed to see action.

Our next step was to study historical figures who took action for justice. I posed some questions for the students: "So what can we do to create peace?" "Do we know anyone who helped to create peace?" Tyrese was hot on the trail; "Martin

Luther King!" he replied. We began critically evaluating Martin Luther King's impact on his community and his overall contributions to our society. I launched a thematic vocabulary study by reading aloud *Martin's Big Words* (Rappaport, 2002), a children's book about how Dr. King used his words to try to change the social structures. Students engaged in our familiar word study process of pulling out "razzlin' dazzlin'" words to add to our thematic word wall. Next, we read Dr. King's "I Have a Dream" speech. The students loved it so much, they asked if we could use it as our shared reading. I was happy to oblige. The students then wrote their own "I Have a Dream" speeches; two of them were honored in the "I Have a Dream" writing contest hosted by our school district.

After writing our speeches, we had the unique opportunity to invite a former secretary for Coretta Scott King (and friend of our literacy coach) to speak to our class. Before Ms. White arrived, the students formulated questions ranging from "What was Martin Luther King's favorite food?" to "Did Martin Luther King ever want to be president?" The students shared their "I Have a Dream" class book with her. Ms. White was able, to a certain degree, to demystify this remarkable man by sharing stories and answering the students' burning questions. Students were awed when she passed around a cutting board given to her by Dr. King himself. As the students passed around the board and touched something that Martin Luther King Jr. had also touched, I felt something magical transpire in our classroom. I watched as some of my usual rowdy, talkative students held the cutting board with reverence. They had a personal connection with Dr. King now, the man they admired for his actions against injustice.

Ms. White would not be the last special guest to visit room 209 that year. We also invited our area's congressman and our city's mayor to speak to the class. By the time we finished our government study, it was election time (not a coincidence). The study of local government leaders led my students to ask to study national government leaders, especially the candidates they saw constantly on television and in magazines. Although my students were "too young to understand the complexity of all the presidential campaign issues . . . they [were] old enough to understand that thousands of people fought for the right to vote. . . . [T]he vote is powerful and . . . exercising it in masse does threaten the status quo" (Cowhey, 2006, p. 102). We studied each of the candidates and their families. Never before have I seen students so engaged and interested in the life and work of presidential candidates. Students brought in *People* magazine issues with articles about the candidates and I brought in *Newsweek* magazines and newspaper articles. These became hot commodities in our class library. Our morning meeting share time shifted from playing video games and going to Chuck E. Cheese to seeing Barack Obama on the news and how their parents let them stay up to see part of the debate on television the night before.

Andrea and I had been talking all along, planning how we might bring our classes together for some sort of shared inquiry. This seemed like the perfect entry point. My kids were so excited that Andrea and I thought we'd put their expertise to use. The students divided up into pairs and my 2nd-grade students taught Andrea's 1st-grade students what they knew about the candidates. On Election Day, I set up a voting booth at the end of our hallway for the students to vote for president. They even had "I voted" stickers to wear. Access to information was indeed leading to an informed citizenry of 2nd-graders.

The election was over but our work was not. Where would we go from here? And who would decide?

CRITICAL LITERACY IN ACTION: EN ROUTE TO . . . PAKISTAN?

Now that the 2nd-graders had worked with Andrea's 1st-graders, we thought our paths should merge. In early February, we combined the two classes for Peace, Power, and Action time twice per week during the last hour of the day. Each 2nd-grader worked with one or two 1st-graders, becoming "Peace, Power, and Action Partners." During the initial meetings, we structured our time together in a workshop format. We brought all the children together to discuss texts such as photographs, books, and so forth. Then they worked with their partner, responding by recording what they saw, wondered, and felt. The sessions ended with sharing time.

Truthfully, at this point in our Peace, Power, and Action work, we got a bit stuck. And though the children were immersed in these big ideas, thinking deeply about text and engaging in discussions, we struggled with how to encourage them to imagine themselves as Peace, Power, and Action actors upon the world. Freire (1999) reminded us, "Human beings *are* because they *are in* a situation. And they *will be more* the more they not only critically reflect upon their existence but critically act upon it" (p. 90). Our hope was that the children would develop some sort of action project, connecting their experiences with our community. We imagined a school-based project such as a food or clothing drive. As Cowhey (2006) asserted, "Young children are capable of amazing things, far more than is usually expected of them" (p. 18). Once again, the children far exceeded our expectations.

Like so many wonderful things that happen in classrooms, the next steps of our inquiry occurred quite by accident. About a month into our workshops together, we read aloud *Listen to the Wind* (Mortenson & Roth, 2009). The picture-book version of *Three Cups of Tea* tells the story of Greg Mortenson's project "Pennies for Peace" (this was before the troubling allegations against Mortenson). Children all over the United States raised funds for the construction of schools in remote regions of Pakistan and Afghanistan. One of our 2nd-graders, Sarah, had been adopted from India 2 years before. Sarah explained:

> When I was in India I learned that kids were in poverty. People were in poverty too. I was in poverty too. I did have not have a car. I did not have a house. I did not have a school. I did not have a bus. I did not have a friend. I

did not have a teacher. I did not have a family. I did not have a building. I did not have pets. Now I am not in poverty any more. Now I have a pet and a family. Now I have friends. Now I have a teacher. Now I have a school.

After sharing the book with the class, the students responded to the text. Dacia wrote, "Dr. Greg made peace by building a school. The kids had to write with sticks. The kids went to school by there self with no teacher." Sophia responded, "Dr. Greg came back to Pakistan to build the kids that didn't have a school one because he listened to the wind like the man told him to do. First they had to build a bridge. He showed action by helping the poor people in Pakistan and by helping the kids in Pakistan that didn't have a school build one."

The Rights of the Child, Article 12 states, "Children have the right to say what they think should happen and have their opinions taken into account." We had provided access to students about others who took action against injustice and were now presenting this same opportunity to their students. Stephanie began the discussion in her 2nd-grade class. They had been learning about the life cycle of plants. The children loved the idea of keeping a garden. Stephanie asked them what they thought should be done with the vegetables, and the children naturally responded, "Let's eat them!" It wasn't until the class watched the promotional movie "Pennies for Peace" that a connection was formed. Stephanie urged, "How could we connect growing a vegetable garden to our Peace, Power, and Action projects?" Ryan exclaimed, "Let's start a 'Plants for Peace' project instead of a 'Pennies for Peace' project!" The next day, the 2nd-graders pitched the Plants for Peace project to their 1st-grade partners; their enthusiasm was contagious. Fortunately, the 1st-graders had been studying the life of George Washington Carver, and had been connecting how he embodied Peace, Power, and Action. Together, we studied *A Weed Is a Flower: The Life of George Washington Carver* by Aliki. We studied how George Washington Carver helped his community, including former slaves, take action to improve their lives by teaching them to grow crops other than cotton to provide food for themselves and their families.

MERGING LANES BETWEEN SCHOOL AND COMMUNITY: THE GARDEN

Our school had a number of raised garden beds, complete with irrigation, which had remained vacant all year. Plants for Peace was a perfect opportunity to put them to good use. We started Plants for Peace by learning all we could about the types of vegetables we could grow, when they needed to be planted, and how to take care of them. We also teamed up with a local service organization that partners with a local homeless shelter, churches, and neighborhoods to grow their own food. The students took multiple trips to visit the community gardens.

As warm weather approached, we invited students from the local university, members of the service organization, parents, and friends to help in planting seeds and seedlings. Over the course of the next few weeks, the children shared the responsibilities, even using part of their recess time, to keep our gardens properly watered and weeded. Although our original intent was to sell the Plants for Peace and contribute the money, the students came up with a better plan. One day while weeding the beds, the 1st-graders started talking about whom the vegetables in the garden should be given to. Christopher said, "To the poor people!" Seth jumped in, "My mom is poor. We could give the vegetables to her." Andrea asked, "Do you think your mom would like to have them?" Without hesitation, Seth replied, "Yeah, she love all kinda vegetables—especially greens like these!" Seth had transferred to Andrea's class in the spring from a nearby rural area. His family had endured a number of recent tragedies, and it was clear that Seth was concerned about his mother. This got us thinking about how we could give the vegetables we were growing in our gardens to Seth's family in a respectful way that would reflect our support, and not feel like charity.

Early one morning, with only 5 school days to go, the principal delivered devastating news. She came to the doorway of our classroom and simply said, "The school was vandalized again last night. I think some of the gardens may have taken a hit." When we got to the gardens, we couldn't believe what we saw. The beds containing lettuces and greens were completely destroyed. Many of the plants had been torn out of the ground and tossed to the side. Some looked like they had been splattered with white paint. Others had been trampled. We were all dumbfounded. A few children cried; a few tried fruitlessly to pick plants up off the ground and replant them.

We were frantic to find a silver lining. We sent out emails to local community groups and friends. The response was overwhelmingly supportive and full of helpful ideas. We brought both classes together to talk about what had happened to our garden. Andrea brought a stack of emails from friends and community members and shared those ideas with the students. Their offers included baking cupcakes with the children, monetary donations, volunteers to assist with clean-up, and food donations from the local farmers market. The students decided to bake banana and zucchini bread to donate to a community center in a neighborhood where many of our students lived. Stephanie's class was very familiar with baking and it took very little persuasion to convince Andrea's class of the value of the project. Along with baking bread, the students decided to write letters to our school superintendent about the project and invited him to help. Unfortunately, neither the superintendent nor the local newspaper responded to our invitations.

However, there was a huge outpouring from the community. Our friends from the local service organization arranged for each of the students to go home that summer with a tomato plant for their family. The students harvested what little was left from our garden. It was fulfilling to watch the students, many of whom have never been near a garden or had fresh produce from a garden, kneeling in the beds picking peas, radishes, and greens and even sneaking a taste of the fresh produce. We felt we were able to turn this tragedy into an opportunity for our kids to learn firsthand about the importance of perseverance in the face of devastating setbacks.

THE ROAD HOME

Some critics of service learning say that it perpetuates social hierarchies of privileged people helping less privileged people, or an "us doing for them" (Hart, 2006, p. 27) situation. While in the minds of the students they were helping others, we decided their project also demonstrated agency, "us doing for us, essentially eliminating the perpetuation of dominant positions" (Hart, 2006, p. 27). Planting the garden was helping the students' own community and their own classmates.

Another responsibility we had as teachers was not oversimplifying the complex issue of poverty. We tried to balance our students' hopeful ambition and meritocratic perspectives with the realities of structural inequalities. Todd's writing portrayed this difficulty:

> You never give up. If you are in poverty you should never give up. Even if you don't have a house you can work for it. One day you can have a house if you work hard and save your money. If you are in poverty you should never give up. If you are in poverty your family can help you. If you are in poverty your mom can help you and your dad can help you too and your brother and your sister can help you too. Families can take care of each other.

We were troubled with the idea that some students like Todd came away with the notion that if you are affected by poverty or your family experiences some tragedy, all you need to do is work hard, pull yourself up by the bootstraps, and it magically gets better. We struggled with how to balance allowing the children to make meaning of their own lives, without subscribing to naïve beliefs in American meritocracy.

Despite the barriers encountered in the Poverty and Peace, Power, Action inquiries, we saw firsthand the power that comes as students read, reflect, and then act upon their world. This idea of "empowerment means not only helping students to understand and engage the world around them, but also enabling them to exercise the kind of courage needed to change the social order where necessary" (McLaren, 2009, p. 74). The knowledge acquired in the classroom enabled these students to then "participate in vital issues that affect their experience on a daily level" (McLaren, 2009, p. 74). Although we began with children's right "to get information that is important to their health and well-being" (Article 17), and our invitations focused on the rights to nutritious food (Article 24) and an adequate standard of living (Article 27), this inquiry grew to include other Rights of the Child. As students began to respond to the texts read in the classroom, we incorporated a child's "right to express his or her views" (Article 12), including "the right to share information in any way they choose, including by talking, drawing or writing" (Articles 13). And as we searched for ways to conclude this critical inquiry, we turned to our students because of our belief that "children have the right to say what they think should happen and have their opinions taken into account" (Article 12).

We have great hope that our students are better equipped to critically engage the world around them, to take courageous action, and to persevere on their journeys despite the inevitable discouragements. As Todd urged, "You never give up."

3

It's Not Easy Being Flat

A 3rd-Grade Study of the Rights of Students with Disabilities

Tonia Paramore

Invitation to Explore:
The Rights of Students with Disabilities

Initiating Experience:

My 3rd-grade students in this rural, Title 1 school came from El Salvador, Mexico, the Philippines, and West Africa as well as Georgia. They included those identified as gifted, English Language Learners, and special needs. Each year, like students in countless elementary classrooms, we read *Flat Stanley*, created our own Stanleys to send out to friends, and waited for our Stanley to return bearing photographs and letters. This year, our challenge was how we could look at this text from a critical literacy perspective with a focus on the Rights of the Child.

Invitation to Inquire:

I invite with you to join my students and me in a critical examination of ability, disability, and the rights of children through a critical inquiry into *Flat Stanley*. Students explored four critical inquiry invitations: Being a Good Friend, Overcoming Obstacles, Discovering Types of Disabilities, and Rights for Everyone. Think about what invitations you might create. Raise issues related to sensitive issues such as students studying the disabilities of peers. Think with me about how we might take action based on what we learned.

Suggested Questions as You Read:

1. How can teachers guide students to critical literacy projects when we also want students to initiate and inquire into issues that are important to them?

2. How are the Rights of the Child similar to the Rights of the Disabled? How are they different?

3. Where do you see possibilities for a study of the Rights of the Child that connects with mandated curriculum in your school?

4. How can students learn about medical conditions such as autism, Fragile X syndrome, and cerebral palsy faced by students at their school? How does learning about these conditions affect students with and without these conditions?

Texts, Tools, and Resources:

We incorporated children's literature, including narrative, historical fiction, biography, and poetry; participant observation in general and special education classrooms; song lyrics; and Internet resources. We addressed the Rights of the Child Article 23, "Children who have any kind of disability have the right to special care and support, as well as all the rights in the Convention, so that they can live full and independent lives"; as well as Article 19, "protection from being hurt and mistreated," Article 24, "the right to food, water, and health care," and Article 28, "the right to an education."

Flat Stanley is everywhere. He travels the world to the delight of elementary children. But through our critical inquiry into the Rights of the Child, my students traveled new territory with Flat Stanley. Although our initial conversations about children's rights centered around Article 19 (protection from being hurt and mistreated), Article 24 (the right to food, water, and health care), and Article 28 (the right to an education), we eventually moved into a discussion of the Rights of the Disabled, which are guaranteed for children under Article 23. As a result of these conversations, my students took Stanley on a very different journey, a critical examination of ability, disability, and the rights of all children.

THE ROOTS OF CRITICAL LITERACY

On Columbus Day during my first year as a teacher, a veteran teacher informed me that I "must" teach my students about Christopher Columbus. She handed me a pattern of a ship and some popsicle sticks. I stuck them in the file cabinet. Instead, I read Jane Yolen's *Encounter* and engaged my students in a conversation about how her portrayal of Columbus differed from what the students had learned previously. The students adamantly defended the Taino tribe and were concerned that Columbus and other explorers adopted such a cavalier attitude toward Native

Americans. I took some satisfaction in fighting rather than perpetuating those stereotypes that I learned in elementary school, when I, too, undoubtedly made miniature ships.

That was my first foray into teaching critical literacy. Maureen McLaughlin and Glenn L. DeVoogd (2004) drew on the work of Paulo Freire to define critical literacy:

> Critical literacy is not a teaching method but a way of thinking and a way of being that challenges texts and life as we know it. Critical literacy focuses on issues of power and promotes reflection, transformation, and action. It encourages readers to be active participants in the reading process: to question, to dispute, and to examine power relations. (p. 150)

From that initial inclination to lead my students in becoming more critically aware, I have sought to become a critical educator. In this chapter, I share how my students and Flat Stanley led me.

BECOMING EXPLICIT

In my eighth year of teaching, I joined a group of colleagues from the Red Clay Writing Project to read about and discuss issues of literacy, social class, race, and social justice. The wealth of ideas we shared helped me define the change I wanted to see take place in my classroom, but I was still struggling with how I would bring it to fruition. When we began to explore the idea of using the United Nations Declaration of the Rights of the Child in our classrooms, I began to see how this document could open up the type of critical inquiry I wanted in my classroom.

Third-graders are adamant about fairness, and they are acutely aware that their voices are not always taken seriously. What better way to allow my students to become agents of change than to study children's rights? However, the year didn't exactly go as planned. I gave birth to a child instead of a new curriculum.

The birth of my son reinforced how important the idea of teaching the Rights of the Child was for me. I wanted my son to live in a world where people stand up for their rights as well as the rights of others, and I assumed that other parents wanted their children to learn to do the same. It became crucial that my students learn about their rights in order to protect themselves and my son from the injustices in our world. I began the next school year with a clear purpose in mind: My children were going to become educated beyond the state-mandated, No Child Left Behind curriculum. They were going to understand their rights, and I was going to help them take a critical approach to learning about these rights.

READING OUR RIGHTS

Typically, students in my rural elementary school are rather quiet on the first day of school. Not this year! My 3rd-graders came in ready to learn and share, as eager as wriggling puppies. The children came from many different academic and cultural backgrounds. There were students identified as gifted, English Language Learners, and special education. There were students whose families came from El Salvador, Mexico, the Philippines, and West Africa. I began the year with 14 boys and seven girls, and it often felt as if the girls and I could barely get a word in edgewise. The children were eager and willing to learn, and I was hopeful that a discussion of our rights would be a topic that would engage and excite them.

I wove the study of human rights into our reading throughout the year. In the 3rd-grade curriculum, we studied the levels and branches of governments, focusing on documents and books related to the rights of American citizens. We also studied famous African Americans and spent several weeks researching the life of Dr. Martin Luther King Jr. and discussing how his work and the work of Mahatma Gandhi could inspire our understanding of human rights. The teachings of Gandhi and King became central to our classroom discussions and served as a teaching tool during times of conflict in our classroom. After reading a biography of Gandhi and engaging in a discussion of his methods of using nonviolence to inspire change, the students began to think about his actions when they interacted with others. One student in particular often shoved others out of the way to be first, and the students began to step aside to allow him in front. They would then tell him how his shoving made them feel.

The Georgia Performance Standards also included biographies of Paul Revere, Susan B. Anthony, Harriet Tubman, Frederick Douglass, Lyndon B. Johnson, Franklin D. Roosevelt, and Eleanor Roosevelt. By reading about the lives of other Americans who had to fight for rights, the students began to connect the importance of human rights in the creation of our country to human rights in our own classroom. My students were beginning to internalize the idea set forth by the 14th Dalai Lama:

> All human beings, whatever their cultural or historical background, suffer when they are intimidated, imprisoned or tortured. . . . We must, therefore, insist on a global consensus, not only on the need to respect human rights worldwide, but also on the definition of these rights . . . for it is the inherent nature of all human beings to yearn for freedom, equality and dignity, and they have an equal right to achieve that. (Dalai Lama, 2009)

As my students developed an awareness of their rights as American citizens, the classroom culture began to change. This was a group with strong personalities. There were tears on the playground and arguments over who lined up first. But the students began to take care of each other more in these situations. They helped each other navigate difficult parts of the day and were quick to defend their classmates to others.

For example, on Pajama Day, Michael wore his footed Pokemon pajamas. In the cafeteria, a group of 4th-grade students were making fun of Michael when my students came to his defense. "We told them it was his right to wear any pajamas he wanted to!" Yelitza said. Michael could have felt embarrassed by his pajamas, but instead his classmates made sure he knew that he had the right to make that choice. That day, my students learned about standing up for themselves and each other, and Michael learned that his classmates would defend him.

By spring, we were ready to explore the idea that even though we are guaranteed certain rights by the government of the United States, there were also protections the United Nations felt were necessary for citizens of the world. I read aloud *We Are All Born Free: The Universal Declaration of Human Rights in Pictures* and we created a chart on which children listed the rights they were able to recall from the text. Education was the first item they included on the chart; the idea that education is a right had become a central part of our classroom dialogue. Yelitza's journal entry seemed to summarize many of the students' feelings:

> It is important to have an education. Without an education, how would we learn to read, write, and spell. If we didn't have an education, we would not know anything. We would just be living in a house and not know that your parents have to pay the bill for your tv and the electricity you use. If you didn't know all that stuff and you move in to a house and didn't pay your bills you would not have any light or power.

The idea of relaxation and play being a right was also important to the students. They had never thought that play and relaxation are not a regular part of many people's lives. The children added the rights of choosing religion, receiving fair treatment, having jobs, and being able to receive a fair trial. With rereading and further discussion, they were eventually able to connect to the idea that food, clothing, and clean water should be considered basic human rights as well. Oscar wrote, "Without clean water, you will be sick. Without water you will be dead. You need water so you can be energized."

However, few of the children picked up on the idea that clean water, food, and shelter were among the rights of all humans. It had never occurred to them. I puzzled over this in my journal.

> It made me wonder why this most basic of needs was not seen as a right. I assume all of my students have food, water, and shelter readily available, and as such they don't see it as a necessity. It would probably be a good idea to study issues of water, hunger, and shelter to help them see that many children are denied these basic needs.

As I troubled over my students' lack of information on issues that confront people living in poverty, I realized that I needed to do more to push their thinking about the rights of people, especially children, beyond the walls of our classroom. The children lived comfortable lives. They played sports, engaged in church activities, and enjoyed time with their families. In this particular group, poverty was not an issue, and they had a difficult time understanding that all children did not lead lives of similar privilege, even in our school. Similarly, I had no idea what it felt like to lack access to clean water, shelter, or food. I grew up in an upper-middle-class home where I also took these basic needs for granted. Who was I to help these children understand what I, a 31-year-old, was still struggling with myself?

EXPLORING HUMAN RIGHTS AND THE RIGHTS OF THE CHILD

As much as I wanted to commit my students to finding some project to change the world, I wanted them to seek it out themselves. How could I move forward with learning about the Rights of the Child, and help the children discover the roots underlying lack of food, clothing, and shelter when I did not completely understand these myself? The words of teacher Vivian Vasquez gave me some comfort: "Critical literacy does not necessarily involve taking a negative stance; rather, it means looking at an issue or topic in different ways, analyzing it, and hopefully being able to suggest possibilities for change or improvements" (Vasquez, 2008, p. 30). Vasquez gave me the courage to move on toward our exploration of the Rights of the Child. It was my hope that in guiding my students we could reach a greater understanding together, and they would begin to find their own way to make their voices heard on issues they cared about.

As we studied the Declaration of Independence and the Bill of Rights earlier in the school year, one group of students had written a rough dialogue to explore the idea of children's rights.

"Hello, young men, what's your names?"
"Max and Michael."
"Does kids have rights?" said Max.
"No, they don't," the man laughed.
"Why?"
"Well, they can't do anything."
"Well, I should have a right," said Michael.
"Why can't we have rights?" said Max.
"Please."
"OK."
"Yes, but what is it?"

"You have the right to be free."
"We never thought of that," said Max and Michael.
"Well, at least kids have one right."

I love the simplicity of this piece of writing. Max, Michael, and Yanaisa spent a great deal of time looking at the Constitution, and they kept asking why children were left out of the text. This initial conversation was repeated by many of the students throughout the year. Many of my students began to ask, "Are the voices of children less important than the voices of adults?"

With this question at the forefront, we moved from basic human rights to specifically discussing the Rights of the Child. Since the Georgia Performance Standards required the students to learn about Eleanor Roosevelt, the students had a rudimentary knowledge of the United Nations. We discussed the idea that the United Nations had worked together to create a list of rights they believed all children should have. To connect to our earlier discussions, I asked the students, "What does it mean to have rights?" I was not surprised when Christa, a spunky student who occasionally had difficulty getting along with others, spoke up, "It means no one can tell you what to do."

My teacher antenna flew up as I envisioned 17 students going home and answering their parents' requests to clean their rooms with, "Mrs. Paramore says we all have rights. That means you can't tell us what to do." I had anticipated this comment. I grabbed a piece of chart paper and wrote "Human Responsibility" in the center. "What do you think the world would be like if everyone did exactly what they wanted all the time?" Hands flew up, and children began to call out.

"People wouldn't get along."
"There would be lots of messes because no one would clean up."
"Everyone would fight all the time."
"No work would get done."
"The world would fall apart."

I then asked the children again, "Are you saying that we can't always do exactly what we want?" I was met with a chorus of yeses. I then pointed to the chart, and asked the children about responsibility. We discussed the fact that a responsibility is something we must do in order to get along in the world. I referred the children back to the Human Rights chart we had generated the day before, and then asked them to think about the responsibilities that go along with having rights. The children generated a list of responsibilities:

- To help others
- Not to call others names
- To get an education

- To work
- To keep our planet clean
- To respect the language and culture of others
- To obey laws
- To be kind
- To stand up for the rights of others.

Once I felt some satisfaction that parents would not think I was advocating anarchy, I asked students to think specifically about the rights children should be granted. I urged them to think back to all of our discussions throughout the school year and to work in small groups of their choosing to create a list of children's rights. The purpose for doing this before I introduced the Rights of the Child was to allow them to connect their prior knowledge to the work we were about to do. If they could create a list of rights and find some commonalities between their list and the UN list, I hoped they would realize that children all over the world had the same needs as children in Winder, Georgia. The students' lists included the following rights:

- We should have the right to have an education.
- We have the right to eat when we want to.
- We have the right to wear what we want.
- We should treat everyone the same as they treat you.
- We should all get medical care.
- We should have the right to practice our religion.
- We should all have the right to have a shelter.
- Kids should be treated fairly at school.
- Kids should not be beat up because of their skin color.
- We have the right to live.
- We have the right to work.
- We have the right to write.
- We have a right to not get abused.
- We have the right to medicine.

THE RIGHTS OF THE CHILD IN CHILDREN'S LITERATURE

Their list indicated that the students were beginning to understand that many of the rights they took for granted were not as readily available to other children around the world. Their perspective of these rights was based on the literature we were reading and the discussion we had engaged in throughout the year. In order to help the students begin to realize which of the Rights of the Child were at play, we discussed several read-alouds, specifically addressing which rights children in the books did or did not have.

For example, when we read *Listen to the Wind* (2009), Greg Mortensen's picture-book version of *Three Cups of Tea* about building schools in Pakistan, we discussed Article 28, "Children have a right to a primary education." Eve Bunting's book *Fly Away Home* (1993) about a father and son who do not have a home led to a discussion of Article 26, "The government should provide extra money for families in need," and Article 27, "Children have a right to a standard of living that is good enough to meet their physical and mental needs. The government should help families who cannot afford to provide this." *Fly Away Home* was a particularly powerful text since the boy and his father looked like so many of them—European American and middle-class, which was not their image of a homeless family. Although my students seemed to lead lives of privilege, I suspect the economy had been a topic of discussion in many of their homes as it had been in mine that year of the Great Recession. They began to talk about what it would be like to have to search for a safe place to live.

After exploring some of the rights in literature set in modern time, we explored the Rights of the Child using the historical fiction text *The Butterfly* (2000) by Patricia Polacco. The students were drawn into the struggles of Monique and her mother as they attempted to help Sevrine, a young Jewish girl, escape Nazis in France. The students felt fear for the girls, but they were also firm in their beliefs that it was within their right to choose their own way to worship despite the tyranny of Hitler. During this time I also read selections from the poetry collection written by the children at the Terezin concentration camp, *I Never Saw Another Butterfly*. There was a strong sense of injustice as my students realized that there have been times when children have been forced away from their homes and families and even lost their lives as they struggled for freedom.

A NEW PERSPECTIVE ON A CHILDREN'S CLASSIC

After we read several texts that explicitly addressed the Rights of the Child, I introduced a text that many would view as safe and with no connection to human rights: *Flat Stanley* by Jeff Brown. Stanley, a European American boy, becomes flat when a giant bulletin board falls off of his wall during the night. Stanley's new state of being flat allows him to have all sorts of adventures and tribulations. He is mailed to visit a friend in California; his brother, Arthur, uses him as a kite and allows him to become stuck in a tree; and he even helps a museum curator catch a gang of thieves. Some colleagues in our Rights of the Child study group had their doubts about using *Flat Stanley*, not seeing the "critical" potential, but I knew Flat Stanley was a favorite of students this age, and was eager to take a critical approach.

In previous years, we had read the book together, created our own Stanleys to send out to relatives and friends, and waited for our Stanley to return bearing photographs and letters. Countless teachers and students throughout the country engage in similar Flat Stanley projects. Much like my students, Stanley appears to be a boy who has it all. Suddenly, a poorly hung bulletin board changes his fate. My goal was to take a seemingly innocent children's book and place it under a critical literacy microscope with the Rights of the Child as our focus.

Before reading, we discussed how family and friends would treat you versus how strangers would treat you if you suddenly became flat. The students all agreed that strangers would treat someone who is flat negatively. They equated being flat with weakness and fully expected that others would "talk and share rumors or laugh at you" or "try to harm you." One group of students thought a flat person would be treated "nicer because you are different and they may think you are sick." Others felt that they would be called names such as Flatty McFlat. I speculated that these feelings were similar to those the children found themselves feeling when they were with others who were different or if they found themselves feeling different from others. As we began reading the text, I urged the students to look for places where they had questions about the rights of the characters.

I divided the book into two parts and allowed the students to decide whether to read with a partner or independently. As the students read, I urged them to make predictions, ask questions, and write responses in their reading notebooks to help guide our group discussion. After 2 days of reading and responding, we came together as a whole group to discuss the first three chapters of *Flat Stanley*. My students gathered in their usual enthusiastic way, squirming and whispering. We summarized the first three chapters, and the children all seemed to agree that being flat would have been fun at first. Christopher pointed out, "Stanley was helpful." When I asked for examples, Jarrett recalled when Stanley allows his mother to lower him into a grating after her wedding ring fell into a hole in the sidewalk. As she guides the shoelace attached to Stanley, a crowd gathers, including police officers. The officers call Mrs. Lambchop a "cuckoo" and threaten to arrest her when she explains why her son is lowered into a grating.

This situation sparked a conversation about rights that had never occurred before, which I attributed to our study of child rights.

MICHAEL: The police were insulting her because they called her loony.
MAX: Yeah, you know, you don't judge a book by
    its cover. She really wasn't crazy.
LEIGH: It's kind of like that lady on TV, you know, the singer. (This
    conversation was occurring just as the Susan Boyle story was breaking.)
    People thought she wouldn't be able to sing when she got on stage
    because she didn't look beautiful. When she sang, though, they were
    surprised. This is like the police should have looked at Stanley's
    mom different just because she had a shoelace down a grating.
CHRISTA: It's like Shrek, too. He was ugly and scared people,
    but when they got to know him, he was really nice.

The students decided that the police judging Mrs. Lambchop was equivalent to how we often judge others based on appearances, and they felt the lesson we should take from the first three chapters was that one should not judge a person or situation without having all the facts. To be honest, I had never thought of this situation with Stanley's mother as any more than a humorous incident in the text. However, my students had taken a critical literacy approach to this text without any prompting from me. Primary grade teacher Mary Cowhey (2006) described critical teaching as a process that "listens to and affirms a minority voice that children challenge the status quo. Instead of forcing assimilation and acceptance of dominant culture, it reexamines cultural assumptions and values and considers their larger ramifications" (p. 13). My students' ability to think beyond the humorous incident and to critique the words of the police officers demonstrated that they were developing critical literacy skills without my prompting.

Two days later, the students had finished reading and reflecting on the book and we gathered again to discuss *Flat Stanley*. Our initial conversation around the final two chapters focused on how the museum did not do very much to prevent the "most expensive painting in the world" from being stolen. Eventually, our conversation turned to Stanley's change of heart about being flat, and suddenly the talk took on a very different tone. In the text, Stanley begins to tire of being flat and is made fun of by his friends. Since children often find themselves the victims of taunts and bullies, this was a subject my students quickly latched onto.

CHRISTA: Everyone laughed at him and made fun of him.
DANIEL: You know, one of our rights is to be treated kindly, and Stanley didn't have that right.
MAX: Yeah, he was different on the outside so people picked on him.
OSCAR: It wasn't his fault. God made us that way.
ME: What way?
OSCAR: We're all different.
KELLIE: But we all have feelings.
CHRISTA: We all have hearts.
ME: Why do you think people were mean to Stanley?
YELITZA: Maybe they didn't have any reason. Sometimes people are bullies because something is wrong at home.
KELLIE: Stanley had a couple of disabilities. He was laughed at like some kids laugh at other kids with disabilities.

The remainder of our conversation centered on the idea of Stanley as having had a disability, and the entire class agreed that Stanley's flatness could, in fact, be considered a disability. I felt more confident in my next steps now, and I jumped into planning the next phase of our inquiry into the Rights of the Child.

AN INVITATION TO CRITICAL INQUIRY:
THE RIGHTS OF FLAT STANLEY

As my children were discussing *Flat Stanley*, I kept thinking about a new situation that was about to occur in our classroom and all of the students' comments related to Stanley's flatness being a disability. A student with autism who had been coming to my classroom for math all year was about to join my homeroom class. This would be his first experience spending all day in a general education setting, and it was an exciting opportunity for all of us. I decided to follow the students' strong feelings related to Stanley's disability, so I developed a series of curricular invitations to help the students explore this possibility.

Katie Van Sluys (2005) described curricular invitations as inquiry that will "promote the social aspects of learning by taking up issues in students' lives and placing inquiries within social contexts" (p. 6). My student Leigh described invitations this way: "An invitation is learning about different topics. Along with learning about people with disabilities, our group got to decide how to present what we learned to our classmates. We got to read about the disabilities and put it in our own words so we could understand it better."

My students explored and then chose from four different invitations: Being a Good Friend (Figure 3.1), Overcoming Obstacles (Figure 3.2), Discovering Types of Disabilities (Figure 3.3), and Rights for Everyone (Figure 3.4). I grouped them based on their first or second choice. Each invitation included informational and narrative books along with copies of the Rights of the Child and the Rights of the Disabled (www.un.org/disabilities). They had access to the Internet to research questions that arose as they read and discussed their invitation.

I always issue new invitations to the students by introducing the invitation along with the resources that accompanied it. The students had time to think about their interests and to list their top two choices. By this point in the year, the students understood the importance of working as a group, and we had developed routines for gathering supplies and asking for help. The students worked for 30 to 45 minutes each day on their invitation, and many of them also chose to work during recess or in the morning after completing morning assignments. When the groups met initially, I asked them to think about the roles they would play in the group and to determine how they would go about the work. Since the invitations were fairly open-ended, the groups typically began by dividing up the materials to read and reporting back at the end of class to the group, although some groups preferred to do everything together.

I rotated among groups each day, providing help when needed. Students had to think about when they needed to access the computers because we only had two computers in the classroom. They were very focused when they had computer time and used their time to find the answers they needed. As the students read, they made notes in their journals or asked questions of their classmates. It was rare

Figure 3.1. Invitation 1: Being a Good Friend

> *Just as they got down on their knees to reach for the lilies, there was a PLOP in the water. The water rippled into circles, one inside another. Eddie Lee pointed to their reflections and laughed.*
>
> *"You look funny, Christy."*
>
> *Christy's face in the water mirror was distorted by the ripples. She put her hands to her cheeks to hide the crooked image.*
>
> *"That's okay, Christy," he said. "I like you, anyway." He grinned his wide grin and put his right hand over his heart. "It's what's here that counts."*
>
> *(From* Be Good to Eddie Lee *by Virginia Fleming)*

In the book *Be Good to Eddie Lee,* Eddie Lee taught Christy an important lesson about friendship after she and JimBud did not treat him nicely. You are invited to explore these books about being friends with children who are disabled. As you read and work with your group, think carefully about what you could do to be a good friend to everyone, including students who are disabled. Questions to consider:

- What does friendship look like?
- In what ways are the children in these texts good friends?
- Are there times that children felt uncomfortable or treated their friends unkindly?
- Were there situations in these books that reminded you of situations you have experienced?
- Are there ways you can think of to be a good friend that were not mentioned in these books?
- Can you think of times that you have been uncomfortable around someone who was disabled? How can you overcome these feelings?
- What rights do individuals with disabilities have? Are there any rights they don't have that they should have?

Resources

Books:

Since We're Friends: An Autism Picture Book by Celeste Shally and David Harrington
My Friend with Autism by Beverly Bishop
Andy and His Yellow Frisbee by Mary Thompson
That's What's Different About Me by Kathryn Robbins
Captain Tommy by Abby Ward Messner
Be Good to Eddie Lee by Virginia Lee
I Can Hear the Sun by Patricia Polacco
Thank You, Mr. Falker by Patricia Polacco
Through Grandpa's Eyes by Patricia McLachlan
Peg by Maddie Stewart and Bee Wiley
Rules by Cynthia Lord
A Corner of the Universe by Ann M. Martin

Song:

Don't Laugh at Me by Allen Shamblin and Steve Seskin

Figure 3.2. Invitation 2: Overcoming Obstacles

"Most of our obstacles would melt away if, instead of cowering before them, we should make up our minds to walk boldly through them." —Orison Swett Marden

People with disabilities have many ways of overcoming the difficulties they face in their everyday lives. You are invited to explore the following texts that focus on the many ways the disabled have of meeting the challenges they face each day. As you read, think about these questions.

- What challenges do the characters in these texts face? Do they face other challenges besides their disabilities?
- Do the characters in these books have particular characteristics that help them overcome their challenges?
- What lessons can you learn about overcoming your own challenges from the characters in these books?
- What types of prejudice do you think children with disabilities face? How can you change these feelings in others?
- Are there other examples you know of people overcoming challenges despite physical or mental disabilities?
- In what ways can we support others as they overcome challenges in their lives?
- What rights do individuals with disabilities have? Are there any rights they don't have that they should have?

Resources

Books:

Special People, Special Ways by Arlene Maguire
Let's Talk About It: Extraordinary Friends by Fred Rogers
Don't Call Me Special: A First Look at Disability by Pat Thomas
Moses Sees a Play by Isaac Millman
Moses Goes to a Concert by Isaac Millman
Moses Goes to the Circus by Isaac Millman
Helen Keller: A Light for the Blind by Kathleen V. Kudlinski
When Learning Is Tough: Kids Talk About Their Learning Disabilities by Cynthia Roby
Let's Talk About Needing Extra Help at School by Susan Kent
Helen Keller by Christy DeVillier
Helen Keller by Margaret Davidson

Figure 3.3. Invitation 3: Discovering Types of Disabilities

Autism, Fragile X syndrome, Angelman syndrome, cerebral palsy, Down syndrome . . . all of these are disabilities faced by students right here at Johnson Elementary. In order to help us better understand our classmates, we need to learn about these disabilities. You are invited to explore various resources that discuss the types of disabilities these children face. As you explore, think about the following questions.

- What are the similarities and differences between the various disabilities?
- What should schools do to help children with these disabilities?
- What should families do to help children with these disabilities?
- What are the challenges children with these disabilities face?
- What can you do to be a good friend to other children with disabilities?
- What are the prejudices students with disabilities face? How can you stop these from occurring?
- What rights do individuals with disabilities have? Are there any rights they don't have that they should have?

Resources

Packets about Dravet syndrome, autism, cerebral palsy, Down syndrome, Fragile X syndrome, and intellectual disability

Books:

Be Quiet, Marina! by Kristen DeBear
My Brother's Keeper: A Kindergartener's View of Autism by Jace Richards and D.R. Richards
Look Mom, No Words! by Kathlyn Gay
Russell Is Extra Special: A Book About Autism for Children by Charles A. Amenta III, M.D.
Mom Can't See Me by Sally Hobart Alexander

Figure 3.4. Invitation 4: Rights for Everyone

By now, we are all aware that the United Nations adopted the Convention on the Rights of the Child in 1989. We are also aware that all human beings have rights. The United Nations has also been looking at rights that are granted to the disabled around the world. You are invited to explore the Convention on the Rights of Persons with Disabilities along with the texts I have provided. As you explore, think about the following questions.

- How are the Rights of the Child similar to the Rights of the Disabled? How are they different?
- Why do you suppose we need documents discussing Rights for Children and the Disabled?
- Can you think of instances when the rights of a disabled person might have been violated?
- In the books, were any of the rights of the characters violated? Did any of the characters choose to exercise their rights either as a child, a disabled person, or a human being?
- What rights do individuals with disabilities have? Are there any rights they don't have that they should have?

Resources

Internet:

Photo Journals: http://www.unicef.org/explore_3890.html
Rights of the Disabled: http://www.unicef.org/explore_3888.html
Rights of the Child: http://www.unicef.org/voy/explore/rights/explore_rights.php
Copies of Rights of the Child and Rights of the Disabled

Books:

Peg by Maddie Steward and Bee Willey
The Printer by Myron Uhlberg
Dancing with Katya by Dori Chaconas
Thank You, Mr. Falker by Patricia Polacco
The Hickory Chair by Lisa Rowe Fraustino

that I was needed or had to solve a conflict. They had taken to heart so many of our lessons that this time in our classroom was incredibly smooth. It was a joy to watch them so engrossed in their work.

In addition to the print resources, I provided time for students to go into our self-contained special education classes to work with the children and to see the types of things they were learning and were capable of doing. This was quite possibly the most powerful piece of the inquiry. It allowed the children to take on the role of observer, interviewer, and helper, and to demystify special education classrooms. I had originally scheduled half-hour increments for the visits, but almost all of the groups were gone for more than an hour. When they returned, they were filled with passion for the work they had observed. One teacher of students with severe disabilities asked my students to help with the morning calendar time. She was excited because my students helped her students make hand motions for the morning songs. The students were proud that they could help; they commented that all of the students tried to make the motions and sing along even if they could not say all of the words. The special education teachers were impressed with the level of questioning and their interactions with my students.

The students completed a reflection sheet after their visit to help them think about the issues that had been raised in their groups before, during, and after their visit. All of the children indicated they had positive experiences even if some of them felt uncomfortable at times. Several of the students described an incident where a student played in the sink and got angry when he was redirected as being uncomfortable, and some also talked about not understanding what the children were saying. Percy wrote that it "felt good to help" during circle time, and observed, "I think what stood out to me most was that the teachers cared about them."

I asked students to think about the rights of the disabled and to pinpoint those they felt were the most important. Kellie said, "All students have the right to be treated kindly. Special ed kids should have the right to be in real classes." When I asked her what she meant by the term *real classes*, she indicated that she thought they should be able to spend time in classes with other children their age. This was around the same time our new student had joined the class, and Kellie, along with the other students, was learning about autism and enjoying getting to know Zach. LeShon also indicated the need for children to have friends and to receive an education. The students all felt strongly that they needed to set an example for others as to how we treat students with disabilities, and they also felt that the rights of the disabled to receive an education were just as important as their right to receive an education.

Katherine summed up this experience for the children when she wrote, "Why do people make fun of people with disabilities? They preach and preach about this, but people still don't listen. They just judge people by what they look like on the outside."

SHARING OUR WORK

Once the students had completed their inquiry, they began to think about how they would share their work with their classmates. Since each invitation was different, they chose different ways to present their topic.

Kellie, LeShon, and Ramiro explored the invitation "Discovering Types of Disabilities" and organized these into a tree map with the name of each disability followed by a brief description to help their classmates understand the disabilities that affect students in our school. One of the disabilities they described was Angelman syndrome. They described children afflicted with this syndrome as having "normal features, no speech, seizures, hypopigmented skin, and a happy demeanor." These descriptions helped students understand the difficulties these students face and how their appearances and actions were often not what one would expect. Students went to the special education teachers to clarify any of the descriptions they did not understand, and they would often ask me to remind them which students had each particular disability in order to help them understand the characteristics.

Michael, Leigh, and Christa approached their exploration of the invitation "Rights for Everyone" by creating a picture book called *James Long*.

> James Long had cerebral palsy. When he was born he could not walk like other babies. He rode in a wheelchair most of his life. It was James first day of kindergarten and he was nervous. When he went in to his classroom his teacher said "Welcome to room 3.B." As he rode in people stared at him and people began to whisper. At lunch he ate by himself, and as people walked by they called him names. At recess he wanted to climb the monkey bars because his chair can go up high so he can play. People said you will never do it no legs. One day when a kid got stuck on the monkey bars. People tried to help him get down but they couldn't do it. When James said he will help he raised up his chair and help that kid down. After that people called him a superhero. People also treated him differently from that day on.

The students were filled with pride. They had created a story relating to those rights that they had deemed important for all children: the right to be treated fairly and to have time to play. This text certainly could have addressed those students who called names, but I felt like they showed how James took control of his situation and saved the day even when his classmates made fun of him.

Max, James, Percy, and Yelitza, who completed the invitation "Being a Good Friend," created a list of ways students could be a good friend, such as "If they are lonely, we can play with them or read to them." They concluded their presentation by performing the song "Don't Laugh at Me" (Seskin, 1999), which they had discovered on the Internet. The students practiced for days and were still off-key, but their words resonated:

Don't laugh at me, don't call me names.
Don't get your pleasure from my pain

Their inquiries drew to an end as the school year was winding down. Fortunately, I was able to loop up to 4th grade with most of the children, so I had the opportunity to see how these inquiries helped my students consider their interactions with each other.

MOVING FORWARD: LET'S TALK ABOUT HISTORY!

As we have moved into the new school year, we welcomed two students with autism into our class. My students treated each other with grace and dignity, and I attributed some of this to our critical inquiries the previous year. Organization is difficult for both of my students with autism, and their classmates helped them get started in the mornings and pack their book bags in the afternoon. Many days I saw a student or two sitting head to head with Zach, reading a book. There were times Zach ran to line up next to his friend, and my heart swelled to see how he had become a part of our classroom.

One of the most important lessons I learned as a critical literacy educator is to trust my students to guide their learning. I had never anticipated their recognition of Stanley as being disabled, or their defense of his rights to be treated fairly and with respect, Article 23 of the Rights of the Child. There was not only increased engagement, but there was also a level of camaraderie among my students that followed us into our new classroom. I was filled with pride whenever they reminded me that someone's rights were being violated as we read a book. We continue to approach texts with a critical eye and to think deeply about the choices authors make in their portrayals of characters. This is particularly important as our students learn about historical figures and time periods. We must work hard to see history from different angles and to take a fresh look at the old stories we have been told.

Our 4th-grade curriculum focused on early American history. As we were coming in from recess one day, Jason asked me, "Mrs. Paramore, do you like Christopher Columbus? Mrs. Ballard says you think he wasn't always a nice person." I paused for a moment and thought about what I had taught my students about valuing multiple viewpoints before answering.

"Do you remember how we talked about looking at a topic from multiple perspectives last year? Have you ever looked at Christopher Columbus from the perspective of the Native people?"

"Well, Mrs. Paramore," Jason said, "I haven't thought about it that way before."

As we settled into the classroom, I said, "Come on, let's talk about history. Let's talk about rights!"

4

Latinos for Involvement in Family Education

Parents Promoting Educational Goals That Respect Their Values and Culture

Stephen Lush and Lindsey Lush

Invitation to Explore:
Respect for the Values and Culture of Parents

Initiating Experience:

"My child needs to learn to read in Spanish and English." Many schools have large immigrant populations, and there, the need for policies and programs for involving families may be obvious. But is it any less important in a school where only a few students in each class bring a language and culture different from those of the majority? Article 29 of the Rights of the Child states in part that "education should aim to develop respect for the values and culture of their parents." We started the monthly LIFE (Latinos for Involvement in Family Education) meetings to bring Latino families, and their values and cultures, into the life of the school; they brought the meetings to LIFE by setting the agenda for how the school could better serve their children, including a new library of bilingual books.

Formal Invitation:

We invite you to think about the families in your school community. Who feels welcome, valued, and part of the community? Explore with us how a parent group might be structured to reestablish trust among families who are outside that community. You may want to challenge the assumption that a separate group is a better starting place than efforts to bring families into the existing organizations such as PTO. And you will certainly ask, as we do, what difference such a group makes for the children.

Suggested Questions:

1. How can teachers build community based on trust and respect with families who have been marginalized based on ethnicity, language, and culture?
2. How can teachers who are LTEP (limited to English proficiency) work effectively with Spanish-speaking family members?
3. What difference does an empowered Latino parent group make for student learning?
4. How is the experience of these teachers and families similar to your own? How is it different?

Texts, Tools, and Resources:

Family funds of knowledge were our primary resource. We addressed Article 29, "Children have a particular responsibility to respect the rights of their parents, and education should aim to develop respect for the values and culture of parents" and Article 17, "increase access to information . . . in languages that minority and indigenous children can understand. Children should also have access to children's books."

————————

Surrounded by a swirl of laughter and rapid Spanish, people talking in groups and greeting each other from across the room, I (Lindsey) quickly lose track of what they are saying. Stephen and I glance at each other, shrug, and wait patiently for someone to translate what they are saying. The talk is about the role of our Latin@ family group, LIFE (Latinos for Involvement in Family Education), in the school's Fall Festival. LIFE family members want an increased role in the festival. They are debating how best to advertise a booth to sell *elotes*, a Mexican meal of roasted corn on the cob smeared with mayonnaise and chili powder, among other options. The conversation moves to the purpose of Fall Festival, although Stephen and I, both teachers at the school, are not leading the discussion. This happens every once in a while when the families really get invested in a topic, and we can't keep up, given our meager Spanish. We wait patiently, knowing they'll explain to us, speaking more slowly, in a few minutes.

THE NEED FOR LIFE

After nearly 4 years, the voices of families in LIFE meetings have grown in number, confidence, and fervor. LIFE began as an attempt to form a community of

Latin@ families within a predominantly European American rural elementary school in Northeast Georgia. Stephen founded the group to provide a vehicle for the school's Latin@ community to work together to address needs specific to their children and families. In addition to school-related issues, he hoped that the group would build a network within the Latin@ community to help with issues of transportation, health care, and learning. From the beginning, the group functioned democratically, giving the families the ultimate say on the issues addressed and the format of each meeting.

So, why this school? What would inspire a novice, Anglo teacher in rural Georgia who taught two, maybe three, Spanish-speaking children a year to start a group for Latin@ families? Stephen saw Jefferson Road Elementary as a prime example of the need for a family support group like LIFE. At the project's initiation, the population of Jefferson Road consisted of 6% Hispanic students, with 21 of those students being served by the English as a Second Language program. Even with these small numbers, Stephen witnessed that important information was not being communicated effectively between home and school. Teachers were frustrated when papers went unsigned and parents did not attend parent-teacher conferences, academic support team meetings, or special education meetings. Teachers' reports that children weren't reading at home or completing homework often went unanswered by families.

For some teachers, this lack of communication led them to believe that the families didn't care about their children's education. Others took responsibility for their own lack of communication skills with Spanish-speaking families and felt guilty because they weren't providing these students and families with equal access to information and support. Even those who felt guilt rather than contempt seemed largely unable to do anything to change the situation. Papers sent home were written in English; often, no one was available to read and translate information. Families felt discouraged from attending school events, conferences, and meetings because they had no guarantee that they could communicate with school faculty once they got there. Short of learning to speak Spanish, a daunting task for most teachers, what else could teachers do to communicate more effectively? At the time, our school did not have any resources in place to support communication with families whose first language was not English; however, teachers were expected to do so and the students were being held to the same standards and expectations for achievement.

This trend is not unique to Jefferson Road's teachers and Spanish-speaking families. Often, a school does not address language and cultural issues until it is overwhelmed with a population that has a specific need. Other schools in the surrounding areas have resources such as Spanish-speaking family engagement specialists and receptionists, but our district didn't provide these services because of our school's small ESOL (English for Speakers of Other Languages) population. Since our small Latin@ population did not pose a huge problem in terms of test scores and funding, this group's needs were put on the backburner.

For this reason, Jefferson Road seemed like the right place for a group like LIFE. The Latino families in the area were marginalized within the school community, but even more disconcerting was how they were largely isolated from each other and often unable to discuss problems and offer support. They didn't have the numbers or political standing to pressure the school to address the issues they were facing. English-speaking families were able to address the teachers and administrators with questions of homework, assessments, assignments, behavior, and so forth. Many came forward when students were being bullied on the bus or were having trouble getting along with a classmate. Many were aware of standardized testing, or could read information sent home or contact teachers to inquire about grades, standards, or their child's academic standing.

While we recognize that Latin@ families are not the only ones who struggle with home/school communication and that factors other than language can create a gap between home and school, we saw this as a particularly pressing need. How isolating to not only feel cut off from the school system your child attends but to live where there are few opportunities to talk with others who share your grievances. We had long argued in school leadership meetings that our school was unique because of the physical geography of the county. The rural structure consisted of scattered homes and neighborhoods separated from each other, with the school the only hub. Community events, church meetings, sporting events, and festivals all took place on the school grounds. Families in need of assistance often used the school to make the necessary contacts.

Few of the Latin@ families were part of these community activities. Yet Article 29 of the UN Rights of the Child states in part that "education should aim to develop respect for the values and culture of their parents." We wanted our school to show that respect for Latino families. As the LIFE families established the agenda over the next few years, they would also identify a strong need "to increase access to information . . . in languages that minority and indigenous children can understand. Children should also have access to children's books" (Article 17). With the creation of the LIFE group, we hoped to bring together a cohesive group of Latino families who felt welcome in their school, and who could participate in educating their children in ways that respected their values and culture.

THE BEGINNINGS OF LIFE

In the spring semester of 2006, I (Stephen) took a Service Learning class set up for college students to get involved in helping in the community, while also learning from their involvement. I chose to work with families who had been on my mind a great deal.

I had always been intrigued by Latin@ culture. Since I began taking Spanish classes in high school, my curiosity and knowledge of the culture has increased. As a teacher, I saw firsthand how some Latin@ students struggle with being immersed in an entirely new language while being held to the same expectations of those who are fluent in the English language. I had heard many a teacher comment on the frustration they felt in attempting to communicate with families who did not speak English—which was not surprising, since all communication from the school was written in English. Students were often overwhelmed by new vocabulary and unable to access information about a new concept at the same time. Students came to school not yet knowing how to read or write in their native language, yet they were expected to read and write on grade level in English.

We needed to establish an effective method for providing families equal access to school information that affected the well-being of their children (Article 17). We needed an avenue to help students develop proficiency in English while retaining their native language and culture. To this end, I wanted to form a community meeting where these issues could be discussed and problems that arose could be addressed by the community.

The first step was to email the faculty with my plan. I told them my idea and asked for feedback on issues to be addressed from their perspective. Here is one response I found particularly encouraging:

> Stephen,
>   I would like to thank you for the program you are trying to launch for Hispanic parents/families. I have three Hispanic children in my classroom, all of which have parents who do not speak English. One of my students does not speak English either, so there is no one in the home who does. I think this program could be very beneficial to them and help them feel more comfortable with our school as well as be more informed about their child's education. I know that other teachers of Hispanic children will be as grateful for the help in communicating with their ESOL students' parents.
>   Thank you.
>   T. S., 2nd Grade

In addition, teachers expressed concern about homework, unsigned paperwork, and the school's attendance policy. We based the first meeting on the teachers' feedback.

The next step was to survey the families (in English and Spanish) to determine a good time for the meeting, number of attendees, if they'd like to bring a covered dish, and whether they spoke Spanish, English, or both at home. I received 14 letters back with about 30 people in all expected to come. A day before the meeting, I phoned each attendee personally. I made it through all 14 phone conversations in Spanish without having to use the language line. This is a system that provides the school with an interpreter over the phone if needed. Funding for this service is provided by our school, so bilingual communication has not been completely ignored; further, the use of this resource has increased in recent years.

This accomplishment was thrilling to me. Being able to communicate in Spanish, both by making myself understood and by understanding others in another language was so empowering. This, the *learning* element of my self-assigned Service Learning project, was to learn to communicate with the families in their language rather than the one I am responsible for teaching to their children. I felt a tremendous feeling of pride that I could communicate with the families, and that the families knew that it just wasn't about learning English, but about really wanting to communicate.

In the meantime, I arranged for a local Mexican restaurant, the Agua Linda, to make 20 large quesadillas for the meeting. The county's central office reimbursed the expenses and the Agua Linda provided a discount on the food. Delicious food became integral to our LIFE meetings. Certainly, a big Latin@-style dinner stocked with homemade flautas, tamales, salads, and dessert is something Lindsey and I look forward to each month!

The day of the first meeting, the thought of having nearly 30 people in attendance was awesome, but also a little scary. The agenda for the meeting was to convene as a whole group and share food, then go to the library and give a presentation on the CRCT (Criterion Referenced Competency Test, Georgia's state test) in Spanish. Because our first meeting took place in March, very near the statewide accountability tests, this was the most pressing issue of the moment, for teachers at least, and likely a large concern for families and students. After the presentation, we would hand out papers that listed many of the doctors in the area who take Medicaid and Peach Care, as well as a list of local places that offered English classes. Finally, we would hold a town hall discussion that would provide an opportunity for families to express their issues and concerns and determine if and when we would meet again.

The time finally arrived and one family came early to help set up the food. Señora Melendez was extremely helpful, and was always asking if she could help me in any way between the time of the survey and the meeting itself. As one of the bilingual parents, Sra. Melendez served as a valuable resource, translating the state-mandated, high-stakes CRCT information as well as handling the introductions. Another helpful resource during the initial meetings was Ms. Carson, the county's migrant education representative.

In total, six families of the 14 came to the meeting. Of the six, two were bilingual and one spoke Spanish only. The rest knew a few words of English, but didn't feel they knew it well enough to speak comfortably. Three of the families volunteered to be a mentor family, that is, to provide their phone number so that other families could call them to help with school issues such as homework or translating notes, assignments, or other general information.

During the dinner, I spoke with all the families in Spanish. My Spanish is mediocre, but I felt it was important to do my best to communicate what I felt was important about the meeting and to just have dialogue with the families to build rapport and trust. Families were always helpful when I got stuck on a word or phrase. They suggested that the potluck dinner may have scared away some of families who weren't able to make something. However, everyone had enough to eat and the mood during dinner was light.

Next, we went to the library to do the CRCT presentation. The presentation went over really well and many of the families asked questions and wanted to know how to help their children study for the exam. We suggested study strategies and explained the main content of the test. Ms. Carson and Sra. Melendez helped with most of the explanations and questions in Spanish. We concluded the first meeting by handing out the information sheets and asking the group about any issues that they thought were important to address.

Here was the moment I had built up in my mind. In my vision, the town hall discussion would elicit a wealth of topics, concerns, and suggestions for future meetings. Families would voice their concerns to me, so that we could continue in a democratic fashion with our subsequent meetings. Instead, as I opened the floor to family input during the final minutes of the first meeting, barely anyone asked questions or made suggestions. Families seemed to be looking at us to provide them with information. They evidently intended to take what we gave them and do with it what they could. I tried to stress the importance of community involvement and that I was there to support them, not just to press information on them, but to learn from them. Still, the minutes ticked on and the group was reluctant to speak. Finally, one member suggested learning some strategies for behavior issues. Unanimously, the group agreed to hold another meeting. Many promised to speak to members of their neighborhoods about the meeting and encourage more people to attend. They all expressed appreciation for the meeting and said they were looking forward to the next.

After reflecting on the first meeting, I decided that we teachers would provide food for the subsequent meetings to avoid the pressure of bringing food to share, and the next meeting would be more of a social event rather than an informational one. Although we would provide information about the end of the year events and perhaps some testing results, for the most part, it would be to get everyone together and discuss ways to help each other help the students. Because LIFE began in the late spring, very near the end of school, we had only two meetings in that first year. The second year began in September, shortly after the start of the school year, and continued each month until summer break. Lindsey, another Anglo teacher at the school (and my future wife), joined the project with just as much enthusiasm, if less Spanish, as she'll describe later in the chapter.

LIFE FOR STUDENTS AND FAMILIES

With the help of our school's After School Program, we were able to provide free child care for the meetings. One evening a month, our school's After School Program director and several program employees would join us for LIFE dinner and, prior to the start of the meeting portion, take the kids outside to play, then to the computer lab or library to watch a movie. We believe this is a critical element to our group's success. At first, we only wanted to alleviate the struggle to find and afford child care, but we found other positive results as well. For many families, the children became the main catalyst for coming to "The Meetings," as they came to be called. Students would stop by my classroom door daily to ask, "When is the next meeting?" "Are you coming to the next meeting?" or "Can my friend come to the meeting, too?" Families commented that spending time with other Spanish-speaking children of different ages was beneficial for their children. In a survey we gave in the third year of LIFE, families noted:

> "The meetings have helped my child make more friends to play with"
> "Happier with going to school"
> "Pleasurable time after school with kids of different
>   ages who speak their same language"

Not only did the children find support and friendship with the group, but many parents and families began to speak of LIFE as a family within the school. We began to see familiar faces inside the school, in the lunchroom eating with students, and at afterschool events, both fun and official kinds. Jefferson Road was becoming a safe, friendly place for these families and, in turn, school information that was constantly circulating was becoming increasingly accessible.

This progress did not happen all at once. At times, we'd sit in meetings of only three or four families, frustrated by low attendance but encouraged by the presence of the few determined families and enthusiastic children. We knew that community building would take time and some families were faced with circumstances that prevented them from attending such as work, transportation (which we would assist with whenever possible), and factors that would keep anyone from spending a Friday night at school. In addition, we struggled to get new families to attend. While we were excited and comforted by the familiar faces, we were aware that many families were still unable or unwilling to attend. Some, we imagined, were reluctant to come because they faced negative past experiences with schools. Individuals vowed to knock on doors and make calls to get more people to come. Attendance began to grow.

READING FOR LIFE

After 3 years, our original goal of increasing the families' access to information that is important to their children's "health and well-being" (Article 17) was going well when families voiced a specific need. Interestingly, Article 17 goes on to say, "Mass media should particularly be encouraged to supply information in languages that minority and indigenous children can understand. Children should also have access to children's books." We would soon find out how much families valued access to children's books—in both English and Spanish.

Parents and families were becoming regular visitors to the school, attending conferences and meetings with increased regularity, and participating in extra-curricular events. We had begun the process as information providers. Parents made requests; we supplied the knowledge. Eventually, as we had hoped, the LIFE families took ownership. The tone at the LIFE meetings began to change. In prior discussions, families often sounded fearful as they shared concerns over school performance, homework, teacher communication, and, most acutely, perfor-mance on standardized tests. The concerns mirrored the problems teachers, coun-selors and administration regularly voiced.

The LIFE families knew that we were there to help, but they also were aware that we were, after all, members of the teacher group who had been expressing concern about their children's academic performance. Previous meetings had addressed behavior management at home and school, homework assistance, and standardized testing. These concerns remained for teachers, students and families alike. However, we heard a shift from the fearful tone of trying to catch up to the school's expectations to a tone of confidence. Families began asking, and in some cases demanding, that the school acknowledge their concerns.

At a meeting in September of the fourth year of LIFE, in a wagon wheel discus-sion triggered by the question *"In what ways can we help the school?"* someone boldly stated, "My child needs to learn to read in Spanish and English." As others chimed in and nodded in agreement, the conversation focused on the need for increased bilingual education. "We could come to school and read with students in Spanish, do writing conferences in Spanish," suggested one parent. Eyes turned to us, as if to say, *"So what are you going to do about it?"* Families expressed their expectations of us, the teachers at Jefferson Road, to help their children become not just literate, but bil-iterate. In addition, they saw themselves as significant contributors in this endeavor.

Following the discussion, we suggested that we spend the money raised at the Fall Festival on bilingual books. We could start the LIFE Bilingual Library. Families talked with great excitement, generating and providing answers to many ques-tions: Where would the books be kept? How would they be checked in and out by students and families? Who should be permitted to use LIFE Library books? LIFE families determined the who, where, and when. Our job was to make it happen. Luckily for me (Lindsey), the families granted me full rein of what books would be purchased, at least for now. And for me, the book lover, it was a dream come true!

Months later, at nearly 9:00 on a Friday night in February, I sat at a table in our school library. Books were spread out across four tables. Children zipped from table to table, examining covers, flipping through pages, calling to each other, and filling their arms with books. As Moises staggered over to me and my makeshift checkout station, books stacked nearly to his chin, I asked him, "Moises, are you really going to read *all* these books?" Eyes wide, he nodded, "Yes! I have to work on my Spanish!" As I finished typing the previous child's selected titles into the computer, his older sister, Alondra, a quiet, thoughtful girl, surreptitiously instructed him to return several books and he obeyed. Still, he took home 11 new Spanish books. Six other children left with nearly half of our newly acquired collection. Since the opening of our LIFE Library, the children meet me in the media center to check out books at the end of each meeting.

However, when many students were told they could check out books in Spanish, they responded, "I don't know how to read in Spanish." They did not connect the reading skills they'd learned in school to reading Spanish, and many assumed that reading in English would not translate to reading Spanish. These children, despite their command of verbal Spanish, had not been taught or encouraged to develop Spanish literacy. For them, reading was associated with school, and school was associated with English, not Spanish. Even though our school library had a small section of bilingual and Spanish books, many of the LIFE students had not accessed them.

The expressions of shock and joy the first time they read the page of a Spanish book was indescribable.

Since the opening of the LIFE Library, we have had two Read-In Days, where rather than the adults meeting as usual while sending the kids off to play, we spread books out on all the tables and families stayed together to read. During last year's Read-In Day, Silva sat side-by-side with her 1st-grade daughter as she read aloud. Silva looked up, her eyes filled with tears. "I didn't know she could read so good in Spanish," she whispered. As teachers, we tell parents that reading at home is valuable to a child's development. But the pride and delight that Silva expressed surpasses anything we have experienced from a reading test score.

Even several months after starting the LIFE Library, students still came to me to check out books. If I had a newly purchased stack in my room, we would peruse them together and I would remind them that there were even more bilingual books in our school library. But for now, many students saw me as "the Spanish Book Lady." Others were walking proudly into the library and checking out their customary two library books, *plus* one or two Spanish/bilingual books, boasting to their classmates, "Mrs. Lush said it was okay for me to get extras because we are learning to read in Spanish." The pride they felt in their Spanish books demonstrated the importance of our efforts to develop the LIFE children's respect for the culture and values of their parents. Could they begin to view their Spanish language and culture as a fund of knowledge rather than a deficiency in English and a stumbling block in school? Could their pride and self-esteem for their culture also create that sense of respect in other students and teachers?

Regardless of their current comfort with checking out Spanish/bilingual books or their command of reading in Spanish (or English for that matter), all the LIFE children showed a significant interest in the LIFE Library. Parents recognized this interest in a survey taken shortly after the opening of the library.

"My children are enthusiastic about reading Spanish."
"Taking books home has motivated them to read."
"Every day her kids read more Spanish, kids like reading Spanish."

Of course, it's not just the students who are enthusiastic about the books we share. Recently, I sat side-by-side for nearly an hour with LIFE parents browsing Spanish and bilingual books online. We were choosing how to spend the money LIFE had earned at our Fall Festival booth. Although parents were content to purchase more books, I wanted more feedback from them on what books they'd like to see. In our first batch of books, students were thrilled to see familiar characters such as Junie B. Jones, Clifford, and the Arthur series. Pleased as I was for their enthusiasm, I was feeling that something was missing. Was a LIFE Library of books in Spanish really enough? What about Article 29 of the Rights of the Child that states in part that "education should aim to develop respect for the values and culture of their parents"? Junie B. Jones might be speaking in Spanish in the book, but she is not a Mexican. I realized that we needed to increase the volume of Mexican children's stories rather than European American stories translated into Spanish. I presented this issue to the families and they agreed. Our search began.

They were curious about what books children in Mexico were reading and thinking back to stories they heard as children growing up in Mexico. We found many classic rhymes and fairy tales from Mexico. I researched Latin@ authors such as Alma Flor Ada, Yuyi Morales, Pam Munoz Ryan, and Carmen Lomas Garza, and winners of the Pura Belpre Award, which is presented annually to a Latin@ writer and illustrator whose work celebrates Latin@ culture. We chose books such as *¿Qué puedes hacer con una paleta? (What Can You Do with a Paleta?)* by Carmen Tafolla, *Tan to Tamarind: Poems about the Color Brown* by Malathi Michelle Iyengar, and *My Diary From Here to There/Mi diario de aqui hasta alla* by Amada Irma Perez because they seemed to mirror the lives and experiences of our LIFE families.

Reflecting, I feel embarrassed at my initial satisfaction and pride in our first batch of books. Had I not missed the point a bit? I try to see each experience as another step in our collective Service Learning project. In each round, we find space for improvement and learn a little more.

PUTTING LIFE INTO THE FESTIVAL AND FAIR

As we mentioned, the money for the library came partially from funds raised during the school's yearly Fall Festival. This event is sponsored by the PTO and serves as their main fundraiser. When the Fall Festival came up at the first meeting of the fourth school year, many LIFE members expressed surprise that this was a fundraising project. One parent explained that in Mexico schools send home a collection envelope to raise money. They believed that the flyers and talk of a "festival" did not register for many Mexican families as a fundraiser, and for that reason many did not participate.

LIFE families felt that they needed to clarify for Spanish-speaking families that attending this event would help raise money for the school's needs. They also felt that, since we, LIFE, were in need of funds for books and other materials, we should have a booth. One parent commented, "They never say, 'Let the Mexicans get involved with Fall Festival,' they just say, 'Come to Fall Festival.'" We decided to sell *elotes*, corn on the cob with sides of mayonnaise and chili powder. Our small booth had an enormous response from the LIFE families and eventually grew to include four batches of corn, fruit salad, *chicharrón* (fried pork rinds) drizzled with hot sauce, and Mexican sodas and snack foods. The LIFE booth was a favorite for many families, regardless of heritage. One European American family who had moved to Athens from California years before was delighted by the traditional Mexican dish and came back again and again throughout the evening. We walked away with over $200 that night, not to mention a little bounce in our step over our success and big plans for next year!

At the end of our fourth year of LIFE, Jefferson Road held its second annual Multicultural Fair. Our school does not boast very diverse demographics, as we've mentioned. Our student body consists of about 79% White, 9% Black, 9% Latin@, 2% American Indian, and 1% Asian American, primarily Hmong families who have immigrated from Laos and Thailand. Many Hmong students are involved in a traditional Laotian dance group. They performed at our first Multicultural Fair wearing traditional costumes. Another parent brought in Native American artifacts from her ancestors. Each family contributed a dish to our Family Traditions potluck. Although the 20 people who attended the first year had a good time, this year the LIFE families decided they wanted a little more say. Surprised?

The Laotian dancers returned for another performance as did the school's Select Music Ensemble. The LIFE children gathered a group of dancers to perform a traditional Mexican dance, complete with costumes. Silvia, a LIFE parent of two current Jefferson Road students and one graduate, was a member of a traditional Mexican dance troupe. She modeled traditional Mexican dress at fairs and events. After seeing the Laotian and Indian performances the previous year, she asked to do the same with our LIFE children. The children practiced at several LIFE meetings as well as outside of school time, then presented a joyful and colorful Mexican dance. The response to this year's Multicultural Fair was overwhelming. Our small cafeteria was filled with faces of teachers, students, parents, grandparents, and guardians of various ages and ethnicities.

Again, we learn from each new experience with our LIFE families. The success of the second Multicultural Fair in comparison to the first speaks loudly for what opens the door to the families. In fact, one of our LIFE regulars had come late to the first festival. When we greeted her, she admitted that her family had arrived much earlier but looked in the window and saw only White people, so they left. The Multicultural Fair, despite its intentions, was not universally welcoming. When Latin@ families had the opportunity to participate rather than just attend, our fairs and festivals became true *community* events.

LANGUAGE AND POWER

LIFE's success has been made possible with contributions from many dedicated people both at Jefferson Road Elementary and at the district level. We benefited from financial support for food and child care as well as guidance from our system's migrant educator. Many LIFE parents and family members played roles beyond being attendees, particularly during LIFE's floundering beginnings. Stephen was the initiating force and continuing drive going into and beyond LIFE's sixth year. Lindsey served as note-taker, calendar keeper, and organizer, mostly with the help of a translator in the beginning years. Professors from the neighboring university provided talks and occasionally attended meetings. Our school counselor and intern attended regularly, despite minimal Spanish proficiency. Jefferson Road Elementary has one part-time ESOL teacher who often comes to dinner to spend time with students and families. Our principal and assistant principal dedicate one of their Friday nights each month to eating dinner with LIFE families, again despite their inexperience with the Spanish language. All of these attendees have worked to make a valuable and valued school group.

The greatest recognition, however, must go to the dedicated families who attend meetings whenever possible. Despite the restrictions of work, family, and obligations, these families consistently take time to come to school for LIFE meetings. They believe in the importance of the meetings and have therefore made the meetings a priority. One parent member in particular has played a significant role in the establishment of LIFE. Luciane Wetherington supported three of her children through school at Jefferson Road. She speaks Portuguese, Spanish, and English and became an invaluable resource for LIFE meetings in the second and third years. After being employed by the district as a bilingual support teacher for the school's prekindergarten program, she also spread LIFE meetings to two other schools in the county.

Each of these contributors brings a different perspective to the LIFE experience. In the next sections, we describe our individual experiences with LIFE over its first 5 years, learning that we take with us as LIFE continues to develop and thrive.

Stephen's Retrospective

My intention was to serve a need in my school while learning about teaching those whose culture or language differed from my own. What memories stand out, and what have I learned in the past 5 years? Those memories are the ones that will stick with me, the ones most important to me and the reasons I will continue with the LIFE group in the future.

Consider the meeting that took place at the end of the first full year of LIFE: our standardized testing meeting. I dreaded this meeting. The idea of standing in front of the families spewing information about test scores, passing or not passing, summer school, and retests distressed me. But, then again, the meeting was not for me. The families requested the information. We had more participation at that meeting than at any of the other meetings throughout the entire first year. The library was packed. I just sat there, looking at all the faces in the crowd, and was moved almost to tears. The experience was like the sweet taste of a ripened fruit after months and months of watching it grow on the tree, and I savored every second of it. The families were here. They had come because they clearly felt a need for the testing information and we had provided a forum for them to acquire that information.

But was that a learning experience? I knew that the families wanted to know about these tests because doing well had been heavily emphasized by teachers. If I didn't know already, I certainly learned how high-stakes tests burden both families and students with excessive stress. The room full of anxious faces spoke volumes. The barrier between school and home for many of these families prevented them even more than English-speaking families from having a clear understanding of the content of the tests and consequences of scores.

My deepest learning was at an event very different from the testing meeting. In year 3, Estella, the daughter of one of the LIFE families, was turning 15. I don't remember my 15th birthday, but in the Latin@ culture the 15th birthday is a big deal. Families save for years to provide their daughters with a huge party on their *quinceañera,* ushering them into adulthood. The family invited Lindsey and me to participate in this event.

Neither of us had ever been to a *quinceañera,* so we entered the huge, rented party building a bit tentatively. We were greeted immediately with tons of food and drink, a live mariachi band, and nearly a hundred people talking and dancing. A large portion of the evening was dedicated to a choreographed dance where Estella, with the help of her many attendants, all dressed in brightly sequined gowns or tuxedos, was twirled and lifted into the air.

Many of the families from LIFE were there that night, and so were many of the students. This time, we were in their world. But for me, that was the special part, that we were invited into their culture. It was a window into their lives that I don't see at LIFE meetings. In that moment, I truly felt accepted by the families. Maybe it didn't hurt that Lindsey and I were the first couple to start dancing when the band started to play cumbia music! I was learning every second that night, being on the inside of the culture I wanted to teach and learn from, seeing things from their side, instead of my side.

The cultural experience really excites me, for this is where the learning takes place. Listening to the stories and history of the families, getting close to them—that is what it's all about for me. Last year, I tutored one of the LIFE children after school. The family didn't have transportation, so I took the student home each week. As it happened, each time I dropped the student off, dinner would be just about ready, and the family would invite me inside to partake of delicious, homemade food.

I believe it was a way for the family to express their gratitude to me for helping their child. But the hours I spent talking with the mother and father at their table meant the world to me. I talked to the father about fishing, the mother about living in Texas, and all the jobs they both had over the years. With a seemingly unending supply of flautas, the time flew by, but the value of those experiences will last a lifetime.

Lindsey's Retrospective

I speak from the perspective of a minimal Spanish speaker. My position represents that of many of my teacher peers who struggle to communicate with Spanish-speaking families and who feel infinitely more frustrated with our own limited Spanish than resentful of the families' limited English. Regardless of my limitations, I sit across from moms and dads, uncles and grandparents, each month and make conversation over my heaping plate of chips and salsa. Our conversations consist of a lot of one-word sentences such as the following:

> SILVIA TO EVA: *La maestra no está comiendo mucho esta noche.*
> ME: (noticing that they are speaking about me and
>   understanding that they are saying something about
>   eating or not eating) *Pollo* . . . I don't eat the *pollo.*
> SILVIA: *Usted es un vegetariano? No comer carne?*
> ME: *Si! No carne!*
> EVA: *Porque?*
> ME: I know that word! I have high cholesterol. I don't
>   eat *carne* or *queso* or . . . *como se dice* milk?
> EVA: *Leche.*
> ME: *Si! No leche.*

The conversation continued in this way for a few minutes, a combination of English, Spanish, and my "Spanglish." We made it work. Eva's and Silvia's English is significantly better than my Spanish, but all of us seem equally insecure about attempting the other's native language.

After several years with these families, I began to feel more and more comfortable. We smile and wave when we cross paths in the halls as they visit their children or outside school at the local flea market. Still, striking up a conversation always sparks that sense of nervousness. Often, as I sit across from a familiar face at a LIFE dinner, I struggle to start a conversation. *C'mon, say something!* But my mind feels blank, searching for even one Spanish word to open a conversation. I feel awkward and embarrassed, even a little rude. *Why can't I think of anything to say?* Slowly, each month, we break through the barriers with our single-word and sign-language conversations, eventually getting our thoughts across the narrow table and the vast ocean of language.

I wouldn't trade these short conversations for anything. As I sit there, lost in a sea of words I can't comprehend, I am vulnerable. And I'm the teacher! And it's my school! Yet I am not the one with the power of communication here. Silvia and Eva could simply turn to each other and carry on a conversation without me. In the school environment, the teachers, administration, and staff have a great deal of collective power that results from sharing the same language. Many members of LIFE do not have the power to communicate with that group. Each month at our LIFE meetings, for those 3 hours, families hold the power of language. Each month, Spanish becomes the language of power.

Even when I do understand snippets of a seemingly rapid-fire conversation, my brain takes so long to process their words, think of my own comment, then roughly translate those ideas to some slightly comprehensible form of Spanish, not to mention to build up the courage to try these words aloud (I think *comer* means "to eat," or is it "to walk"?) that by the time I'm ready to speak, the conversation has moved on and my comment is irrelevant. It's exhausting.

How often do our Spanish-speaking parents and students experience this dizzying struggle to communicate? How often has a child simply not had time to comprehend and formulate a response to our question, but the teacher assumes s/he doesn't know the answer? How often has a Spanish-speaking parent's failure to respond to a teacher's letter or phone call been insecurity with English? And most important, what can I, as a teacher, do about it? I certainly haven't found the answer to all my questions, but I do feel that by putting myself in that position, I can begin to understand the relationship between power and language.

Most recently, I sat across from Rosa at a student-led conference. Rosa has been a LIFE regular for 4 years; her eldest son was in my 5th-grade class 2 years earlier and her son Steven is currently in my 3rd-grade class. Rosa has been learning English through the Rosetta Stone program the school made available. She can access the program from home, so she practices on her own time. We began the conference with Steven describing his work in school, first in English then in Spanish. Eventually, the conversation moved to mostly English. Rosa was nodding along and occasionally responding in English. After Steven had finished going over his conference points, he moved away to play with his little sister. Rosa and I continued to talk about Steven's progress in school, his father's work, and Steven's health. Most of our conversation was in English, with pauses while one of us searched for the right word. The discussion was slow, but not awkward or forced.

Near the end of the conversation I told Rosa, "Your English is too good now! I didn't get to practice my Spanish at all!" She argued that her English wasn't good and that writing and reading in English is still very hard for her. We shared our frustration of comprehending more of the foreign language than we can speak. She told me, "I understand everything you say but I'm not able to think of the words to say back. I have to think first in Spanish, then to English." I knew exactly how she felt! We laughed and commiserated over our language struggles. That day, we talked for over an hour.

In the end, we concluded that even when we learn another language, it's hard to speak to native speakers because we feel shy and embarrassed about saying the words wrong. This conversation was made possible not only by Rosa's determination to learn English on her own, but by the relationship we've established through LIFE. Both of us were able to be vulnerable with a new language, and that made communication possible.

When we sit across the conference table with Spanish-speaking parents and families, maybe we really don't know how much of what we say is lost in the sea of apprehension. LIFE has taught me that language itself is really only one element of communication. So much of our success with LIFE families and with our language learning has been developed from community, trust, and respect for each other.

LIFE GOES ON . . .

As LIFE continues, we cannot help but get a little uneasy about the future of our LIFE families. Our state has passed damaging and intimidating anti-immigration laws. We never inquire about how families arrived in the United States; we are only aware if they tell us. The anti-immigration legislation threatens the trust between us and the faith that the school is a safe place for all families. We feel for the families who are constantly on edge, worrying that they or other family members may be deported, or that their own children are not welcome in this country. Their worries also make us fearful, hesitant, and concerned. The fact that these families are so involved in their children's education takes away some of the uneasiness. With each meeting, bilingual book, home visit, and *quinceanera*, we are overcoming some of those fears, and providing a future generation of students with the resources to be successful.

A second concern has to do with the very success of LIFE. As LIFE gained numbers and voice, we began to assert ourselves within the school. More than once, we have felt a twinge of discomfort that we were creating a bridge between school and home life for some, while deepening a cultural divide. A snapshot of PTO and LIFE says a lot. The brown-skinned faces of the LIFE families contrast with those of the PTO, comprised of White members, with one or two Black parents, a ratio consistent with the school's population. On one unfortunate occasion, we planned a LIFE meeting on the same night as a PTO meeting followed by student square dancing. The LIFE families had no knowledge of the PTO meeting. PTO had seldom even been mentioned in LIFE meetings.

Should we work to combine the efforts of these two valuable parent and family groups in our school? Would it be detrimental to the cohesion of LIFE families if Anglo families were invited to attend? At the same time, can we really ask LIFE members to double their contributed time and also attend PTO meetings? Our (now) 9% Latino population is represented monthly by up to 30 people, whereas the remaining 91% of the school is represented by 6 or 7 dedicated PTO parents. PTO controls a great deal of money and organizes the majority of the extracurricular events and fundraisers for our school. Should LIFE only be looking out for our own? Perhaps families are feeling that same separation and are concerned as well. Families have voted for funds raised from this year's festival to go toward the school library as a whole, rather than specifically Spanish books. Perhaps they are beginning to see themselves as advocates for our whole school, not just for our Latino population.

Our original goals from the UN Rights of the Child were to increase access to information and to develop respect for native culture and values. With the monthly LIFE meetings as the catalyst, information led to actions that led to the development of cultural awareness and respect (including a library of culturally relevant bilingual books), both for the LIFE families themselves and for the teachers, students, and families at Jefferson Road Elementary. The empowering effect of that information compels us forward, to solve these problems and to learn with and from families.

5

Protection from Deportation and Family Separation

Middle School Students Explore Their Rights as Recent Immigrants

Kelli Bivins

Invitation to Explore:
Protection from Deportation and Family Separation

Initiating Experience:

Many of the middle school students in my urban Title 1 ESOL classes are undocumented, living in the shadows of an increasingly hostile society. I wanted to create a pedagogy with my students in which they could examine their oppression. I decided to explore some of the "enduring understandings" in Social Studies, as well as writing narratives as required by the Georgia Language Arts standards, using the Rights of the Child as a catalyst. Each student chose the right s/he would study. The next semester, students continued their inquiries through Freire's Cultural Notebook process.

Formal Invitation:

I invite you to explore connections as well as disconnections among your own curriculum standards, the enduring understandings that guide social studies teachers, and the UN Rights of the Child. Think about what mini-lessons you would teach to link critical inquiries and state-mandated curriculum. Raise concerns you might have about encouraging students to write about sensitive issues such deportation or kidnapping. Join me in creating and critiquing critical pedagogy with English Language Learners.

Suggested Questions:

1. How can teachers enact critical pedagogy when required to follow a state-mandated social studies and language arts curriculum?
2. How can teachers bring a critical pedagogy lens to writing personal narratives through Freire's Cultural Notebook process?
3. Which rights are most important to students who are recent immigrants?
4. What are the benefits and dangers for students, families, and teachers who "tell family stories" and inquire into injustices in their lives?

Texts, Tools, and Resources:

Students interviewed family members as primary resources. We examined all the Rights of the Child; many students focused on Article 10, "If you live in a different country than your parents do, you have the right to be together in the same place to maintain the parent-child relationship" and on other articles related to their rights as recent immigrants.

———————

I witnessed and experienced many injustices in the small, Southern town where I was raised, including child abuse, racism, and sexism. I often saw KKK members on street corners fully cloaked and handing out leaflets to spread their hateful propaganda. These things left an indelible mark. At the time, I didn't know about personal and civil rights. I just knew hateful things were being done to people in my community, to poor people, to African Americans, and to women and girls, including me. Over the past 2 decades, many Latin@ families have moved to north Georgia to fill the need for labor in poultry processing plants, carpet mills, and related industries. I see many parallels between the three generations of European American women from my family who worked in poultry plants and the mothers of my Latin@ students who work in similar plants. I also see parallels between my life and those of my students, who hope, as I did, to be first-generation college students.

Latin@ students are not faring well in the United States as a whole. The dropout rate is 17% for Latinos in U.S. high schools, more than twice as high as for non-Hispanic Whites (Pew Hispanic Center, 2009). I teach emergent bilinguals (García & Kleifgen, 2011) in a Title 1 middle school with a 99% free and reduced-price lunch rate. The school population has changed from mostly European American and some African American students a decade ago to its current demographics of 60% African American and 40% Latin@. Many of my students are first-generation immigrants, most from Mexico, El Salvador, Guatemala, and Bolivia. They live primarily in crowded mobile home parks and ride buses to a school nowhere near their neighborhoods. Due to high-population-density neighborhoods, they are statistically "urban students." However, unlike true urban students who benefit from public transportation, commercial centers, and cultural assets such as museums and libraries, my students are isolated, with not even a park or business in walking distance.

Unfortunately, the racism I witnessed toward African Americans during my childhood is now often directed at my Latin@ middle school students. I sense their disgust and paralysis in a local and national society that has positioned them as "illegal." I wanted to work with my students on these issues, and found in the Rights of the Child the critical content framework I needed. It was particularly helpful that those of us in the study group went into the classrooms using the Rights of the Child, as we provided support for one another.

For these reasons, I chose the Rights of the Child to teach my students how to recognize and name the injustices they witnessed and experienced. It was my hope that with the naming would come solutions and healing.

INQUIRING INTO THE RIGHTS OF THE IMMIGRANT CHILD

This inquiry project was a collaboration with my friends in the Rights of the Child Project and others dedicated to serving and educating children who come from economically impoverished homes. With them, I learned that there is transformative power in words, especially when students write their own stories and address oppression in their lives (Freire, 1970). I also had the benefit of working with Professor Ruth Harman and graduate student Mary Alvarez from the nearby university, who volunteered to record and work through the unit with me. With our Institutional Review Board approval in hand, we set out to educate the students about their rights and the rights of other immigrant students.

Planning with Paulo Freire

In my working-class family, there was little time to think about why people were in the situations they were in. Frankly, my parents and others like them were too exhausted from work to think of ways to systematically change the nature of an oppressive society. I am thankful for the hours they spent toiling for me to have an education, for now I have had the privilege to study educational theorists such as Paulo Freire and can make sense of larger issues such as human rights and how some groups have their rights denied. Likewise, examining my teaching practice critically and identifying the theories underlying my practice as well as the nature of society at large helps me to name oppressors and oppressed in order to arrive at transformative teaching and learning outcomes for myself and my students.

Paulo Freire, the Brazilian educator expelled from his country due to his radical (and successful) education of the poor, guided my work. Freire stated that teachers who delivered lectures turn students into receptacles to be filled by irrel-evant information. This pedagogy dehumanizes students. Freire argued instead for a shared inquiry between students and teacher,

> a pedagogy that must be forged *with*, not *for*, the oppressed (whether individuals or peoples) in the incessant struggle to regain their humanity. This pedagogy makes the oppression and its causes objects of reflection by the oppressed, and from that reflec-tion will come their necessary engagement in the struggle for their liberation. And in the struggle this pedagogy will be made and remade. (Freire, 1970/2000, p. 48)

Critical pedagogy is a humanizing teaching philosophy (hooks, 1994) in which students and teachers co-investigate their experiences in order to challenge and transform unjust social conditions. While "banking education" replicates the status quo by "depositing" information into students' supposedly empty minds, critical inquiry has the potential to transform students (and teachers) into agents of change who interrogate the interconnections among culture, language, power, and established institutions (Freire & Macedo, 1987; McLaren, 2009). English Language Learners and economically disadvantaged students perform better with teachers who practice a critical pedagogy (Zou & Trueba, 2002), which values stu-dents' culture, language, and experiences and seeks to interrogate and reveal the underlying power structures of society (Giroux, 2009). I employed Freire's vision of critical inquiry.

In addition to Freire's educational theories, I employed critical action research as a way of documenting and understanding human action and interaction. I teach my English Language Learners to become critical researchers who look deeply and critically into their lives and surroundings. Not only does this empower students and frame them as experts, but it is also an effective way to teach social studies, research, and literacy skills. Students research their own lives and write up their insights and findings. My student researchers, equipped with notebooks and pens, used interviewing and observation as they documented the Rights of the Child and how they applied or were denied in their lives.

Rather than prescribing a particular right for us to focus upon, I presented all the UN Rights of the Child to my students and let them choose those most pertinent to them. This selection process developed ownership of the project and motivated the students to investigate an area of personal interest—all within our required curriculum.

Situating the Rights of the Child Within the State-Mandated Curriculum

My "non-negotiable teaching contract" requires that I teach our state social stud-ies curriculum. In order to pass to the next grade level, my students must pass the same state-generated tests as other students, regardless of when they entered the country and began learning English. Therefore, I do teach the state curriculum and standards, yet I pay close attention to the academic, social, and emotional needs of my emergent bilingual students. Thus, I look for ways to connect the standards to the lives of my students in order to make learning meaningful.

The state social studies curriculum includes 18 enduring understandings (Wiggins & McTighe, 1998), global themes to encourage students to connect with issues in their lives, including:

Beliefs & Ideals: The beliefs and ideals of a society influence the
   social, political, and economic decisions of that society.
Culture: The culture of the society is the product of the religion,
   beliefs, customs, traditions, and government of that society.
Distribution of Power: This is a product of existing documents and
   laws combined with contemporary values and beliefs.
Individuals, Groups, & Institutions: The actions of individuals,
   groups, and/or institutions affect society through
   intended and unintended consequences.
Movement/Migration: Movement or migration of people
   and ideas affects all societies involved.
Production, Distribution, & Consumption: The production, distribution,
   and consumption of goods/ services produced by the society are
   affected by the location, customs, beliefs, and laws of the society.
Time, Change, & Continuity: While changes occur over time,
   there is continuity to the basic structure of that society.

These enduring understandings reflect a move away from "one right answer" instruction to critical thinking about social issues, patterns, and actions. Noting many connections between the enduring understandings and the UN Rights of the Child, I created a framework for critical inquiry consistent with our social studies standards.

Before we began, I worried that teaching about human rights might be difficult because rights are not tangible, not something new language learners can easily describe such as writing about a pet or a field trip or even about an event in history. Yet I quickly learned that even students with minimal English know about rights. Perhaps rights are intangible for children who have always enjoyed their rights. However, because many of my students have been denied certain rights they understood the seemingly abstract topic. For example, some of my students knew firsthand the value of clean water, since they remember when their villages in Central America got a community well. It was easy to connect their prior knowledge of gaining access to clean water to the enduring understanding of Scarcity, technological innovation, and distribution and to UN Article 24, which stipulates that children have the right "to safe drinking water."

Critical Inquiry: "Children Have the Rights to Have a House, Learn, and Have Fun"

We engaged in this inquiry during the 3 weeks leading up to state-mandated, standardized testing in the spring. During that time, students were confronted with banners in the hallways counting down the days until *The Test*. Everyone from students to teachers to administrators were on edge, and the pressure to do well on the high-stakes test took on a life of its own. My students knew that if they failed the test in 8th grade they would not graduate to high school. The pressure was on. No one wants to be 16 years old in middle school. I began the Rights of the Child inquiry to lessen the test-prep tension and to help my students think critically about big ideas. I did have to couch it in terms of test-prep on my submitted lesson plans.

Two classes of 7th-grade students and one class of 8th-grade students participated in the Rights of the Child inquiry. The unit lasted nine class sessions, interspersed with mandatory test-review lessons. Each day began with us viewing images projected on the board from a UNICEF photo essay on the Rights of the Child from their website (http://www.unicef.org/photoessays/30048.html). Students wrote and discussed what they saw in each photo. The purpose of this activity was to "stir up" students' thoughts and prior knowledge and to learn the vocabulary associated with the Rights. While discussing the photos, I read the description of the Rights as written on the photo essays. I paraphrased at times because the language was not always accessible. I also asked for volunteers to translate. When we were unable to translate, we referred to the Rights in Spanish, which I had printed out ahead of time.

I told the students, "On May 5, we will have a party to honor the Rights of the Child. I want you to help other people (adults and students) understand about your rights. To do this, you will choose a Right that is most important to you. You will write about this Right. Then, you will create a piece of art depicting this Right." To begin each class, and to get the students in the "Right" frame of mind, we looked at Internet images related to student rights. We discussed the image and co-wrote a summary of the image and how it related to the Rights. These short writing assignments, guided by mini-lessons on summarizing, provided a foundation for their longer essays.

A new student joined our class midway through the inquiry. I viewed this as an opportunity to assess how students were thinking about and understanding the Rights of the Child. I asked them to explain to our new student about the Rights, and several of them eagerly filled him in:

"Children have the rights to have a house, learn, and have fun."
"The Rights of the Child is to have a house, school, a bus, and a
     home with books."
"Children should have a school, food, water, and a house. They should
     not be drinking beer or sniffing glue and should not have guns."

Visiting graduate student Mary Alvarez led a mini-lesson on writing personal narratives. She told two stories from her own life. Students listened intently as Mary told us about how her parents (even though bilingual) didn't teach her Spanish on the bad advice of a teacher, denying her right to her home language (Article 30: "Minority . . . children have the right to learn about and practice their own culture, language and religion"). Her second story was about her brother-in-law, who was living without documents here in the United States because he didn't want to leave his wife and children, who are U.S. citizens (Article 10: "Families whose members live in different countries should be allowed to move between those countries so that parents and children can stay in contact, or get back together as a family"). The students were keenly interested because Mary's stories dealt with language discrimination and deportation—topics my students tell me they think about often. The students chose for Mary to write her brother-in-law's story. Mary did a think-aloud/write-aloud of her story, while I charted points on the board.

We then asked students to explain how the Rights of the Child applied to Mary's stories. This led to students discussing the Rights we'd been viewing and writing about. Each student then chose a Right that spoke to them, one they felt was important in their lives. Below is a summary of the articles from the Convention on the Rights of the Child and the students (all pseudonyms) who selected each:

> *Article 10:* If you live in a different country than your parents
>   do, you have the right to be together in the same place
>   to maintain the parent-child relationship. (Pepe, Isabel,
>   Emiliano, Yessenia, Jorge, Tania, Alex, Allie, George)
> *Article 12:* You have the right to give your opinion and for adults
>   to listen and take it seriously. (Jésus, Johnny, Margarita)
> *Article 15:* You have the right to choose your own friends and join or set
>   up groups, as long as it isn't harmful to others. (Emmanuel, Mary)
> *Article 16:* You have the right to privacy. (Lisa)
> *Article 19:* You have the right to be protected from being hurt and
>   mistreated, in body and mind. (Jessenia, Gabriela, Lisa, Elvira)
> *Article 30:* You have the right to practice your own culture,
>   language, and religion. Minority groups need special
>   protection of this right. (Maria, Yaneth)
> *Article 31:* You have the right to play and rest.
>   (Jaime, Alexander, Emiliano, Ian)
> *Article 33:* You have the right to protection from harmful
>   drugs and the drug trade. (Elisbeth, Juan)
> *Article 34:* You have the right to be free from sexual abuse. (Gabriela)
> *Article 35:* No one is allowed to kidnap or sell you. (Elvira)
> *Article 38:* You have the right to protection and freedom from war. (Donny)

For the remaining days of the inquiry, the students worked on this piece of writing through peer-editing and teacher conferences. Each class began with us looking at picture that invoked thoughts about rights of children. We chose each picture to launch into a mini-lesson about writing, either style or convention, then had writing and conferencing time. The classes ended with students and adults sharing the learning and writing that had occurred during the class period.

As a teacher, I had the luxury of two other adults (Mary Alvarez and Ruth Harman) in the room to conference with students. When students were not working with an adult or writing individually, they were working with a partner to figure out ways to improve their writing. Students added detailed language, descriptive terms, and transition words to their drafts with the help of adults or peers. The students who were newest to the country often worked with a bilingual peer and an adult. All the students seem to benefit from these one-on-one conferences with classmates and adults. Through reading their drafts aloud and answering questions about their writing, students developed more complete pieces. One student with a learning disability connected strongly with Ruth and looked forward to her arrival each day so they could work on his story. Both student and professor often looked surprised when the bell rang because they were so engaged in the writing.

Finally, the students typed their essays on our classroom computers, which also necessitated a few mini-lessons in word processing. Each student printed his or her writing and illustrated it by hand or with pictures found on the Internet. Our classroom transformed from writing lab to art room for the final few days of the inquiry.

Several girls who finished their essays and art began planning our party to inform quests and to celebrate the Rights of the Child. They created a large poster and rewrote the Rights in their own words. They also created and sent invitations for the celebration.

Connecting the UN Rights with Our Rights

"I like this class," remarked Jaime confidently, "because I feel smart in here and I say smart things."

Seventh-grader Jaime, who rarely talked in other classes, shared this thought with us during the final days of our Rights of the Child study. Other students made similar statements indicating that they felt empowered as they learned about their rights. They produced several essays with illustrations to depict how the Rights apply to their lives. Together, we categorized their writings according to which right they studied.

Jaime and two other boys wrote about the right to play. Sadly, many of my students have P.E. only one semester a year, due to scheduling constraints. We were deep in the "needs improvement" stage of school reform since we had never made Adequate Yearly Progress according to No Child Left Behind. Interestingly, these three boys were some of my newest arrivals to this country. Each had told stories about interacting with the land in their native countries. Emiliano, for example, had a farm; he was in charge of tending to most of the livestock. Ian lived in a rain forest and hunted iguanas daily in the jungle as a food source for his family. These boys missed being outside in nature and chose to identify a child's right to play for their projects.

Several of the students wrote about Article 10, which deals with a child's right not to be separated from his or her family. Almost all of my students are undocumented; those few who are documented have parents and/or siblings who are undocumented. There is a palpable and pervasive fear of immigration officials. Stories circulate in the community of friends, neighbors, and family members being picked up and deported. There is even a word in Spanish (*conagra*) denoting a raid on a poultry processing plant. The name comes from the poultry producing giant "Con Agra."

Elvira wrote about Article 35, a child's right to not be kidnapped. Elvira often gave us news reports on the large numbers of kidnappings in her native city of Juarez, Mexico. She recounted how kidnappers infiltrated her cousins' school, taking several children as hostages for ransom money. Donny, writing on Article 38, which protects children from war, told about how his family was on the losing side of the civil war in El Salvador. He told many sad stories of child soldiers and murdered family members.

The Rights of the Child unit engaged my students in real issues in their lives, built on their cultural and experiential knowledge, made the enduring understandings of the social studies curriculum alive and relevant, and led to increased quality and quantity of writing. I wanted to continue and extend this kind of critical pedagogy. Fortunately, I had the opportunity to teach many of the same students the following year in an every-other-morning "remedial" 55-minute period called Extended Learning Time. I would be able to teach literacy lessons of my choice.

YEAR 2: CRITICAL PEDAGOGY AND CULTURAL NOTEBOOKS

During the summer following the inquiry into the Rights of the Child, I realized that many family stories—those like the ones Mary Alvarez shared—are silenced due to fears of deportation. People living in the shadows of society do not have the same right to tell their family's story; it could cost them dearly. Yet my students needed a venue to tell important family stories, and our society needs to hear the stories. As Nieto (2002) explained,

> The major lesson that I would encourage teachers to think about is that curriculum and pedagogy can either reproduce the inequality with which students are confronted

every day, or they can have transformative power for both individuals and institutions. In the case of language minority students, using their language and culture, encouraging them to tell their own stories, and engaging them in critical discussions about the issues which are most important to them—whether these be about racism, the importance of their language, or the central role of family—can all lead to a pedagogy that uses students as experts rather than as walking sets of deficiencies. (p. 172)

Like Nieto, I wanted a curriculum with transformative power based on the students' language and culture.

Freire's Cultural Notebooks

To develop a transformative pedagogy, I turned again to Paulo Freire. Rather than viewing learners as deficient, Freire honored their home language, culture, and experiences, and used them as points of departure for teaching literacy skills. He encouraged students to read their worlds. As students "read" their worlds, narrating their lives, their teachers documented their words and local stories because ". . . the people should be the subject of the knowledge about themselves" (Freire & Macedo, 1987, p. 46). Teachers compiled the local histories and family narratives, bound them in Cultural Notebooks, and housed them in popular libraries, or ". . . a cultural learning center, and not just a silent depository of books . . ." (Freire & Macedo, 1987, p. 45). Cultural Notebooks became a crucial element of liberatory education in community literacy programs. I was struck by the connections to Article 29, students' right to education that respects "the values and culture of their parents."

As I developed a Cultural Notebook unit for the fall, I approached the process of writing Cultural Notebooks as a form of oral history research (although Freire and Macedo did not call it this). I saw oral history research as a critical approach to literacy that encourages students to be active historians. Oral history researchers attempt to understand specific aspects of participants' lives, such as an event, issue, time, or place, in relation to wider social contexts through narrative and ethnographic data collection techniques (Cole & Knowles, 2001). I taught my students to become oral history researchers, building on their interviewing and observational skills developed the previous year.

Most of my students and their families lived in the shadows of society. They were called illegal, aliens, undocumented. Many wouldn't even call 911 in an emergency for fear of deportation. There is no wall on the border commemorating the people who crossed into the United States the way we now celebrate immigrants who entered through Ellis Island. The Cultural Notebooks unit was for and about the stories of my students, wonderful young people full of promise, who are neither "illegal" nor "alien." They have names, families, and stories they will share with you in this chapter.

**Situating the Cultural Notebooks Unit Within
the State-Mandated Curriculum**

Just as I connected the Rights of the Child inquiry to the social studies enduring understandings, I wanted to situate the Cultural Notebooks within the state
English/language arts (ELA) standards. I realized during the Rights of the Child
inquiry that although I felt comfortable with teaching history and writing related
to historical events to my students, I needed to rethink how to teach narrative
writing. Instead of assuming that the students would know how to write dialogue,
for example, I realized that I needed to teach this skill explicitly.

Each year, the first few weeks of the middle school reading/language arts curriculum is devoted to writing narratives. Then, the curriculum shifts to another
genre. I wanted to slow down the state-mandated curriculum in order to maxi-
mize learning for my students. I wanted to allow my students the opportunity to
linger in the narrative genre, hoping for depth of literacy learning. I had the support of my principal, but I had to defend this choice on several occasions to our
literacy coach, who was unhappy that the students were not "further along."

I decided to devote half of the year to narrative writing and the other half to
informational writing. The class was made up of 6th-, 7th-, and 8th-grade emergent bilinguals. I followed the 7th-grade ELA/Writing Georgia Performance Standards; the 6th- and 8th-grade standards were very similar.

ELA7W2: The student demonstrates competence in a variety of genres.

The student produces a narrative (fictional, personal, experiential) that:

1. Engages readers by establishing and developing a plot, setting, and
   point of view that are appropriate to the story (e.g., varied beginnings,
   standard plot line, cohesive devices, and a sharpened focus).
2. Creates an organizing structure appropriate
   to purpose, audience, and context.
3. Develops characters using standard methods of characterization.
4. Includes sensory details and concrete language to develop
   plot, setting, and character (e.g., vivid verbs, descriptive
   adjectives, and varied sentence structures).
5 Excludes extraneous details and inconsistencies.
6. Uses a range of strategies (e.g., suspense, figurative
   language, dialogue, expanded vocabulary, flashback,
   movement, gestures, expressions, tone, and mood).
7. Provides a sense of closure to the writing.

The student produces *informational* writing (multi-paragraph expository composition such as description, explanation, comparison and contrast, or problem and solution) that:

1. Engages the reader by establishing a context, creating a speaker's voice, and otherwise developing reader interest.
2. Develops a controlling idea that conveys a perspective on the subject.
3. Creates an organizing structure appropriate to purpose, audience, and context.
4. Develops the topic with supporting details.
5. Excludes extraneous and inappropriate information.
6. Follows an organizational pattern appropriate to the type of composition.

From the standard, I devised a list of topics that I taught through a series of mini-lessons (see Figure 5.1). To illustrate these topics, we read several chapters of Paul Fleishman's *Seedfolks* as a mentor text. After discussing these chapters, the students worked in small groups to locate examples of the literary elements we were focusing on that particular day. For example, students found examples of sensory detail, metaphors, dialogue, and colorful adjectives. We kept a classroom notebook for these examples so the students could refer back to them when they were writing their own narratives. I also created a "narrative checklist" for students from these standards.

Early in the fall semester, we talked as a class about the function and importance of oral history within families and our society. The students fondly recalled hearing family stories and were eager to collect a story to share with the class. Each student interviewed a family member for a story that could be shared in class. Students then handwrote the stories and read them to a class partner. Next, the students honed their writing skills through a series of mini-lessons focusing upon what good writers do. Each time we studied a new literary element, such as plot development, dialogue, or creating believable characters, the students revisited their stories and identified the element in their stories. If the element was missing or needed work, the student revised. Some students illustrated or brought in pictures, and some translated the stories from either their native language into English, or from English into the native language.

The class ranged from newcomers to those who were born here. Thus, each was at a different speaking, reading, and writing stage. The first example is from a child who would be considered a newcomer. The first draft is written primarily in Spanish with a few words in English; the final draft is written in English (Figure 5.2).

Figure 5.1. Sample Mini-Lessons for Cultural Notebook Writing

Develops plot

Beginning
Middle
End

Creates an Organizing Structure

Chronological order
Cause and effect

Setting

Who
What
When
Why
How

Uses Descriptive Language

Sensory details
Colorful adjectives
Vivid adverbs
Beginnings and endings

Develops Character

- Physical
- Emotional

How? Detailed, vivid descriptions, dialogue, character's
thoughts, actions, reactions, and motivations, as
well as the reaction of other characters.

Uses Figurative Language

Similes
Metaphors
Personification

Develops Conflict & Resolutions

Human versus human
Human versus nature
Human versus self

Develops Complex Characters

Uses authentic dialogue

Figure 5.2. Newcomer's First Draft and Final Draft

Emilio Navarro   9-21-09 7

my   Aguelito   me   diso   que

La   llorono   salio

en   Mexico   y   los

Dogs.   te   nian   miedo

Because   gritaba   muy   resio

y   abuelo   ABentava   valasos

Para   que   sefuera

The Story of La Llorona Part Two [Final draft]

My grandfather told me that La Llorona left Mexico. My grandfather's dogs scared her by barking very strong. My grandfather also shot his gun in the air to scare her away. La Llorona never went back to Mexico.

—Emilio

The second story, a detailed accounting of the family's move to the United States, comes from a child who had been in the country for 2½ years. This is her final draft.

When We Came to the United States
I was nine or ten years-old when we started in Zitacuaro, México to go to the United States. Zitacuaro was a big city near my house. I was sad because I wanted to stay with my big sister, Esbeidy. She stayed behind.

We were twenty-five people who took a bus going to a town called Miguel Aleman to get another bus. Next, we got to another bus and eventually, we had to get off the bus for the night. The man who was taking us north took us to a hotel to stay the night. The next morning the man came to get us. We had to walk four hours. We had to cross the Rio Bravo in a little boat. I saw a crocodile. I was crying, because I was so scared.

We continued walking until we reached a town called Makalen. We stayed in an apartment that belonged to the people who were helping us cross. The next day, the man took us to a Chinese Restaurant. That was the first time I ate that kind of food. I thought it was weird, but I ate it and liked it. Then, we went to the park. It had a playground. This was my first time being in a park and on a playground. It was exciting! All my life I wanted to play on a playground. I played there with my sister. We spent the whole day in the park. At the end of that day, we went to another house to go to sleep.

The next day, we crossed into the United States. First, we went in a car for two hours. Then, we had to walk forty-two hours. I was so tired. My mom, who was pregnant, was tired, too. I wanted to sleep. I was also thirsty. They gave us a bag of food. Every two hours we had to drink water. It was in the summer, and it was so hard.

Everywhere I looked, there was just sand. I was scared!

I jumped over a little fence, and the thirty of us got in three cars. There were so many people packed in these cars! My sister was crying because a fat lady was sitting on her. Then they stopped and moved the woman. I was on top of everybody.

We were in those cars for 7 hours. It was so hot! Some men took all their clothes off, except their underwear. The man driving bought us some chips and soda at a gas station.

We went to another apartment to stay the night. The next day, my aunt, named Maria de Jesus, came to pick us up. I was so excited because all my cousins were there. They gave us a tour of stores. It was cool. We stayed at her house for eight months. Then, we came here to [this town]. That was three years ago.

By: Michelle O.

The last story comes from an 8th-grade student who was born in the United States and was poised to exit ESL. He wrote all drafts in English and published the final version with a hand drawing of the story's climax.

My Great Grand Pa
A story that my family tells is that my great grandpa, a tall and very thin man, went down to the city on horseback one evening. While he was in the city taking care of some business, it started raining. As a result, the river started to grow beyond its banks. My great grandpa decided that it was time to go home. When he got close to the river, the horse started acting different and scared. Right before crossing the river, the horse stopped and laid down. My great grandpa tried everything he could to make the horse cross the river. Still, the horse didn't move. My dad says my great grandpa got his gun out and *boom*! My grandpa got home alone as the horse floated in the river.
    —(Anonymous)

Once the students had completed their 24 family stories, we decided on the printing layout of our book. After reading all the stories, the students identified three global themes: families, scary stories, and migration. Within the theme of families, five of the stories were about grandfathers and five were about other family members. The next six stories were scary, several about the legendary Mexican legend of La Llorona. The final eight were about migration and the difficult choices families made to pursue better opportunities. The book included all the students' stories, some with their names, some "by anónimos." A university colleague printed multiple copies of the books.

The day of the celebration, the students stayed after school to help decorate the cafeteria, transforming it into an art gallery with student work taped to the walls. Local restaurants donated food, and we arranged the tables in front of the stage so that visitors could eat while listening to the students talk about their work. We also had a dessert station with two large sheet cakes that had the student-created party invitations grafted to the top in edible icing. Between the tables we made a small playground area for the youngest visitors; too many times parents feel forced to leave school functions to tend to their little ones who do not want to sit through presentations. Parents took advantage of this makeshift playground, complete with tumbling mats, games, and tents, and were able to listen to the entire ceremony as their little ones played. In addition to many family members eager to see the unveiling of our cultural notebooks there were professors, our superintendent, and even a music group composed of uncles of former students.

Juan, a Latino college student who mentors some of our students after school, led the program bilingually, addressing all members of the crowd, and explained the itinerary, which included a pre-party soccer match with university students and community members from 4:00 to 6:00. As people entered, they saw photographs of students in a PowerPoint slide show, heard music by local musicians Incatepec, and filled their plates. Juan introduced the ceremony and explained the purpose of the evening, which was to celebrate a year's worth of inquiry and writing by our students. Next, several students, along with Ruth and me, presented our cultural notebooks to the community. As we had just received the box of printed notebooks, we were excited to see the final book. The girls had written a poem about our work during the year, which we read as a group. We then informed the audience that after the ceremony, they would each get a copy of our Cultural Notebooks. They were, after all, from the community and for the community.

With the help of our emcee, I explained that next we would be playing a game called Passport. Each table set up in the back of the cafeteria highlighted some aspect of our work together. A student ambassador would be standing at each table to explain the work involved. Visitors would collect stamps at each table to fill up a paper passport. At the end of the evening, following dances and a history lesson, visitors with complete passports, those who had visited each table and spoke to student ambassadors, had the opportunity to win prizes that has been donated by local shops and businesses.

Several parents of students eagerly pointed out their student's work in our printed anthology. The students beamed with pride. I particularly enjoyed listening to one of the 8th-grade girls try her best to explain to the superintendent and his wife that the phantom La Llorona was real as she read her entry in our Cultural Notebook.

The first page of our anthology is my letter to family members, students, and other "Fans of Our ESOL students." It says, in part, "Stories have many purposes; they entertain, pass on vital information, educate and influence. Stories told within a family reinforce identity and heritage. After all, as our principal Mr. M often says, we are the stories we tell and retell." After explaining the interviewing, drafting, and revising processes, I showed how our work met the Georgia Performance Standards and also honored "the vast knowledge students and their families bring to school."

AN ENDURING UNDERSTANDING:
THE RIGHT TO TELL ONE'S OWN STORY

Working with the Rights of the Child encouraged my students to ask hard questions about enduring understandings of social studies, including distribution of power, human environmental interaction, and issues related to movement and migration. They came to new understandings of these big ideas in both in their own lives and the lives of others. From their study of the Rights of the Child, especially those related to the lives of recent immigrants and their families, and the enduring understandings, students were able to move the next semester to collecting, appreciating, and writing well-developed cultural narratives, honoring the voices of their families and recounting some of their immigrant experiences.

There is a raging, often rancorous, debate in the United States about human rights, specifically about the rights of immigrants who live in the shadows of our society. As I write, legislators are proposing rescinding the right to citizenship for immigrant children born in the United States to undocumented parents. At a time when such rights are under attack, it is more important than ever for students to study the Rights of the Child, and to write the stories of their families. Perhaps UNICEF should add Right 55: the right of children to tell their own stories. As Freire wrote,

> Human existence cannot be silent, nor can it be nourished by false words, but only true words, with which men and women transform the world. To exist humanly, is to *name* the world, to change it. Once named, the world in its turn reappears to the names as a problem and requires of them a new *naming*. Human beings are not built in silence, but in word, in work, in action-reflection. (Freire, 1970/2000, p. 88)

It is through this naming of the violation of the rights of undocumented people that we can envision and create a space for all voices and people, not just those with official documentation.

6

"I Need a New Way of Lyfe"

High School English Students Inquire
into the Right to an
Adequate Standard of Living

Lois Alexander

Invitation to Explore:
The Right to an Adequate Standard of Living

Initiating Experience:

> My inquiry started the day Adrian got kicked out of school. He left behind the echoing lines of his poem: *I cry out "I want to Change"/ I am a person who needs a/ New way of Lyfe.* Students in my 10th-grade collaborative Literature and Composition class were predominantly African Americans, with some Mexican and Cuban Americans and a few European Americans. We addressed some of the issues in their lives, including poverty, racism, and other forms of oppression, during an inquiry on poverty.

Formal Invitation:

> I invite you to think critically about poverty in relationship to culture, identity, and community and to explore the effects of poverty. Explore with us how poverty affects a community and how students read their world through responding to relevant literature, inquiring into local poverty conditions, and by nurturing their reflections on the world by writing about it. Raise issues about the potential risks, benefits, and ethical questions of asking students to evaluate effective and detrimental parenting—including their own. Join us in taking a critical approach to high school literature and composition.

Suggested Questions:

1. How do high school students inquire into the UN Rights of a Child as they pertain to issues of an "adequate standard of living" (Article 27) and "the right to education" (Article 28)?
2. What is the connection between critical thinking and critical inquiry?
3. What connections and disconnections do you make with the students you teach who are in special education? General education?
4. How can teachers create options for critical inquiries that give students genuine choice and maintain academic rigor?

Texts, Tools, and Resources:

Students gathered local newspapers, church bulletins, and photographs. We read novels, poetry, adult nonfiction, and political commentary, a history of the local African American community, and August Wilson's play *Fences*. We addressed Article 27, the right to "an adequate standard of living," and Article 28, "the right to education."

It was the beginning of the fall semester at Meadow Brook High School, a campus drawing students from many neighborhoods affected by poverty. The mini-lesson in writing workshop was on "I Am" poems. Adrian, an African American male, came through the door on time. On most days, he was tardy from hanging out in the bathroom, a haven for the weed smokers. His bloodshot eyes and wide grin were evidence of his early activity. Most of the time, he clowned around the room for a good 5 minutes before settling down to work. When he was absent from class, we missed him. We had come to love him, along with his impractical ways.

Acknowledging me with a smile, he slid into his seat, looking at the door and around the room. He gave Antwon, his best friend, a nod and asked about the assignment. After the mini-lesson, he silently wrote and every now and then looked up at the door. There was a knock and the assistant principal entered the room: She needed Adrian to come with her. Adrian stared at me as he pleaded with the assistant principal. "Please let me stay and finish. I am just about through." "No, you must come with me," the AP said firmly. " You can finish the assignment there and I will give it to Ms. Alexander."

This was the last time that I would see Adrian. When I walked to the office at the end of the day, I found Adrian's poem in my mailbox. I smiled as I read his poem. I couldn't wait to share it with the class.

The next day, Antwon came in eagerly, excited to tell me that Adrian wanted to know what I thought about his poem. I replied, "I love it. Please let him know that he can continue to write with us." I then shared Adrian's poem with my class.

I am a person who needs a new way of
    lyfe
I wonder where I will be 10 years 4rm
    Now
I hear a voice in the thin wind saying
    "U can do it"
I see another way but don't want to
    Take it
I am a person who needs a new way of
    Lyfe
I pretend to fit in and know the
    Fit
I feel I am getting older to represent
I touch the top of my goals
I worry that I won't change
I cry out "I want to
    Change"
I am a person who needs a
    New way of Lyfe
I understand that it's possible for me to change
I say I believe in myself
I dream that it's a nightmare
I try to keep focus
I hope I will be successful
I am a person who needs a new way of
    Lyfe

CRITICAL INQUIRY INTO CHILDREN'S RIGHTS: POVERTY AND RESILIENCE

In education, we strive to teach our students how to read their world (Freire, 1970). As a veteran African American teacher who grew up in circumstances similar to those of many of my students, I try to bring in the issues of students' lives, including poverty, racism, and other forms of oppression. I try to help students read their world through responding to relevant literature, inquiring into local issues such as poverty, and by nurturing their reflections on the world by writing about it. My goal is that by reading their world, students will learn to communicate effectively and become change agents in challenging issues of oppression. Adrian's writing showed his insights into himself and his world; his poem demonstrates remarkable resiliency for a student who knew he was about to be kicked out of school.

"I need a new way of lyfe" is a common phrase used in this community where poverty presents daily challenges.

In this chapter, I share the journey of my high school students as they read the word and the world in our critical inquiry into issues of poverty in our community as well as globally. This 10th-grade collaborative (general education and special education) Literature and Composition class was composed predominantly of African Americans, with some Mexican and Cuban Americans and a few European American students. Collectively, the group had many labels, none particularly positive. Further, the high school graduation rate for this county was the third-worst in Georgia, which has one of the nation's lowest graduation rates. Far fewer African American, Latin@, and poor and working-class students graduated than their European American and affluent peers.

The students and I addressed the UN Rights of the Child articles pertaining to an "adequate standard of living" (Article 27) and "the right to education" (Article 28). We inquired into issues of poverty, that is, the denial of an adequate standard of living, using the themes of identity, community, and culture, which are themes of the district's 10th-grade curriculum. I invited the students to spend a semester inquiring into the issues of poverty through multiple resources, including novels, movies, poetry, and Internet resources. This process allowed the students the opportunity to read the world and make connections in order to gain an understanding of their roles within their community, and how they co-exist in a society that oppresses some of its citizens.

For several years as the director of Red Clay's Project Outreach, I have explored ways to support the resiliency of students like Adrian by helping them take ownership of their learning. This chapter is divided into phases of the students' inquiry into defining what poverty is and how it influences their identity, culture, and community. I examine the revelation that many of the students would be considered to be living in poverty, question this revelation, and take a critical stance toward studying poverty. The tools I used to motivate student participation in the process, along with some of their work, are included.

Invitation: Thinking Critically about Poverty

The focus on issues of poverty grew out of the Red Clay's Project Outreach, which I directed, as well as a local focus on the complex issues of the county's high poverty rate. Our community had been involved in wide-ranging discussions about how to reduce poverty in an initiative called People for a Prosperous Athens (http://www.prosperousathens.org/about-ppa). This initiative generated a great deal of discussion in the newspapers and in various adult groups, so the timing seemed right to get students involved. I created the invitation (Van Sluys, 2005) (see Figure 6.1) and shared it with students. They could choose either this invitation or one on genocide. Eventually, we connected the two.

**Figure 6.1. Invitation: Thinking Critically About Poverty
as It Relates to Culture, Identity, and Community**

---

*"I write books to change the world. Perhaps I can only change one little piece of
that world. But if I can empower teachers and good citizens to give these children,
who are the poorest of the poor, the same opportunity we give our own kids, then I'll
feel my life has been worth it."*

—*Jonathan Kozol*

*"A genuine framework for understanding poverty prepares us to be change
agents . . ."*

—*Paul Gorsky*

You are invited to think critically about poverty in relationship to culture,
identity, and community and to explore the effects of poverty. How can we as
productive citizens help with the reduction of poverty?

Possible discussion questions:

1. How do we link culture and poverty reduction in our community?
2. Generational poverty: How do we stop the cycle?
3. What are some of the problems of the working poor?
4. What are living wages? How will living wages
   reduce poverty in a community?
5. What are the effects on identity in relationship to youth and culture?

Possible topics to consider:

1. Poetry, literacy, and empowerment for communities of poverty
2. "Responding to the values of the poor"
3. Generational poverty
4. Youth, identity, and culture

Resources:

1. The local newspaper online website
2. Forum: "Anti-poverty plan needs 'living wage'" by Ray MacNair
3. *A Story Untold: Black Men and Women in
   Athens History* by Michael Thurmond
4. *There Are No Children Here* by Alex Kotlowitz
5. *Schoolgirls* by Peggy Orenstein
6. *The Minds of Boys: Saving Our Sons from Falling Behind in
   School and Life b*y Michael Gurian and Kathy Stevens
7. *Sienna's Scrapbook: Our African American
   Heritage Trip* by Toni Trent Parker
8. *Protecting Young People Living in Urban Poverty Today and in the Future*
   http://www.unfpa.org/swp/2007/youth/english/story/preface.html
9. *Overcoming the Silence of Generational Poverty* by Donna M. Beegle
10. Talk to someone in your community about living in poverty
11. Web resources: www.onlineathens.com, www.prosperousathens.org, www.
    nydailnews.com, www.povertyinamerica.psu.edu, and www.heritage.
    org/research/reports/2004/01/understanding-poverty-in-america

The Poverty Inquiry learning center began with a focus on the students' communities: Students brought in obituaries of their family and friends, newspaper articles, church bulletins, and other items to show what the students valued in their community. A bulletin board displayed the quotes from the invitation, the essential question, and photographs students and I took of both positive and negative aspects of the community, e.g., a mobile home park where some of the students' playground is near a solid waste site, students playing in subsidized housing green spaces, the Boys and Girls Club, and the Eastside Community Center. The classroom library showcased the books listed on the invitation plus additional texts such as *Amazing Grace: The Lives of Children and the Conscience of a Nation* by Jonathan Kozol, and *The Working Poor: Invisible in America* by David K. Shipler.

The invitation generated some interest, but I knew I needed to help students get into the inquiry in ways that connected directly to their lives, as well as to explore poverty as a global issue. I decided to start with the Rights of the Child.

Hard Times: Culturally Conscious Learning About Poverty

Dre, an African American football player in dingy gray sweats and Eduardo, a Mexican American baseball player in jeans and a t-shirt with the school's insignia blazing across the front, entered the room, high-fiving each other while hastily moving to the back corner to sit near the window together as other students arrived. Joyce, an African American female who is trying out for the school's step team, has burgundy micro braids flowing over her shoulders; Rosa, a Cuban American female who is a member of JROTC, joins the duo in the back sitting near Dre. I started with whole-group discussion of Article 28: "All children have a right to be educated."

ME: All children have a right to learn . . .
DRE: We don't want that right.
ME: Why wouldn't you want that right?
STUDENTS: Because it's boring.
EDUARDO: Man, y'all need to turn around and be quiet.
ME: Eduardo, please go to the board and write the word *rights* on the board and put a circle around it. I want each student to associate the word *rights* to anything you know in your life.

The students were eager to share their connections. The word splash generated many words and phrases: Martin Luther King, vote, choose my own clothes, stay out late on a week night, choose my own friends, go anywhere, live or die, who I will marry, where I go to school, where I hang, be in a gang or not, religion. . . . The board was soon covered.

I seized the moment to introduce the Rights of the Child. The students viewed the UNICEF Convention on the Rights photo essay that introduced each article with photographs symbolizing the theme. After some discussion, we watched a video on the UNICEF Rights of a Child/Somalia. Somalia is the only country besides the United States that has not signed the Rights of the Child. The video showed children playing outside in shanties, garbage blanketing the ground along with discarded building materials. There were children in line for meals, flies gnawing on them as if they were carcasses while a soldier stood nearby with a gun. Children with skeletal frames were wandering down dusty roads.

My students engaged in a culturally conscious dialogue on why Somalia—and especially the United States—didn't adopt the rights.

DRE: You know they don't care about us . . .

JOYCE: You have to go through so many things to receive
    help. I know. I've been with my mother . . .

EDUARDO: We only got our neighborhood cleaned up when
    the Olympics came to Atlanta and Athens . . .

In the vignette above, the students revealed that they didn't want the "right" to a boring education, but they became quite engaged when the topic was important to them and they could get actively involved. This discussion seemed to move many students emotionally; they learned a new perspective on the plight of children around the world and began to consider degrees of impoverishment. Sonia Nieto (1999) pointed out that culture is not a static condition, but is evolving and multifaceted. Likewise, poverty is not a static condition; it, too, is multifaceted, and is constantly evolving based on social and political conditions. My students needed to inquire into different cultures to gain an understanding of the many faces of poverty and the social and emotional issues raised as poverty evolves in various cultures. I call this phase of the inquiry "culturally conscious learning."

During this phase of the inquiry, students looked at the politics, religion, social class, race, and gender of the people in an impoverished country (Somalia) and tried to understand how the people felt about their situation. In the UNICEF video, one child asked, "Other children around the world have rights—why don't we?"

The next step was to facilitate the students in connecting to their own community. The students continued their search via books, interview transcripts, and online journals to learn about rights allowed students in other countries. To better understand the local community, the students studied parts of *A Story Untold: Black Men and Women in Athens History* by local author and political leader

Michael Thurmond (2001). This book opened the students' eyes to local African American history, education, religion, and politics. In culturally conscious learning, it is imperative that students see themselves in the books that they are reading. Harris (1993) stated,

> An argument can be made that the culturally conscious books are essential for African-American children specifically and for all children generally.... If African-American children do not see reflections of themselves in school texts or do not perceive any affirmation of their cultural heritage in those texts, then it is quite likely that they will not read or value schooling as much. Children need to understand the languages, beliefs, ways of life, and perspectives of others. White children and other children of color need to read African American literature because notions of cultural pluralism are becoming more important as cultural, economic, and geographical barriers are eradicated. The task confronting educators, then, is to provide all children with opportunities to hear, read, write about, and talk about literature, especially literature that affirms who they are. (p. 180)

Thurmond's book sparked a great deal of interest. I asked students to look for church bulletins, newspaper articles, magazines about Athens, and anything else they could find where they could see themselves in the information.

As we talked about Article 27, students questioned what an "adequate standard of living" meant. The article says, "Children have the right to a standard of living that is good enough to meet their physical and mental needs. Governments should help families and guardians who cannot afford to provide this, particularly with regard to food, clothing and housing." Eduardo tried to make meaning of this definition in his own life.

EDUARDO: Does poverty means we don't have food, clothes, and a home . . .
ME: No, it means that you don't always have enough money to
    pay for those things. You know, when your mama says we
    got to stretch the dollar or wait to the next pay period?
ALL: Yeah, I know what you mean.
JOYCE: So this means that my parents lived in
    poverty? Why didn't they get out?
ME: Like many of you, your parents didn't call it living in poverty. They
    may have called it having "hard times." (The children nodded in
    agreement.) I want you to continue looking for ways people are
    affected by poverty. If you have any questions about poverty, write
    them down to share later with your group. For example, we can talk
    about foods we eat because of not having enough money. When I
    was growing up, my mother would cook breakfast food for dinner. I
    remember one night sitting around the table and we asked, almost in
    unison, "Why are we eating breakfast for dinner?" The hurt expression

on my mother's face told the story as she silently walked away. Now
what are some of the foods you have when grocery money's tight?
DRE: Bologna sandwiches.
JOYCE: Hey, any kind of sandwiches—tomato, mayonnaise.
EDUARDO: *Frijoles!* A lot of rice and beans.
DRE: Kool-Aid when you can't buy drinks. No-name drinks.

The initial inquiry into poverty allowed the students to think about their own lives in a community with one of the highest poverty rates in the nation. Most people don't say that they live or grew up in poverty. I really didn't understand that other people saw my family as poor until my childhood friend Porscha told me. She explained that her mother would allow her to play with me, but no other "project children." I questioned Porscha about the statement. She replied, "Only poor people live in the projects." This was an epiphany for me because I didn't know that other people thought that it was awful to live in government housing.

As students explored resources to find anything they could on poverty and their community, Tanya, a shy African American student, found an article online: "How Poor Are America's Poor? Examining the 'Plague' of Poverty in America" compiled by the U.S. Bureau of the Census. She called out, ecstatic, "Ms. Alexander, I found Clarke County where we live and our information."

Other students looked at Tanya's information and complimented her. Rosa, a recent immigrant, turned and looked at Tanya. "Keep looking, Tan, you're doing great! See if you can find something about my people."

The last 20 minutes of class, students reflected in writing about their experience. Jason wrote the following, referring to his brothers, who were incarcerated:

When you don't have anything to say
Sometimes I don't know what to do when I just
    start thinking about stuff in my life
no future
Sometimes people ask me do I care about anything?
Sometimes I say yes, because there is something inside that makes you.
I can't take my problems out on the whole world
So I just chill with my brothers
'Cause I won't see them until I am about 39 or 40 years old
So that is another monkey on my back.

On the other side of the room, an African American student wrote,

My name is CiCi and I am a young mother who has a very tough life. During my pregnancy, it was very hard. I never knew how I would make it by being so young with a baby but I always kept God as my right hand man and made it through it all. I answered all of my own questions by staying in school and making something out of my life, and I figured that's how I'm going to make it for me and my son. But as each day go by, it is not easy because every day we live in poverty . . .

Jacqueline's reflection was both personal and poetic.

Poverty why do you hurt so many people?

Generational

Family or survivor

Living wages

Not enough money

Teen pregnancy

People are getting infected

Poor health

People are dying.

The students now seemed deeply invested in their inquiry into the nature of poverty. They were making connections to their lives, and at the same time seeing poverty as a global issue. They had no idea where their inquiry would take them, and neither did I.

"We Need a Better Question": Inquiries Lead to More Questions

I wonder if his mother is going to die. It's not fair that she has to go and clean her own bed after waiting four days to receive help from the doctor! What kind of world do we live in? Life just isn't fair.

—Dre

Dre is reading *Amazing Grace* by Jonathan Kozol. He is sitting on top of the desk with Jacqueline, Rosa, and Joyce nearby. He continues to read with his iPod draped around his neck, no earplugs in his ear, just reading. Rosa and Jacqueline are looking at the Internet research information to choose writings that are related to generational poverty, while Joyce is writing a poem about a girl living in the streets. At this point, she has written three stanzas and doesn't quite know which way to go. I quickly walk over to see why she has stopped writing.

JOYCE: This is very hard.
ME: Why?
JOYCE: It seems so real. I have so many problems with girls, my hair, and just life. Ms. Alexander, you just don't know how girls get together

and just keep up this mess about boys. They're supposed to be your
best friend, and when spring rolls around, they come up pregnant
with your boyfriend's baby, just baby mama drama. They don't
have a job because they are living day to day just to get by.

ME: What would you like to say to the girls?

[Joyce puts her head on her desk. Pulling on her burgundy braided
weave, she looks in my face, stress showing in her pleading eyes.]

JOYCE: You mean I can put stuff like that in my poem?

ME: Yes, it needs to be real.

[Joyce begins to write:]
An African-American female,
In the streets
Doing Nothing
A life time
Can anyone afford it?
In the streets
No jobs, no life
Can God make a way?
How are they going to afford it?
In the streets
Umm! I wonder!
It's time to make a change
What's wrong with these people?
In the streets
Stop! People
You can have a wonderful home
Make a change in your life.

Joyce incorporated an incident in her life that affected her identity within her
social community of female peers as she explored the connections between poverty, teen pregnancy, and her friends. Once she made this connection, her writing
flowed. Culturally conscious learning—explicitly connecting learning to her cultural influences—allowed Joyce to connect in substantive ways.

Having resources available is critical for students to make personal connections and share their inquiry with students with similar interests. As the students
pulled together information, they shared, questioned, discussed, and reflected.

DRE: You know this is crazy. They have teddy bears and flowers
on the street where people have died. . . . Can you imagine
sleeping on the floor afraid of bullets? Now they are giving
out needles to druggies on different time shifts.

JACQUELINE (a Mexican American student): What is your question?
DRE: How could the world get so bad?
JACQUELINE: We need a better question. What happens to
    a community when the government allows drugs to
    flow freely and assists people with needles?
DRE: I don't know, but I'll keep reading . . .

Inquiries are addictive. Students eagerly kept searching because they wanted to know more. This is the essence of the invitational process of inquiry. Dre brought in the other members of his group by reading orally in disbelief. Students worked independently by gathering data, synthesizing the data, and sharing the data with other members of the group. When the students came across information that piqued their curiosity, they created questions to continue the research. As students researched and questioned their findings and shared information, the suspense wrapped itself around all of us.

Fences: A Dramatic Connection

Students had been reading August Wilson's play *Fences*, and I wanted them to examine some of the themes in the play in relation to their inquiries. We talked for a few minutes about Cory, who wanted to play football in the play, and about his father, Troy.

ME: Today, we are going to look at our parents' role in the family.
    We will address both sides. How many of you know a family
    where there is only one parent in the household?
[Most of the African American students are
    waving their hands energetically.]
ME: How many of you know of a single-parent household where the
    father is not present and there is not a relationship with the father?
[Again, most of the African American students' hands are raised.]
ME: We are going to draw a large T on the board to analyze
    what makes a good and bad parent. First we are going to
    look at the good side of parenting. What are they?
DRE: A provider!
ME: Of what?
JOYCE: Food, money, clothes, a lot of stuff.
DRE: Protector.
ME: Of whom?
DRE: Family, wife, children, uncles, aunts, and anybody in our family.
EDUARDO: Loving and caring.
JACQUELINE: Problem-solver, somebody you can tell your problems.

EDUARDO: A good listener.

ME: Okay, let's go to the other side. What makes a bad parent?

JACQUELINE: Child abuse!

ME: What do you mean?

ROSE: Sexual abuse.

DRE: Beating and cussing you out.

JOYCE: Selling the food stamps and then there's no food.

EDUARDO: Homelessness.

ME: But what if they lost their job? Does that make them
    a bad parent?

DRE: Sometimes, yes, because they won't get up and go to work.

The students by this time were yelling additions to the list. I stopped the brainstorming and moved to their own analysis. "Now, we are going to address the character Troy and his role as a parent. You may have a partner, but both of you must have equal input."

The students used the "T" format to analyze Troy's attributes as a good parent/bad parent. Most of the students identified Troy with physical abuse because he swings a bat at Cory to intimidate him. Most did not understand why Troy refuses to allow Cory the right to play football. At this point, they had not connected to Troy's perception of his world. Dre wrote,

> Troy knows how important it is for Cory to play football. All fathers know this. Times are not like they use to be when he was a boy. He is just pushing Cory away from him and he is going to leave and never come back.

The students' connection to Cory in the story demonstrated a strong interest in issues of parenting and how time, place, and culture influence parental decisions. Dre and Eduardo identified with Cory because of their sport affiliations, as well as having similar economic issues at home. However, they did not understand Troy's decision to make Cory quit the football team and return to his job at the grocery store. They identified with Cory so much that they didn't give credence to Troy's fear that Cory's dream of playing college football would be squelched, just as Troy's dream of playing major league baseball was. Troy was in the Negro Leagues but never got a chance to play in the Major Leagues because he was too old when Major Leagues began accepting Black players.

To help students see the complexity of parenting, I posed some questions: What did you learn from deconstructing the role of Troy and issues of poverty? Did you see changes in Troy, changes in the relationship between Troy and his son, or changes in the way you viewed the role of poverty in the plot? Students used a graphic organizer to chronologically trace these issues. I asked them to analyze whether Troy had changed by the end of each act. If the character had changed, they had to explain why. They used the organizer to record direct and indirect traits, as well as supporting quotes. They then wrote a character sketch of Troy using the chart.

The analysis led to many spirited discussions between partners. At the end of the class, the students shared their insights.

DRE: Troy cares about his family. He cares too much that he won't let
    Cory play football because he is afraid Cory will be just like him,
    playing full of hopes, but suddenly blocked and feeling helpless.
EDUARDO: Troy's got too much mouth. It's a wonder he didn't get
    Bono in trouble, too.
DRE: He's just like my daddy . . .
ROSA: We like this story.
ME: Why?
ROSA: Because it's just like us.

The next day, the students wrote about Troy and his connection with his world and family. Students who normally struggled to write seemed to connect to the issues in *Fences*. Dre brought the issue of making it in the competitive world of college sports into poetic form as he wrote about a friend.

Young John

With the local football club he plays under fourteen
In their football colors the blue, orange and white
He dreams of the NFL and how he will start one day
Against Georgia's finest he will be picked to play.

Every time I see young John he's with the egg shaped ball
Playing by himself or with other boys in the jungle and for his age he is big
His dream is to play as number one for Ohio State his favorite team
Enjoying a great victory as he sings the Club song.

Most boys of his age have a wish or a dream
To win a gold medal or play with a top football team
But not all dreams do come true everyone can't know fame
Still it is nice to dream of great things just the same.

He is at the top of his football team
And as a player of promise he knows local esteem
But few good juveniles grow into great players
And young John he still has a long way to go.

Throughout the semester students wrote essays and poetry during writing workshop. Each student also chose a poet and created a poet study, explaining why they chose the poet and his or her style of writing, how they used poetic devices in their work, and how they incorporated those devices in their own work. Through their reading and writing of plays, poems, essays, and a variety of informational texts on issues of poverty, students for the most part stayed engaged throughout the semester. How, I wondered, could I help them bring this sweeping inquiry together?

BRINGING IT HOME:
LEARNING PROJECT OPTIONS AND EVALUATION

I created a Tic-Tac-Toe format to allow students to demonstrate and connect what they had learned in their inquiries (see Figure 6.2). Working in groups, they could choose any three squares on the Tic-Tac-Toe menu; however, they all had to go through the center square because a major focus of the 10th-grade curriculum was on persuasive writing. Of course, some students wanted to choose an option that wasn't a straight line, so I let them maneuver throughout the Tic-Tac-Toe and included another option: "Design your own performance task." I made sure students had daily writing workshop time and instruction to fully develop a persuasive paper and all the other learning products in the Tic-Tac-Toe. I helped them create a schedule of everything they were responsible for doing.

The students were excited about the final project. All of them wanted to do the multimedia presentation, an electronic portfolio. It was much easier to manage a project of this magnitude when students found common ground; we were able to do several targeted lessons on designing and presenting e-portfolios. Dre's group chose to go down the middle of the Tic-Tac-Toe. They completed a PowerPoint

Figure 6.2. Tic-Tac-Toe Learning Projects

Design an End-of-Course Test	Anthology of Poems on Poverty	Scrapbook
Visual Display	Persuasive Paper	Community Project
Photo Essay	Illustration on Poverty/ Political Cartoon	Multimedia

presentation with an anthology of poems completed throughout the semester. They each wrote a persuasive essay addressing different themes in *Fences*. Each also created a political cartoon. I was disappointed that none of the children chose the community project. However, they did say that they would speak with a group of teachers who were working on similar projects.

We developed rubrics that helped guide the development as well as evaluation for each kind of project (see Figure 6.3). Although the point values and ranges of projects varied, we used a consistent definition for evaluation:

5   *Excellent:* Quality of work exceeds target
    (above and beyond requirements)
4   *Good:* Quality of work somewhat exceeds target (all requirements met)
3   *Fair:* Quality of work meets target (missing one requirement)
2   *Needs Improvement:* Did not meet target
    (missing more than one requirement)

"I'M NOT AFRAID BECAUSE I LEARNED SOME THINGS": SHARING EXPERIENCE

It's Saturday, and my student Chad and I are driving to JoBeth Allen's house to talk with the Rights of the Child teacher study group.

ME: How do you feel?
CHAD: I'm straight. I'm not afraid because I learned some things.
ME: What are you going to share?
CHAD: I am going to share my essay on Black on Black crime
    as a form of genocide and how it relates to poverty.
ME: Why is this so important to you?
CHAD: Well, when I was younger in my neighborhood, I saw these two
    men hugging each other in Red Spruce apartments and I didn't
    think anything about it. But what was actually happening, one of the
    men shot the other. That bothered me for a long time to see another
    person get shot. I told my mother what had happened. I couldn't
    sleep at night thinking about the blood and what had happened.
ME: Wow, I can't wait to read your paper. We're here.
    Let's go inside. I have your back and if you don't feel
    comfortable sharing something, don't share it.
CHAD: I'm not afraid. Let's go.

Chad first read some of the other students' poems and essays. He then read his essay on Black on Black crime as it relates to poverty and genocide.

Figure 6.3. Evaluation Form for Learning Projects

Visual Display (25 Points)	Points Earned	Comments
# of slides (15 required) (15 points)		
Layout (5 points)		
All Elements Present (5 points)		
Total:		

Speaking (15 Points)	Points Earned	Comments
Volume (5 points)		
Pace (5 points)		
Posture (5 points)		
Total:		

Requirements: Students will present a 3- to 5-minute PowerPoint or Photo Story presentation reflecting the themes explored throughout the semester: culture, identity, and community in conjunction with poverty. The reflections should reveal the inquiry process and thoughts on different themes. During your presentation, you must speak clearly and not too fast or slow so that everyone can understand what you are saying. The volume of your voice must not be too loud or too low. The tone must be appropriate, and no laughing unless it is appropriate. Do not stand in front of the display.

Poetry & Essay (60 points)	Points Earned	Comments
Narrative Poem (10 points)		
Question Poem (10 points)		
Two-voice Poem (10 points)		
Other Poems (5 points)		
Poet Study (10 points)		
Essay (15 points)		
Total:		

He answered many questions from teachers who were both interested and impressed. As we walked out to my car, he said, "Imagine me sitting with all those teachers and talking. It wasn't bad at all. I really kind of felt special."

Chad earned a 95 for the semester. He also exceeded the target on the Georgia High School Graduation Test. All students except one passed the state writing test.

For the final exam, each group presented their e-portfolio. Dre's group presented parts of their Tic-Tac-Toe projects. Dre read first:

> I am from Lake Oconee and vegetable gardens,
> To cement playgrounds and hanging out.
> I am from the bling bling on my neck,
> To the old Michael Jordans on my deck.
> I'm from a room with Martin Luther King Jr's picture on the wall,
> To a dusty grey fan about to fall . . .

That day, my students demonstrated growth in critical thinking, inquiry skills, and writing abilities. It no longer mattered that it was a collaborative class whose students had many labels attached to them. Only two students had incomplete projects. The culturally conscious discussions, analysis, and writing reflected in the final projects led students to insights about "hard times" in their own lives and issues of poverty in their community. We had addressed many of the Rights of the Child in our inquiry into poverty, but it was Article 28 that I came back to as I listened to my students. "All students have the right to an education"—a meaningful education, connected to their lives. Still, I had a nagging question in the back of my mind. Paul Gorsky (2007) "spoke" all semester from our bulletin board invitation: "A genuine framework for understanding poverty prepares us to be change agents . . ." (p. 19)

Were my students prepared?

FROM SCHOOL PROJECTS TO CHANGE AGENTS

It is the spring of 2009, and the group returns to work with me during an after-school program. Cindy and Jason, who are African Americans, and Maurice, a Caribbean American, had joined the group. We are discussing how the school will celebrate Black history. The students are accustomed to the traditional "bring our dead ancestors back to life" programs, but I ask them to brainstorm other ideas and share with a partner.

Maurice sits down by my desk to have a private conversation. He is a senior this year and wants to leave a legacy behind to benefit other students. He is tall and slim with a wide Afro. Many days he wears suits to school because he wants to attend Morehouse College in Atlanta. He wants to be a "Morehouse Man" like his uncle, one of Maurice's many mentors.

I introduce Maurice to Dre, who is excited about the upcoming program and intrigued with Maurice.

> DRE: Man, where are you from? You kind of speak differently.
> MAURICE: I am from the Virgin Islands. I don't speak differently. I have an accent.
> DRE: The earthquake hit your country!
> MAURICE: No, the earthquake hit a neighboring country, Haiti.
> DRE: Well, all of you guys live in the Caribbean Islands?
> MAURICE: No, but we are a part of the United States and Haiti is an independent country who was once under the French rule. The people there speak French. But I do feel for the people there because they might lose their identity if a more powerful country comes in to bring their own influences.
> DRE: I know what you mean. We studied identity last year with Ms. Alexander when we studied impoverished communities.
> MAURICE: That's Haiti, one of the poorest Third World countries in the world. Man, they have lost everything.
> DRE: You know, if we came up with a question about how Haiti could retain its own identity, we could do a tribute to Haiti!
> MAURICE: Nah, they want to do the traditional program, remember Martin Luther King, Harriet Tubman, and others. They wouldn't want to pay a tribute to Haiti.
> DRE: Yes, we can. We did it before with invitations last year. All we have to do is issue an invitation to everyone to explore Haiti and how we can serve them. Ask Ms. Alexander.
> ME: Dre and Maurice, I think it would be a great idea to inquire into Haiti and how they can maintain their own identity. How would this relate to the rights of children in Haiti? Dre, explain to Maurice about the Rights of the Child Project we started last year . . .

Dre was ecstatic to share with a senior his experience with the UN Conventions on the Rights of a Child. That day, Dre and Maurice connected to create an invitation to the group to inquire about the rights of children in Haiti.

I thought back to Adrian, and how he had pleaded for a new life: "I try to keep focus/I hope I will be successful/I am a person who needs a new way of/Lyfe." Critical inquiry is a new way of life for many students like Adrian, Dre, and their classmates. It is the promise of a meaningful education, one that engages with the issues of a complex and troubled world. Students like Dre and Maurice might "change one little piece of that world" (Kozol, 1996).

7

Becoming Thrice-Born

10th-Grade History Students Inquire into the Rights to Culture, Identity, and Freedom of Thought

Paige Cole

Invitation to Explore:
The Rights to Culture, Identity, and Freedom of Thought

Initiating Experience:

"I don't believe in religion. I just believe in science because it can somewhat prove what religion can't." Alex shared this belief in the 10th-grade U.S. History class I teach in a culturally diverse, rural, Title 1 school. In creating a dialogic classroom where students take a critical stance toward history and culture, I created learning opportunities reflecting issues of identity and freedom of expression in the Rights of the Child.

Formal Invitation:

I invite you to explore Srinivas's concept of becoming "thrice-born": First, we are all born into our natal culture; second, we explore the lives of others and absorb other culture's ways of being; and our third birth comes when we reflect on our natal culture through new lenses developed from learning in or about other cultures. Join me in thinking about and critiquing our first, second, and third birth processes, as we engaged in Culture Pie, the Culture Project, the *Maus* Project, and other ways of being reborn.

Suggested Questions:

1. How can we help students understand their own cultural influences, especially those students who say, "I don't have a culture"?

2. How can students learn new cultural perspectives from each other in a multicultural classroom?
3. In what ways are my students alike and different from those in this rural, Title 1 high school?
4. How do Web 2.0 technologies support critical inquiry into culture and identity?

Texts, Tools, and Resources:

Families were a primary resource for learning history and culture. The graphic novel *Maus* was a common text; we also studied history texts, historical memoirs, and Internet resources. We addressed Article 8, "preservation of identity"; Article 12, "respect for the views of the child"; Article 13, "freedom of expression"; and Article 14, "freedom of thought, conscience and religion."

———————

I teach in a school that is going through a perpetual identity crisis. We are located in a rural community that is becoming an exburb, absorbed by the suburbs of Atlanta. Many parents of our students commute to work, as do 40% of our teachers, from surrounding towns and suburbs. Our school is not in the center of a town, but off the side of a highway, a highway that symbolically divides the county. The other county high school is steeped in traditions and hometown rituals; we are steeped in transience.

My school is the new school in an old town with a lot of "good old boys." We are a Title 1 school, though the poverty is not as obvious or as concentrated as the poverty of a city school. Many of my students are new arrivals to this community. Some fled the Rust Belt states with their families in search of better jobs while others fled genocide in Southeast Asia or oppressive poverty in Latin America. I teach in the town where Barbara Kingsolver's fictional missionary family originated in *The Poisonwood Bible*. Many of my students are very religious and openly proclaim their love for Jesus; others sit quietly because their shamanistic beliefs do not conform to the mainstream in this highly evangelical community. I'm a European American woman who has explored many religions and claimed none.

I teach 10th-grade U.S. History, general as well as Advanced Placement classes. It can be unnerving to teach historical topics that are still controversial and shape the modern political landscape, such as the Vietnam conflict and *Roe v. Wade*. I used to get rattled when I heard some students' views on issues such as the wars in Iraq and Afghanistan, immigration, and gay rights. The narratives that my students often bring to class are powerful and shaped by forces that I do not always understand or agree with.

As a history teacher, I wanted to include the widely differing and sometimes conflicting beliefs and cultures of my students, and to examine history in light of differing beliefs and cultural norms, but I struggled with how to go about creating the kind of dialogic classroom I valued. Joining the Red Clay Rights of the Child Project gave me a pathway, a critical content framework. Article 8 (Preservation of identity) and Articles 12–14 (Respect for the views of the child; Freedom of expression; and Freedom of thought, conscience, and religion) emphasize that young people must be allowed to form their own views and express not only their views but their identities freely. As I moved forward in my attempt to truly see and hear students, I looked to these rights to help me create a classroom environment that valued students' thoughts and identity while guiding them to listen and act from a place of respect toward others. I thought that if students and I began to question why and how our views were shaped, we might learn to respect how others came to be as well.

In this chapter, I report on my ongoing endeavor to create a dialogic classroom with my 10th-grade U.S. History classes. I asked students to interpret history through their own cultural lenses; to disentangle what they saw from the voices of power, including my own; and finally, to try to understand the perspectives of others.

BECOMING THRICE-BORN

As I began my fifth year of teaching, the concept of becoming thrice-born espoused by Indian anthropologist M. N. Srinivas intrigued me as a way to organize the year with an emphasis on understanding issues of culture and identity within the classroom. Srinivas, theorizing what happens when anthropologists and others do field work in a culture different from their own and then return home, described a process of becoming "thrice-born." First, we are all born into our natal, or native, culture. Our second birth comes as we explore the lives of others in another culture(s). What may have initially seemed strange eventually becomes part of the way we understand the world; we absorb other cultural ways of being. The third birth comes when we "come home" and look at our native culture through new lenses. In this third birth, our natal culture has the potential to be transformed.

This structure appealed to me because I look at studying historical lives as being strongly related to the cultural or ethnographic work of anthropology. This work has the potential to increase understanding; however, one has to go through the processes of understanding how the past has a hold on us to see if we are just coping or instead moving toward the kind of learning that can come from consciously examining the way we see or are situated in the world.

While I was thinking about Srinivas and the way his ideas related to the work we do in my classroom, I was struck by connections with the UN Rights of the Child. My interest was piqued when I read Desmond Tutu's words about the inspiration behind the Rights.

During the Vietnam War, we were shocked by a picture that flashed around the world. It was of a young Vietnamese girl running and screaming. She was naked and ablaze, the victim of a napalm bombing. The picture captured the ghastliness of war and showed dramatically that the vast bulk of victims of war were innocent unarmed civilians, mainly women and children and the elderly—totally unacceptable targets of the weapons of death and destruction even if they were camouflaged as "collateral damage." (Tutu, 2001, p. ii)

The picture Desmond Tutu referenced is one I show every semester in my U.S. History course. I am always taken aback by how deeply this image shocks my students and seems to touch their humanity. I have never known exactly how to channel the disbelief my students feel into productive action. However, I began to see how the Rights of the Child and Srinivas's ideas about being thrice-born could be married to facilitate a series of explorations into issues of identity and culture that could lead to possible action.

The United States has not passed the Rights of the Child initiative, and a fierce debate recently erupted between competing political factions. In promoting a politically charged initiative like the Rights of the Child, I would run the risk of alienating students, many of whom are from political communities that look at the United Nations with suspicion if not outright hostility. Taking my cues from Paulo Freire (1970), I believed that I "cannot expect positive results from an educational or political actions program which fails to respect the particular view of the world held by the people" (p. 95). If I promoted an authoritative discourse, whether it was progressive or conservative ideologically, I ran the risk of stifling discussion.

I also knew that if I wanted students to see the importance of guaranteeing rights to children around the world, I could not do this by just talking "at" them. Vygotsky (1986) believed that it is futile to try to teach discrete concepts devoid of context; at best, students will only parrot back information in a charade of learning. Tolstoy likened it to teaching a child to walk by teaching them the laws of equilibrium. Despite fear-mongering rhetoric that says otherwise, deconstructing and co-constructing knowledge is not intended to indoctrinate but instead serves to problematize the world we live in. Problematizing is not intended to tell students their beliefs are wrong, but instead creates a space where diverse people can engage in dialogue. Until a dialogue becomes internally persuasive or the words becomes *theirs* and *mine*, we operate from very different worlds, where I pretend to teach and students pretend to learn. We began our quest to become thrice-born with the Culture Project, a way for students to examine their natal cultures.

FIRST BIRTH: LOOKING AT OUR OWN CULTURES

On the first day of school, students brought in their summer assignment, a written account of their life story. This assignment's purpose was twofold. First, this was to be their narrative of the way they saw their life. Students could share this with the class if they chose, but most turned them directly into me. I read the stories, which also gave me greater insight into the young people. I gave them feedback but did not give them their papers back. I learned that I had students from Laos, Moldova, and Turkey, as well as South and Central America. I also saw that many of my students were deeply religious and had documented the date they were saved. I kept their stories to give back at the end of the year so they could see their personal growth. Second, we used the life stories as a springboard for the Culture Project.

Defining Culture

One of the first things I do as a history teacher is explore with my students how we are all cultural beings. This means that we are influenced by the time and space we live in. So, just as it may be hard for a Westerner who is fully immersed in modern ideas about love and romance to understand arranged marriages, it is also difficult for my students to realize that culture is not fixed, but a construct that we accept or deny and one that is always in flux. The Culture Project became the venue where students put into writing or visually represented their culture as they saw it. My students tend to excel at these kinds of introspective explorations. Vygotsky (1986) believed that adolescence was "less a period of completion than one of crisis and transition" (p. 141), which makes it a developmentally powerful time to engage in work that explores ideological becoming and is also a great time to reflect and act critically.

I began the exploration by asking students to define culture. First, we engaged in a chalk talk where students silently came to the whiteboard to write what they thought the aspects of culture were. They filled the board with cryptic words and phrases such as *iPhone* and *HALO II*; food, music, and clothing predominated. Once students had responded, we debriefed what we saw. I asked them to think of culture not just as the externals of what we consume but how we see things or respond to people as a part of our cultural lenses. We discussed cultural practices like saying "bless you" after a sneeze or cultures that shake hands versus those that do not.

I also told a story of my own cultural naivety in the way I used to view the head covering or *hijab* worn by some Muslim women. When I was younger, I did not realize that many Muslim women find the *hijab* to be liberating, freeing women from oppressive ideas that women should look a certain way or flaunt their sexuality. I was so immersed in my culture's message that to be a liberated woman meant I could dress like Madonna that I could not see that I was buying into an idea that was being marketed to me and not a truth. Like many young women, I was forced to decide if I was going to accept mainstream ideas of beauty and be constantly sexualized or go my own way. Seeing what influences had a grip on me and how I negotiated this made me start to better understand the complexity of the *hijab*.

Culture Pie

I passed out a piece of paper with the word *culture* written across the top and a large empty circle taking up the majority of the sheet. We generated a working definition of culture: Culture includes "ways of being," "ways of acting," and "ways of knowing." Culture is learned and shared, often unconsciously. Culture is always changing and influenced dramatically by the people you come into contact with. We came to this definition after twhinking about questions such as How do we greet people? How do we dress at a funeral? How do we fix our hair? What is our relationship to time? How do we treat people of different races, genders, and sexual orientations? How do we learn?

Students then independently created their own Culture Pie, basically a pie chart of categories within their culture that shape the way they see the world. They indicated how much influence different aspects of culture have in their life by the size of each slice. While students worked on this, I circulated to help those who were stuck or wanted clarification. When students finished, they shared their Culture Pies with partners. This gave everyone the opportunity to add or subtract as well as re-weight the aspects they listed. I asked some students who were studious and tended to conform to school expectations why they left education out of their culture pie; they seemed to think it was just an oversight. Race and gender were also left off of most students' Culture Pies, but technology, media, and friends, not surprisingly, were staples.

Students then shared with the class and I took notes on the overhead, creating categories including the topics I mentioned in the previous paragraph as well as religion, family, fashion, and sports. This allowed students to see what common themes existed, prompting many students to rethink and reevaluate some of their own choices. Next, students created what was essentially an interactive Culture Pie that they could share with classmates. In the past, students have used Movie-Maker, PowerPoint, and other tech tools to create their Culture Project. However, Voicethread best served our needs for the Culture Project.

Voicethread is a free storytelling tool that allows students to upload pictures and then narrate or write about what the viewer is seeing. Voicethread also allows for multiple voices to share space by creating a dialogue complete with doodling. This tool is free and easy to use, and because students can comment on each other's work, it would lend itself well to the second birth phase. By using a Web 2.0 Internet tool, I realized there was potential for inequity; most but not all of my students had computers and Internet access at home. I tried to counter this digital divide by providing access to the school computer lab during class, although those with home access finished more quickly.

Culture Projects Go Viral

For the next 2 weeks, students worked in slivers of time on composing their Culture Projects while we moved on with course curriculum. We continued periodic peer and teacher conferences. The Voicethreads consisted of 10–12 slides that presented the students' elements of culture as well as explanations and critique. I set up a page on our class wiki, which is coauthored with my students. They posted their work, and I taught the "bless" (asking the audience to tell you specifically what worked well in the writing), "address" (asking the audience to address a specific aspect of the writing you need help with), and "press" (asking the audience to press you on anything they think would improve the writing), a protocol for students to ask for the kind of feedback they wanted their peers to give them.

When I commented on the projects, I was careful to be respectful of cultural aspects they identified in order to create a space where students felt comfortable sharing and commenting. I tried to see everything, even identification with brand names and consumer products, as a part of their natal culture. I put students into feedback groups of about six students to watch and comment on each other's Voicethreads. This intimate space encouraged positive feedback and built community. It illustrated Bakhtin's (1993) claim that "only lovingly interested attention is capable of generating a sufficiently intent power to encompass and retain the concrete manifoldness of Being, without impoverishing and schematizing it" (p. 64). The Culture Project opened the classroom and brought in the voices and Being of all students; it created a space where students were not impoverished and schematized as crude stereotypes. In short, it fostered the students' right to "preservation of identity" (Article 8) through their "freedom of expression" of those identities (Article 13).

What happened next was not planned, but I probably should have predicted it in our YouTube culture. Students began watching other classmates' projects, and not just the people in their groups. Before I knew it, some of the projects had gone "viral" and were being widely viewed and discussed within the class. I was pleased because many of the most frequently watched projects were not created by students with high social capital but by students who were inventive or who discussed unique cultures.

Alex Addresses Religious Identity

Alex's project about his Russian identity and how that influences the way he sees American culture was hugely popular. Alex, a very intelligent and diligent student who moved here from Moldova, was often frustrated by what he saw as a lack of appreciation and work ethic in his peers. This, of course, did not make him incredibly popular. He also found some of the students' evangelical religious views troublesome. However, in his project he made clear how his natal culture influenced his beliefs about religion. "Moldova was Socialist and that still effects [sic] me today because people did not really practice a religion openly. . . . [B]ecause of this I myself am not really Christian though I do celebrate Christian holidays." Alex was an excellent science and math student and used his Culture Project to discuss his attraction to these fields and how they influenced his beliefs about religion. In his project, he explained, "I don't believe in religion. I just believe in science because it can somewhat prove what religion can't."

When Alex shared his project I was little nervous, expecting students to be upset with his views on religion. However, the students accepted what he said and did not try to argue with him. Students seemed to see him as a whole person instead of just a set of beliefs that may have clashed with their own. It was as if the Culture Project put Alex in context. When students saw the complexity and multi-faceted nature of his beliefs and where they came from, they were less judgmental.

Lori Struggles with Consumer Identity

Contemporary American society seems largely driven by consumerism. What we own (or do not own) is often seen as indicating something about who we are. Though I am careful in my critique of a self-and-stuff obsessed culture, I am not comfortable with students using their Culture Project to unquestioningly market what has been marketed to them. As a testament to the power of consumer culture, a sizable percentage of students included clothing brands and other monikers of social standing. However, when students viewed each other's work, I did not have to be the one to initiate a discussion.

A couple of the students who created projects based more around "stuff" such as brand names remarked that they felt that their projects were not very good but could not exactly put their finger on it. One student named Lori talked with me about it.

> LORI: This project is really a lot harder for me
>   because I don't really have a culture.
> ME: Everyone has a culture. Why do you think you don't?
> LORI: Kids from other countries have more culture.
>   We just don't have that much here.
> ME: Susan included traditional Hmong clothing and you also included
>   clothing and even included the brands you liked. Isn't that culture?
> LORI: I guess.

Lori seemed less than satisfied by my explanation. I think she began to see that she was not "normal" with everyone else being exotic but that she was a part of a culture that was distinct and identifiable. I talked to the class about consumer culture and how that absolutely was culture, but I asked, "I think the issue really is, are you comfortable with that?" I pointed out that if they were not comfortable with what they depicted in their Voicethreads they might want to explore where their influences were coming from and the positive and negative ramifications. "Maybe there is nothing wrong with Coca-Cola and Abercrombie and Fitch being significant cultural aspects of your life," I commented. "But many of you seem troubled by this cultural representation."

The Culture Project was a way to investigate and represent students' thematic universes. "The task of the dialogical teacher . . . working on the thematic universe revealed by their investigation is to 're-present' that universe to the people from whom she or he first received it—and 're-present' it not as lecture but as a problem" (Freire, 1970, p. 109). In the Culture Project students investigated the forces that influenced their identity and shaped their culture. They explored the stratification of their lives and how normalizing forces might be working on their perceived reality. I believe the more active role they take in "the exploration of their thematics, the more they deepen their critical awareness of reality and, in spelling out those thematics, take possession of that reality" (Freire, 1970, p. 106). They looked critically at their own projects for themes.

The culture project also offered a chance for students to transact with alien discourses. In this case, an online forum offered a space and time for reflection and to engage with others.

Tyrell Illuminates Racial Identity

One of the most compelling examples of how struggling with another's discourse can be a liberating experience came from Tyrell, a very popular young man who was also the only Black student in his AP U.S. History class. In his Culture Project, he spoke frankly about how many of his family members, especially those who live in the inner city of Philadelphia, were distrustful of Whites. Bakhtin (1981) observed that "the importance of struggling with another's discourse, its influence in the history of an individual's coming to ideological consciousness, is enormous" (p. 348). Tyrell stated in his Voicethread project that "much of my family does not like people of other races, but the part of my family that I was brought up by taught me to be open-minded to all people from all places." Tyrell showed how the discourse on race within his own family is complicated and multifaceted.

Tyrell said what I imagine many White students suspect, that tangible racial animosity flows both ways. Black students are often the minority in my classes, which may encourage some White students to try out their philosophies on things like reverse discrimination in front of peers who are probably not going to seriously challenge them. In my classroom, White students avoid making overtly racist remarks and there is a certain level of respect for Black athletes and other Black students who conform and do not challenge the status quo. However, not far below the surface there is tension. Tyrell's project unearthed what I think many White students feared, that even though Tyrell may conform and "fit in" with the predominantly White class, he is involved in conversations in other spaces that question White people.

Tyrell's Voicethread was a conversation with words and concepts he may have been resisting, but he may have also been "stylizing discourse by attributing it to a person" (Bakhtin, 1981, p. 348) in a kind of double-voiced parody. Tyrell may have used his Voicethread to push students in the class to see that although he was assimilating into the predominantly White class, he was not doing so without recognizing or being conscious of other discourses. No students directly commented on Tyrell's insights about race or about his family's distrust of Whites, but I'm convinced that a dialogue occurred even though it may have been unspoken. I feel that the discourse around Tyrell's Culture Project, though silent, led some to deeper understandings of the reality of racial tension.

I first noticed this when I taught the students about the 1960s riots in Watts and Detroit. These students seemed to grasp the complexity right away, which is unusual because rioting is a complicated socio-political-economic phenomenon that seems paradoxical and can be challenging for adolescents (and adults) to understand. It was as if Tyrell's earlier discourse had become internally persuasive to other members of the class and what was once alien now seemed to make sense. Tyrell put a human face on the frustration and feelings of alienation that many who live in urban areas feel as a result of a lack of jobs and safe neighborhoods. He seemed to make it possible for students to understand how people could be pushed to a point of burning parts of their own communities.

As a White middle-class teacher, I suspect students hear my explanations as empty rhetoric when I try to connect the frustration many Blacks felt at the lack of progress and equity to the riots. In the past, many students had trouble seeing this frustration as a contributing factor to the burning of these cities. However, after Tyrell offered up his own family and their struggles and frustrations, a dialogue began. This was the beginning of a second birth for many of my students.

SECOND BIRTH: EXPLORING OTHER CULTURES

The second birth comes about by exploring a different culture in such depth that what seems strange at first eventually becomes part of the way we understand the world as we absorb other cultural ways of being. Again, we connected with the Rights of the Child. Article 13 states in part that "in exercising the right to freedom of expression, children have the responsibility to also respect the rights, freedoms and reputations of others." Moving from first birth, our native culture, to second birth, exploring other cultures, required that respect.

To take students out of their natal comfort zones and into another cultural space, I started within our classroom community. Tyrell's project was a good example. As we explored each other's culture projects, students began to actively engage with each other's work. They gained respect and openness to new ideas. Through the projects and discussion, students saw a diversity of experiences and perspectives; they were often able to point out what aspects of their own culture made them think the way they did.

We had in-depth discussions about autobiographical and biographical materials that represented different cultures. For example, in studying Native American cultures, we read Dee Brown's classic *Bury My Heart at Wounded Knee* for a historical perspective, then watched a video journal of a teenage girl living on a reservation where she was training as a boxer to support her young daughter (Longman, 2009). This piece opened up a lot of discussion; though this teenage mom was a Lakota, my students had more in common with her than with the wealthy, White teenagers on *The OC*.

As the year progressed, students read, viewed, and entered into dialogue with countless voices representing other points in time and cultural space. One of the most intense voices we listened to was that of Art Spiegelman in *Maus*.

Exploring the Culture of Nazi Germany: The *Maus* Project

After students examined their natal culture, the *Maus* Project was a place to begin to explore the voices they have heard through their lives in more depth. It seemed like a logical progression for students to have a "second birth" by looking at family members whose own process of becoming started at a different time and within different circumstances. It was a smaller step than, say, moving to Nepal.

Maus is a graphic novel by Art Spiegelman that explores the life of Vladek Spiegelman as well as the author's relationship with him. Vladek was Art's father, a Polish Jew, who survived Auschwitz. I chose *Maus* because it is just as much about Art as it is about Vladek. Spiegelman does a great job depicting the tension between his father's discourse and his own. *Maus* served as a mentor text as we began our explorations.

I asked students to interview a family member and create a short graphic novel in which they depicted their family member and themselves engaged in a conversation about an era or period in American history. I wanted students to explore the dialogic tensions in their own lives and to develop their ability to "perceive critically the way they exist in the world with which and in which they find themselves" (Freire, 1970, p. 83) so they could see that the world is in a constant state of transformation. I also asked students to examine how we bring our own lens to all we see and how we construct knowledge—all critical aspects of historical study.

We used the graphic novel format because *Maus* demonstrated that it could be an effective way to depict dialogue and the interview process. I stressed that content was most important and that the pictures could be simple. However, I introduced students to a couple of free comic-making programs online that they could use to tell their stories. I showed them Comic Life, which allows the importation of real photographs and gives them a comic feel. It is easy to use but all of the options intimidated some students. We also looked at Make Beliefs Comixs. Its 15 predetermined characters make it limited but easy to use. Some students chose to hand draw their graphic novels, which I encouraged. Interestingly, Article 13 encourages freedom of expression through "talking, drawing, or writing."

Some of my students immediately knew whom in their family they wanted to interview and what they wanted to talk to them about. However, many felt that because their family members had not survived something like a concentration camp or a war they did not have something worthy of the project. In order to demonstrate that anyone can teach you something or bring a different perspective or cultural framework, I brought my mom in to be interviewed by our class.

My mom was born in 1948, at the beginning of the baby boom and in my opinion was largely influenced by post–World War II American culture. She engaged with the students in a question-and-answer session about how she was told she could be a nurse or a teacher while her brother was encouraged to go into business. She spoke of how things have changed for women and gave examples from her own life. She talked about the pressure she felt to get married and how she felt like a complete failure when she got divorced. She also spoke of her work with Head Start and on the Bobby Kennedy campaign, which put her at the RFK rally in the city of Indianapolis, where he gave the famous speech announcing the assassination of Martin Luther King Jr. However, the students quickly began to ask her about what they were interested in.

> ANN: Ms. Hester, were there gay people when you were growing up?
> [Ann is on the basketball team and is learning how to
>   accept and work with openly gay teammates.]
> MY MOM: I think there have always been gay people but people were
>   just not as open about it when I was your age. I don't even
>   think I knew what being gay was until I was in college.

It should not have surprised me how much students wanted to talk about social issues and gender relations. There was a lot of rich discussion, and the interview process was demystified as students realized there was little difference between a conversation and an interview.

After my mom finished, I asked students to create a four-frame comic strip based on the conversation. The comic was to feature themselves and my mom as active characters advancing some kind of narrative. I collected these as the students filed out of the room and my mom and I enjoyed looking at their impressions. We laughed because my mom talked only briefly about how attitudes toward sex and sexuality have changed since the Sexual Revolution but this was the centerpiece of many of the comics. This closing activity also allowed me to assess if the students understood the bigger project at hand. The next day, I shared student exemplars of the mini-comic to show students that they had not only already completed a comic, but that they had interviewed a regular person and seen the way historical factors shaped her.

I spent parts of the week in short conferences with students about what information they obtained from their interviews and how to go forward. Some students took notes on their interviews and some were able to tape the interviews, which was really helpful. I did not ask students to transcribe word for word what their interviewee said, but instead to take the direct quotes that were most interesting.

Over the coming weeks, students turned in their completed graphic novels. Many of them had taken the task to heart and produced compelling stories that were both inspired and at times heartbreaking. I read about families who came to the United States smuggled by coyotes or fleeing oppressive government regimes. One student discovered that the Nazis had sterilized her aunt during World War II. Another interviewed her parents about the Rodney King beating and their subsequent decision to leave Los Angeles after the riots.

However, the comic that surprised me the most was by Terrence. He had called his grandfather in Philadelphia to interview him about Vietnam. The following is an excerpt from that project.

> TERRENCE: Did you feel like you had a purpose to be in Vietnam?
> GRANDPA: As a soldier, yes. As an American soldier, no, not at all.
> [Terrence then included his own thought bubble that he
>   did not say out loud to his grandfather.]
> TERRENCE: Wow, that's pretty interesting. I guess I never would have thought
>   to differentiate the two. Could you clarify that a little more, please?
> GRANDPA: As a soldier, I simply did what I was told. But as an American
>   soldier, I was supposed to do what was right. And I didn't.

Terrence did not ask his grandfather about what he did that was not "right," but instead changed the subject to when his grandfather came back to the United States. I asked Terrence about his decision not to push his grandfather on this and Terrence told me he did not want to know what his grandfather had done.

Terrence then asked his grandfather if his views of America changed after the war and the effect of the war on his family. Terrence's grandfather, who was living in poverty in Philadelphia before the war, said that after the war, "we did end up having a little more money, but I missed the birth of your aunt and she was three before she knew my name," to which Terrence asked, "So, was the effect mostly negative for you, and not the family as a whole?" Terrence's grandfather agreed that there were benefits to the war for the family, but did not let Terrence oversimplify the situation and instead said, "Yeah, I guess you could say that the family life got better, but I was wounded, missed my daughter's birth, and I had no job to fall back on . . . our family was looked down on by others. It hurt me as a man because I wanted to work."

Terrence wrapped the interview up at that point, but in his comic had a thought bubble that said, "Wow. His demeanor completely changed when his manhood was challenged. Maybe I should finish with this"—but he did not. Terrence may have read his grandfather correctly and wrapped up the interview at the exact right time. However, I think Terrence may have backed away because he was either not able or not willing to take on that kind of responsibility without more guidance and practice.

I think his grandfather may have been inviting Terrence into a deeper dialogue about what it meant to be a man and, more importantly, what it meant to be a man who felt that he could not fulfill his duty to his family, what it meant to be a man under oppressive forces. I also think there was an issue of race that was just below the surface. Terrence and his grandfather are Black, but race was not explicitly mentioned in the interview at all; but that does not mean it was not a part of the discourse. Lastly, I think that Terrence's grandfather was able to have a discussion about his own dehumanization during and after war as well as acts of dehumanization he may have committed against others, but Terrence was not ready to fully hear about it. This does not mean that this exercise was in vain. It may be that this was the beginning of a questioning process for Terrence, just as constructing the Culture Project was the beginning of my own efforts to be more fully human in the classroom.

Reading Historical Memoirs

Students did so well talking to and exploring the lives and humanity of those close to them in the *Maus* Project. I wondered if they could sustain that level of interest and inquiry when dealing with people who were very different from them. In order to get students to stretch a little further outside of their comfort zones, our next challenge was to read a historical memoir. I book talked a number of books, some of which were student suggested, in order to appeal to as wide a range of interests as possible. The only criterion was that they dealt with historical events that occurred somewhere between World War II and the present and had some connection to the U.S. History standards. Students voted on which memoirs to read by narrowing a list of ten student- and teacher-generated books down to three: Tim O'Brien's *If I Die in a Combat Zone*, Philip Caputo's *Rumor of War*, and Anne Moody's *Coming of Age in Mississippi*, the first two memoirs about Vietnam, the third a chronicle of the civil rights movement.

I secured funding to buy a class set of books through my department and a writing project grant. Over 3 weeks, I gave students time to read in class during Sustained Silent Reading (SSR) and Independent Literacy Exploration (ILE) time, a term I borrowed from Janet Allen (2000). When I first started doing the Culture Project, I pretty much marched on with the standards-based curriculum and students read on the side; reading literature, even if it was nonfiction, seemed foreign to what I was trained to do. However, I now do much more reading in my social studies classes, utilizing strategies such as ILE, reciprocal teaching, double-entry journals, and book clubs. As I conferenced with students to see what insights they had about their text, I found that the students were highly motivated to read and discuss the memoirs—and history.

THIRD BIRTH: MAKING CONNECTIONS

The third birth required students to look back at their own culture after the completion of the *Maus* Project and the reading of the historical memoirs. As a kind of warm-up, I asked my students to think about cultural (including economic or political) practices to which we no longer ascribed. I asked, "Did you know that not that long ago there would have been a smoking lounge in the school for you all?" There was a lively outbreak of responses, with some students calling for reinstatement of the smoking lounge. We discussed what had changed and how society now viewed smoking. We also discussed other cultural practices that we now looked at as backward or even barbaric, e.g., why American slaveholders did not question keeping other human beings in bondage. The culmination of this reflective work came in the students' final project.

Community Reflection Forums

I asked students to look back at their life story, Culture Project, and *Maus* Project, and finally to use the historical memoir they had chosen as the basis of the third birth or final reflection. I created three discussion forums on our wiki to house their writing. This gave them a community forum, a larger audience than just me, a teacher who had to have 120+ essays graded in 2 days. The directions were pretty straightforward:

- You will respond to the discussion threads by first finding a quote in the memoir that in your mind responds in some way to each of the three questions.
- You will then need to explicitly write about the connection you are seeing between the quote and the question.
- Your response to EACH question should be between 200 and 400 words and the quote will not count toward the word count.
- Because you all read different books, make sure to include the title and page numbers.

The first discussion forum asked students to reflect: "After revisiting your life story and Culture Project, how do you see this memoir connecting with yourself?" The second forum asked, "What connections do you see between the memoir and the family you come from and their experiences you documented in the Maus Project?" On the third forum, they responded to this question: "Finally, what does this memoir teach you about the world?" I scheduled class time in the computer lab and allowed the students to work at home to give them ample time to reflect deeply and honestly.

Over the last few days of school, which can often feel less than productive, we engaged in work that was meaningful and required focus, reflection, and interaction. I logged on to the wiki at different times, read what students wrote, and then immediately conferenced with them. Using the wiki as a tool was fabulous because the students appeared more invested than just turning in a final essay on the last day before summer vacation. I did not hear one student complain; they just wrote and wrote and poured out their hearts. Students used quotes that they connected to from their memoirs in order to anchor their piece and to give the readers who may have read different books some context. I was surprised at the honesty of the writing and was awed at how they handled complexity.

Student Reflections:
"I can . . . search for a life that is more on the edge"

One student had interviewed her grandfather, a Vietnam veteran, for the *Maus* Project and chose Philip Caputo's *A Rumor of War*. To anchor how the memoir made her reflect on herself, she chose a quote that dealt with Caputo's boredom in the sterilized suburbs. He described it as a place where nothing much happened and how he was ready to get out of that place before he went to Vietnam. Miranda's response moved me, not because of what she said but because of the potential I saw in who she could become.

> I can relate to this quote because I come from a very comfortable, easy suburban life where my parents have instilled a strong work ethic in me to carry on the policy of "work hard to give your kids a better life than you had." I have never had to struggle and work for the greater good of my family, on the contrary; my life is focused on entertaining myself with my parents hard earned money, and the (closest) I come to benefiting my family is working hard in school in order to achieve the same lifestyle I (grew) up around. I have not experienced, in large amounts, the "real world" or the violence and prejudice that many Americans face daily, and I have not had to worry about how I will maintain basic necessities, moreover, I do not carry much responsibility other than to use my common sense. However, the drive to achieve independence and escape to a world that is less serious and more risky and dangerous is very prevalent as I start to get older. Like Phillip Caputo, I can sometimes take how easy my life is for granted and search

for a life that is more on the edge and rebellious so I can have stories to tell, because in my point of view, living a short, adventurous life and having stories to tell is more important than living a long, picture perfect life where your experiences did not impact society.

Another student I got to know better through this process was Nancy, a Mexican American student born in Los Angeles. Nancy and I had a series of bumps over the school year. I found her to be a sweet and sensitive girl who sometimes lashed out at her peers as well as her teachers. Nancy describes herself as a Leo with a personality that leans toward "aggressiveness, a tendency to enviousness, hyperactive, dramatic, protective, risk taking." She wrote, "I don't like talking about my early childhood. It is something I wish to delete from my memory." Nancy read *Coming of Age in Mississippi* and described her connection to a comment that Moody makes about beginning to hate people when she was 15, after the murder of Emmett Till:

> I didn't begin to hate people when I was fifteen, I've always hated people, but when I first arrived in Georgia and saw so many white people I found it odd. Arriving in a rural area . . . I thought that I should have hated white people, because I thought they were the ones who ran everything. Once I went to school and saw more of Barrow county I realized that . . . these white people weren't rich they lived in trailers in dirty houses something that I thought I would never see a white person live in.
>
> I came with thoughts of hating white people, but in time I started liking them more than my own race. My family thought of it as odd, my friends think of it odd, but I have reasons why I separated myself.
>
> I hate the Hispanics who let the white people see them as lazy with the grades that they get and I respect the ones who actually do study because I know they want a future because they're not going to settle for working in a factory or doing manual labor in the blazing heat.
>
> I don't hate white people or Hispanics, but I do have resentment towards Hispanics for not trying to prove the stereotypes wrong.

After reading this piece, I realized I had not fully seen Nancy for most of the school year. Her anger and wish to detach herself from her community was hard for me to accept. I may have been more like Nancy when I was younger than I wanted to admit, and because of this I was impatient with her and wanted her to mature or get past the resentment she felt. Was Nancy still in her second birth? Or was she in her third birth, and seeing herself and her culture through the lens of someone else? Was she internalizing how another culture saw her, and was I complicit in this?

FLOATING BETWEEN BIRTHS

Though the concept of being "thrice-born" was a helpful organizational tool, I realized that my students and I constantly float between births. We may not know from one minute to the next who we are or where we are going. If we do not even understand the past the same way, how can I expect us to agree about how to act upon the future? I hope I am teaching my students to think in a critical manner without breeding cynicism or disconnecting them from the beliefs that sustain them. I want them to have the space to work through their own ideas, and I want to have the patience to support them.

The Rights of the Child protects not only children, but also teachers who are working to support students. Article 8 (Peservation of identity) and Articles 12–14 (Respect for the views of the child; Freedom of expression; and Freedom of thought, conscience, and religion) encourage teachers to work with and learn from students instead of asserting common hegemonic discourses. It would be easy to slip into an authoritarian model that asks students to conform to an identity that the dominant institution supposes for them. Article 14 says in part, "Children have the right to think and believe what they want and to practice their religion. . . . The Convention supports children's right to examine their beliefs, but it also states that their right to express their beliefs implies respect for the rights and freedoms of others."

By using a problem-posing and dialogic methodology to explore this and other Rights of the Child, I was able to explore some of the tensions within the classroom world. As I expanded my teaching practice to include more space for students' cultures, histories, and thoughts, I began to see how much I had been missing. We used personal histories, the *Maus* Project, and the reading of memoirs to preserve identity as well as create a classroom that respects students' expression, thought, conscience, and religion. I strengthened my conviction that optimum educational and human growth takes place when we create spaces that value students' identities.

The thrice-born framework complements the Rights of the Child; it supports the process of becoming rather than a finished product. Like Freire (1970), I believe that "every thematic investigation which deepens historical awareness is thus really educational" and that "the more educators and the people investigate the people's thinking, and are thus jointly educated, the more they continue to investigate" (p. 109). These abilities are necessary in a world that is constantly changing and in a country that must be able periodically to be reborn. My students will, one way or another, shape that rebirth.

8

PeaceJam

High School Student Activists
Work for Human Rights

Lindy Crace

Invitation to Explore:
How Students Work for Human Rights

Initiating Experience:

We live in an increasingly multicultural, globally interdependent world. Hostility and apathy seem to be on the rise, perhaps most of all among teenagers. Service learning has been touted as an effective method for bringing lessons from the high school curriculum into the world outside the classroom so students can develop as critically thinking, compassionate, and empowered humans who speak out against injustice and actively work to create change in their communities. Affiliated with the international PeaceJam program (http://www.peacejam.org/), PeaceJam at our high school is a service learning course and club centered around the study of Nobel Peace laureates' lives, nonviolence, social justice, and community change.

Formal Invitation:

I invite you to explore PeaceJam, the remarkable global movement that connects young people with Nobel Peace laureates. Our high school students will share with you the challenges, frustrations, and rewards of service learning through PeaceJam; the vocabulary and critical thinking skills they developed for self-reflection and future leadership; and the increased sense of community and of common purpose these young activists developed over time.

Suggested Questions:

1. How does engaging in service learning through PeaceJam impact students in a culturally diverse high school? What existing or potential school club or class might take on similar work at schools without a PeaceJam chapter?
2. How do PeaceJam activists approach community social issues?
3. What kinds of creative solutions can high school students design and enact?
4. How do PeaceJam students understand themselves and their roles within their home, school, community, nation, and world?

Texts, Tools, and Resources:

Resources included student journals and interviews; photo and field note documentation of classes and meetings; PeaceJam materials; interviews with representatives from local social service organizations, including Project SAFE, the Economic Justice Coalition, Oasis Católico, Jubilee Partners, the Southeast Region PeaceJam director and assistant director, and two Nobel Peace laureates. We addressed the UN Universal Declaration of Human Rights and UN Rights of the Child Articles Article 2, "non-discrimination"; Article 19, "protection from all forms of violence"; Article 24, "health and health services"; Article 28, "right to education"; and Article 30, the right of "children of minorities/indigenous groups…to learn about and practice their own culture, language and religion."

The PeaceJam chapter at the high school where I teach began as an invitation from a student, in contrast to the invitations issued by teachers in other chapters of this book. Alice, a sophomore at the high school where I teach (all names are pseudonyms, usually chosen by the students), invited her teachers to partner with her on a project she saw as important and necessary: to bring to the students in her community the basic right of every child to an education. Alice described how she first got interested in PeaceJam:

I was tutoring 8th-graders who hadn't passed the [state exit exam] in the summer with NHS [National Honor Society], and I was just noticing that these kids don't know how to multiply because of whatever and then they're gonna drop out of school because there's no way they can catch up and then they're gonna be poor for the rest of their lives and then their children are gonna be poor—so that's a generalization—but that's basically how I was seeing it. . . . I wanted to start this tutoring program that had role models for the middle schoolers and just encourage them basically to catch up, to learn to do well in school, to have people who have an interest in them when they come to high school, to have someone there who they already know who wants them to do well who's not just a teacher because teachers can be unrelatable when you're a too-cool freshman.

Alice learned from a teacher about the PeaceJam program, an organization founded in 1994 to connect Nobel Peace laureates to children around the world and promote the values of nonviolent resistance and community change. Alice said, "The two ideas just kind of merged. . . . I thought they went nicely together." Alice shared her inspiration with me and fellow 9th-grade teacher Ashley Goodrich, and thus PeaceJam at our high school was born. Our local PeaceJam chapter has included students who are European American, African American, multiracial, and Polynesian, as well as students from India, Colombia, Guatemala, Mexico, Peru, and Nicaragua. But it all started with Alice. We had little to go by initially, as we were the first PeaceJam club in the state, but we soon received plenty of guidance from the regional director for our area.

SERVICE LEARNING, THE RIGHTS OF THE CHILD, AND PEACEJAM

Although the term *service learning* is bandied about frequently in the world of education, there is much confusion about what the term means, what its implementation should look like, and how it might differ from other forms of service. According to Billig (2011), "Service-learning typically is comprised of six components: investigation, planning, action, reflection, demonstration, and celebration" (p. 8). In explaining PeaceJam to other adults and to the students, I have struggled to make clear that service learning is not synonymous with community service, which involves volunteers helping to fill a community need. Billig summed up the distinction, explaining, "'Action' is the only component that service-learning and community service typically have in common" (p. 9). The component of reflection becomes just as important as the action itself.

The basis for PeaceJam's international organization is to bring together youth and adult role models who have been recognized for their contributions to community change so that young people are inspired to create real change in their own communities. Gifford (2004) described PeaceJam as a program in which students

participate in year-long, ongoing leadership training, in which they roll up their sleeves and immerse themselves in provocative issues . . . , study the lives of Nobel Peace laureates . . . , attend two-day PeaceJam conferences led by Nobel laureates . . . , learn firsthand wisdom and strategies for dealing with conflict . . . , and implement service projects in their communities. (pp. 3–4)

Each year, students study the life of the Nobel Peace laureate selected to lead the regional conference, so over time our students studied about and worked with Betty Williams of Northern Ireland, Rigoberta Menchú Tum of Guatemala, and Shirin Ebadi of Iran. But this study is just a part of the curriculum, which also focuses on nonviolence and the development of a Global Call to Action. These two portions of the curriculum are purposely interwoven to develop students' awareness of the problems in their community while also prompting them to consider the root causes of these problems and ways the root causes might be addressed. The framework for the Global Call to Action is the United Nations' Universal Declaration of Human Rights, condensed into a one-page handout that students keep in their journals and refer back to over the course of the year.

Though the PeaceJam curriculum includes introductory content that is standardized, after the initial meetings, the direction of group activities and discussion proceeds ideally from student interest. The focus of PeaceJam materials is the Universal Declaration of Human Rights. Sponsors are encouraged to help students see the connections between the rights and their own lives through interpreting and applying the rights from the perspective of young people. Students work through a series of exploratory activities, including research, discussion, and self-reflection, before selecting the local issue they would like to address individually, in small groups, or as an entire club. Students then work on a Global Call to Action, a service learning project designed to both educate and serve.

This PeaceJam framework created a natural tie-in for us to the UN Rights of the Child, which are based in the UN Universal Declaration of Human Rights with specific emphasis on the lives and experiences of youth. Students were drawn each year to think about Article 28 (Right to education) as the setting for these explorations was their school and the greater part of their lives has been spent in similar institutions. However, each year students developed additional interest in local issues related to other rights. For example, during the second year, two students' focus became gay rights, which arose from discussions about several of the articles but most specifically Article 2 (Non-discrimination). Another group that year chose to focus on issues of domestic violence based on Article 19 (Right to Protection from All Forms of Violence). Students in the fourth year found particular resonance with Articles 24 (Health and Health Services) and Article 30 (Children of Minorities/Indigenous Groups).

PEACEJAM YEAR 1: CASTING A WIDE NET

My social studies colleague Ashley Goodrich, having written her thesis on service learning, was the expert on the topic. I brought my experience as an English teacher and my desire to create a space for open dialogue outside the pressures of the state curriculum and standardized tests. We are European American, female teachers in our early years of teaching, with a passion for social justice. After brainstorming a list of students we thought would be interested in PeaceJam or who might benefit from involvement, we cast our net more widely by asking teachers to recommend students. We stressed that we were not just interested in high-achieving students who had already shown leadership ability; we were most interested in recruiting students who might be overlooked or who might themselves be disenchanted with school and existing extracurricular activities.

Ashley and I then issued invitation letters to the students and their parents, explaining the club's mission and laying out plans for the year. We congratulated students on being selected and invited them to become PeaceJam Ambassadors, the official name for high school PeaceJammers. The response was overwhelming. Many students were unable to join because of other commitments, but many others who had not received invitations stopped by our classrooms to ask about joining after hearing about it from friends.

The Tutoring Project

We started with Alice's idea of a tutoring program between high-achieving high school students and underperforming 8th-graders at our feeder middle school. Goodrich and I both taught freshmen and wanted to get them involved, but we felt that tutoring students only 1 year their junior would be inappropriate. Still, we wanted them in on the learning aspect of the project, with the intent that they could join in on the tutoring once they were old enough. So we outlined a plan for a Peacemaker Recognition Program to be implemented by the underclassmen. The underclassmen worked to identify peacemakers in our community whom we could interview and award so that the idea of community change could be located closer to home than the work of Nobel Peace laureates. The upperclassmen and underclassmen worked on their service projects separately, but they all met once a week after school to study the curriculum together.

Alice had tapped into one of the underlying problems at our school, and one that is not unique to our community: a school-within-a-school. Our student population is diverse both ethnically (roughly 50% African Americans, 35% European Americans, 15% Latin@ and students from other ethnicities) and economically, serving the fifth-poorest county of its population size in the nation. The majority of students receive free and reduced-price lunch, but our high school is also home to students whose parents live in the old-money residential areas of town and work as educators at the state university. Our school is located on a block literally between fraternity row and government housing.

Despite this diversity, our classrooms remain segregated by race and socioeconomic class. It is possible for high-achieving students to graduate without any knowledge that poverty exists here, and for students affected by poverty to never have a class with their affluent peers. In a 2-week period, our school was on the front page of the local paper twice, first for being designated by the state as an underperforming school, and next for being among the top 1,000 schools in the nation. Clearly, students' educational experiences were not equitable.

Alice's experience gave her a glimpse into what her teachers see every day, that students experience their town and their schools in quite different and often alienating ways. Our primary goal for PeaceJam was to break down these divisions and bring students from diverse backgrounds into dialogue through weekly discussions.

A Turning Point

One of the most breathtaking moments of the year, one that showed us the transformative power of PeaceJam, happened during a discussion of violence in our community. This was in the second month of our weekly meetings, and we were a bit discouraged at the lack of depth in students' reflections. Students seemed to repeat stereotypes about others and platitudes about violence, race, and poverty without much thought. We were wary of strongly guiding students' thinking because our early attempts had seemed too heavy-handed. We were caught in the same position we often experience in the classroom, with an urge to challenge student thinking in a way that did not take advantage of the power imbalance between a teacher and her students, no matter how open and democratic the environment she creates.

And then a student stepped in. The PeaceJammers had divided into small groups, each of which had a map of our town and some markers to color in the areas of high and low violence. A group of upperclassmen volunteered to share their work first and did so almost dismissively, as if the results were so obvious that they were hardly worth sharing. They had color-coded "low violence" in the more affluent areas of town in which most of them lived or wanted to live, and coded as "high violence" areas in several government housing areas and other low-income apartment complexes. We asked for responses about why these areas were chosen; there was a brief discussion about violence being higher where there's higher poverty. The group members started to sit down.

Then Kara, a freshman girl who had barely spoken since PeaceJam began, raised her hand. "Why did you mark Highland Apartments as high in violence?" she asked. The group members did not respond, instead looking at their map blankly, not certain which area Kara was referring to. Kara stood up, stepped through the students sitting on the floor or on desk tops, and pointed to an area of town just off the main highway. She explained, "This is Highland Apartments, where I live. We just moved there. My mom got another job because she said she didn't want us living in a dangerous place like the neighborhood we used to live in." There was a pause. None of the presenters knew how to respond, and Kara seemed a bit taken aback by her own courage. Then she explained further, "There is some crime and violence where we live now, but it's not the people who live there. It's people coming from other parts of town to do their business in our neighborhood. The people who actually live there are trying to keep the violence out."

It was a turning point for our group. We witnessed the process described by Hart (2006) by which "the dichotomies of 'fortunate helping unfortunate', or 'us doing for them,' are erased and replaced with 'us doing for us'" (p. 27). Suddenly, PeaceJammers could no longer talk about the violence in "their" neighborhoods or the reasons why "they" are so aggressive. That's not to say that every moment from there on out was defined by students critically engaging with complex issues or even fully listening to one another's expertise, but it did start to break down the walls between our students and show us that transformation might be possible.

My greatest regret that first year was that we were not more successful in creating moments like this one. However, I felt students were thinking about root causes in some ways, even though we were not doing enough reflection as a group. For example, when asked what she learned from leading the tutoring program, Alice responded:

> I feel like education is the root of everything . . . that having the basic education where you can get a good job is important. And I think not enough attention is paid to education as the root of every problem in the economy and social problems in our community. The rampant poverty is all attributable to education in my eyes or lack thereof. . . . I just feel like parents who didn't go to school aren't going to read to their children when they're little, and that's important, they're not going to get on them to do their homework. If you're just struggling at a minimum-wage job, you don't have time to help your kids with their homework, and you might not know what they're doing. Parenting is the key to making good children who are educated and you have to educate the parents in order for the kids to be educated. You know, it's a cycle. And it might be too late to help these parents, and that's sad, but it's just true, that they're not in a position where it's their job to learn, but these kids are in a position where they're at school for 8 hours a day, and it should be the primary goal of the schools to make sure that they're getting a good education. You have to work with the next generation that's coming up so all subsequent generations will be better and better as far as education and poverty in general go.

Alice was clearly looking toward larger social forces in trying to make sense of the situation in which she found the students she was trying to help, and she was making some progress. Her conclusions, though, are full of the stereotypes and dichotomies that most of us have blindly accepted when viewing the world through our limited lenses. It disheartens me to know that as her advisor I did not do more to challenge her assumptions so she could better evaluate what she thought she knew.

While Alice was doing some thinking about what she was observing, I fear that many of her peers were doing little reflection, and we adults did not do enough to help guide this reflective work. When I asked Alice about discussions with other PeaceJammers about the reasons the middle school students needed tutoring, she reflected:

> I think we all agreed that a lot of it is just fear of failure and just feeling like you're not good at it. If you feel like you're not good at something, you're not going to try because you will look stupid or you'll feel bad about yourself afterwards. No one likes to do things they're not good at just because it's embarrassing and painful, and when kids get behind early, then in 8th grade you're embarrassed to read aloud if you don't know how to read well or at all.

Despite her insights into the perspective of the struggling 8th-graders, neither Alice nor any of the other PeaceJammers that year really talked with the students they tutored about their own experiences or asked for their perspective. We did little as their sponsors beyond asking some leading questions in discussion. The PeaceJammers often encountered resistance to their offers of help, whether from students who refused to attend or from students who used the time to "goof off." Alice reflected,

> It sounds all like warm and fuzzy and gushy, but there were definitely moments when I wanted to throttle the student I was working with. In my heart, I wanted to believe that they were capable of succeeding and getting this, but sometimes I would feel like, "This is not going to happen, this person is just not going to get it," and so that's where I guess what I felt and what I hoped was just totally distant from the reality of the situation.

As their advisor, this is where I could have been more supportive and pushed the PeaceJammers to question why someone would resist what is seemingly so helpful. What assumptions were we and our students making?

When I asked how she dealt with resistance from the students she was trying to help, Alice noted insightfully, "I didn't develop a strategy or anything, but I tried not to make it into a you-versus-me situation. These kids are trying to be tough and resistant because they're scared." Her approach was "just laughing with them about it or just saying, 'All right, we're going to keep doing this.'" Alice recognized the importance of breaking down barriers between the tutors and the students being tutored, but she relied on her own judgment of how and when to break down those barriers rather than seeing the younger students as equals who could fully participate in the project.

In not promoting more in-depth reflection and challenging students to resist the dichotomies between those serving and those being served, I failed as an educator. According to Cipolle (2004),

> The educator/leader can assist students in moving from a commonly held view of the world (common sense) to a critical view of reality (good sense) through problem-posing and dialectical thinking (Allman; Mayo). Schools then become sites of contestation of the status quo and the terrain for Gramsci's war of position against the dominant culture. (p. 13)

We did not do enough, particularly during the first year, to help our students start questioning their own interpretation of reality. Instead, we allowed them to continue seeing themselves as the do-gooders helping those who needed help.

PEACEJAM YEAR 2: EXPANDING PROJECTS

Based on our evaluation of the previous year, student feedback, and the fact that second-year PeaceJam students were intermingling with new students, we decided to change the format of the program to incorporate multiple projects that were developing through student interests. We decided to meet once a week in the morning to work on these projects and after school to continue our discussions on nonviolence and community change.

More important, we wanted to further develop the critical pedagogy behind the work. Through our discussions with the Rights of the Child inquiry group, we were seeing the need to challenge ourselves and our students to dig into the root causes of social injustice. Too much of the service students had done in the first year fell into the trap described by Hart (2006): "Permitting responsibility and care to serve as the ends rather than the means to civic literacy leaves service-learning as an approach to education that falls short of its promise as a counter normative liberatory pedagogy" (p. 22). The students felt good about their work, many of the students they had tutored were successful in their early months of high school, and there had been some discussion of the forces behind the need for tutoring intervention.

Still, we felt that although students had made some headway, the incorporation of reflective practices had not done enough to close the large divides between the students being tutored and the PeaceJam volunteers. Cipolle (2004) observed that service lacking reflection "promotes a paternalistic, 'better than thou' attitude, reinforces preconceived stereotypes, and precludes the need for social change" (p. 18). Instead, we wanted to create a program that more closely resembled the process described by Hart (2006):

As citizens become aware of how social and political systems work and become conscious of themselves as agents within these systems, they can identify and critique the domination, oppression and authoritative structures embedded within those systems. Critique is seen as the first action toward transformation. Further, critical theory proposed that these conscious citizens must recognize that they are members of a community within which they must come to understand the context in which their actions take place. Through this awareness, a commitment to democracy is enacted through continual social critique and transformation of social, political and organizational structures. (p. 23)

Several of the changes we made were designed to foster more transformative practices. First, we encouraged students to build on their own interests in projects. While the tutoring program continued for students who remained interested, several students were developing areas of personal concern from our exploration of the UN Declaration of Human Rights that were more powerful for them to pursue. We also decided to bring in experts on a variety of issues to pique the interest of students who had not yet found their passion but also to support more in-depth understanding of societal forces influencing the issues students had identified. Among other smaller service projects, the following three student-led, ongoing projects seemed to have the most lasting impact on students.

Gay Rights

Two students became interested in gay rights after expressing frustration with comments about homosexuals made by classmates. We brought in speakers from our local university to work with our students on their role as bystanders. Among other topics, they discussed dealing with feelings of frustration and anger when hearing these comments, effectively letting others know that they did not appreciate homophobic comments, and alternatives to remaining silent when hearing ugly statements or jokes. The two student leaders also attended a 1-day conference on standing up for gay rights and brought back what they had learned. They led discussions for all of us to implement strategies, including using humor, personal identification (e.g., a close family member is homosexual), and comparisons to other oppressed groups. We discussed our progress and use of the strategies throughout the year.

Domestic Violence

Several students expressed interest in working against domestic violence. Avery, a freshman new to PeaceJam, explained, "Domestic violence was an issue that touched me because I know some people personally who have experienced this and I really think it isn't an issue that's addressed enough within the community, or even nationwide." Because high school students were considered too young to work with the local battered women's safe house, interested PeaceJammers instead volunteered regularly at the thrift store whose proceeds went to support battered women and children. Mary, a junior, served as project leader and coordinated this work. She also arranged for several presentations by staff of the safe house to discuss domestic violence and help us explore the causes, prevalence, reasons women might continue abusive relationships, and alternatives.

Several students shared examples of domestic violence from people close to them. Student interest led to a campaign at the school centered on the Chris Brown–Rihanna case that was so much in the news. Several years later, one of the participants, Lulu, reflected on how deeply she was moved by this work and how it affected her career path, writing, "I learned about the issue of domestic violence through PeaceJam, and I feel that domestic violence has to end. No person deserves to be abused by others regardless of the reasons. I feel very strongly about this subject. I am now working on a social work major, and in the future I know I will be involved in this issue."

Project Masada

A third came to be known as Project Masada. During the summer of 2008, Sanjana, a rising junior PeaceJammer, traveled to Masada, her family's village in India, during a monsoon. Returning to the United States, she immediately sent me an email:

> While I was at my village, a flood struck, leaving us stranded for about one week. We had no power and our water supply ran out. . . . I felt pity for the farmers who worked so hard for a whole year just to see all their grains washed away all at once. Worst part was that the flood struck at the beginning of monsoon season, meaning another flood is very [possible]. I was wondering if we could raise money for those poor farmers whose year-long toil and mud houses wash away every time it rains. I thought this would be a good project for PeaceJam.

I applauded her concern and gave her the go-ahead. Sanjana expressed concern to the group about her plan to raise money for the villagers because her family remaining in the village had warned that local Indian officials could not necessarily be trusted to use donations to help the people. We spent the first few months of the school year brainstorming ways to turn this interest into a specific plan of action. Sanjana met with engineers from the local university to discuss building rain gutters to direct excess rainwater out of the village and into nearby rivers. She made presentations to local businesses using pictures of flooding she had taken during the week she was stranded and incorporating historical and geographical data she had gathered. People in our community seemed willing to help, but still the ideas seemed impossible, given the physical distance between our club and the Indian village.

One of the speakers at PeaceJam was from a group on justice and peace I was involved in outside of school. Through a translator, this artist from Nicaragua described his efforts to bring art education to poor children in his country. Sanjana described her response:

> He was using the artwork to educate us about how his children paid for education. Because free public education does not exist everywhere, many children have to use their own talents to pay for their own education. I was drawn to this effort because I realized how much I took my public education for granted. The determination of these children to attend school was so immense that it made me want to do something to help them.

Project Masada was born. Sanjana would lead it for the next 2 years. She made a pitch to her fellow PeaceJammers, using much of the presentation she had put together for community members, and asked for them to join her efforts. Though she still wanted to help the Indian farmers, she turned her attention to schoolchildren from her home village. Like the Nicaraguan children, they were not able to attend school beyond a certain age because of the cost of supplies and travel to a neighboring city. Sanjana and other interested PeaceJammers organized several fundraising projects: sales of Indian sweets Sanjana and her mother baked, for which the group created a brochure and pricing information; a raffle of artwork created and donated by PeaceJammers; sales of PeaceJam calendars with each month highlighting a different Nobel Peace laureate drawn by a PeaceJammer; and direct appeals for donations.

In the meantime, Sanjana created and distributed an application for interested schools in the Masada area. The group chose a primary school that seemed to most need the money for current books and writing tools. The group sent several hundred dollars through a local man traveling from our community to theirs, and the head of the school sent back descriptions of student use of the supplies. PeaceJammers used this knowledge the following year during fundraising efforts. Though other fundraising ideas surfaced, as advisor, I tried to stress the importance of students sharing their knowledge through all fundraising efforts so that their work would be service learning rather than mere service. This year, I felt like this project did help students challenge their beliefs and assumptions, especially early in the project when they were collaborating with people who had been to India, and that they grew in their understanding of the lives of the Masada villagers and some of the causes of poverty in the area

Sanjana wrote, "PeaceJam has made me realize that once you start giving, you are in debt to those who are receiving your gift; they will continue to look for your support. It is not just for one moment; it lasts forever." Sanjana is continuing

Project Masada at the college she is currently attending. She also returned to our school on a break from college to fight through our district's red tape to release the money raised the second year. She succeeded where I failed. Sanjana returned to India to deliver to another school the money the group raised during the second year and see firsthand the effects of her project.

Our First Regional Conference

In late spring each year, the Southeast Region of PeaceJam holds a conference in Tallahassee, Floria. During our first year of PeaceJam, our group was unable to attend the conference, but we raised enough money the second year to make it happen. After this first experience, students began to look forward to these trips. Much of the energy, enthusiasm, and inspiration students gained over the years originated in their time with the Nobel Peace laureates and with other PeaceJammers at these conferences. As freshman Emily wrote, "The PeaceJam conference was unlike any experience I've had before. I've never before been in a room filled with hundreds of people all hoping to teach the same goal: peace. It was inspiring. It made me feel like achieving a level of peace is a possibility, not just a juvenile dream." Fellow freshman Kimberley explained, "PeaceJam has motivated me to take action in [my school and town]. The stories that other people told at the conference about what they had achieved in their own schools made me realize that we could do the same things here."

At each conference students spent time in their "family groups" of about 15 students, none of whom were from the same PeaceJam chapter; each family group is led by two university students enrolled in PeaceJam. During this time, the students and their mentor-leaders shared their personal stories and listened to the experiences of others. Marian, a first-time sophomore participant, reflected,

> Family groups are pretty emotional. Everyone gets really intense and talks about their life and you kind of bond in a really short period of time with the other people, which was nice. I teared up a bit, I'm not going to lie, there were some meaningful things going on. There was a huge sense of togetherness. It was cool to know there are other people that are really concerned about the future and bringing peace and unity that are not just the people from your school.

Students also learned about global issues based in the Universal Declaration of Human Rights. During registration, students selected the issues of most interest to them personally, and those determined which workshops they attended and which protest rallies they participated in. Every year included training in leading protest marches and rallies, which led our students to develop their own protest march during our town's annual Human Rights Festival the following year.

However, what students mentioned most in their survey and interview responses was working closely with the Nobel Peace laureates. The laureates do not just speak to the students and then leave. They make several whole-group addresses and spend the rest of the time interacting personally with PeaceJam students, listening to their experiences, and giving them feedback on the Global Call to Action projects they have implemented during the year. At this first conference, Betty Williams was the laureate, and students responded strongly to her and her story. Freshman Cathy wrote,

> Hearing Betty Williams speak was extremely inspiring; I learned so much about the conflict between the Protestants and Catholics in Northern Ireland and about the importance of starting protests and marches in order to voice opinions and begin making changes. It was very encouraging for me to see so many young, diverse students gathering to learn about peaceful practices and all of the issues occurring today that need to be solved in peaceful ways instead of through violence.

Freshman Leandro added,

> Eight hours in a bus for a PeaceJam conference. Was it worth it? Yes. Betty Williams opened my eyes to how many problems there are in the world and how easy it is for someone to make a difference for the better if they're just willing to not be a bystander.

We returned with energy and resolve.

PEACEJAM YEARS 3 AND 4: ADDRESSING OUR LOW GRADUATION RATE

During Years 3 and 4, PeaceJammers continued the work on previous projects and also began some smaller individual projects. For example, junior Marie took interest in the school's health policy and the selection of items available in the lunch line. On her own, she conducted research about the use of local, fresh foods in school cafeterias and attended a conference on farmer's markets and locally grown food. She then met with our district nutritionist and presented her ideas, which led to the inclusion of locally grown vegetables in the school's salad bar. Marie actually changed school policy, an accomplishment that may lead her to larger successes in the future.

One group of students, frustrated by their perception that some teachers treated students differently based on their race, inquired into the root causes for racism. They read articles, watched film clips and documentaries, shared their own experiences, attended local talks and panel presentations on race, and brainstormed project ideas, including working with younger students to help them explore their own attitudes about race. We felt like the students who participated in this group came the closest of any PeaceJam group to understanding underlying causes of social injustice. Their inquiry and discussions were also important to the large goal the students adopted next.

The most galvanizing project of Years 3 and 4 was the focus on the high number of students, disproportionately students of color, who dropped out of our school.

Learning from Students Who Dropped Out

During the third year of PeaceJam, our school faced a lot of media attention for its continued status as a failing school, with the graduation rate hovering around 60%. At our weekly meetings, students discussed what this might mean in the lives of their fellow teenagers and for our community. Many PeaceJammers personally knew people who had recently dropped out or adults who had not earned a high school diploma, although many of them could not even imagine not earning college degrees, much less not finishing high school. Through their sharing of personal experience, students were able to speak to one another in ways more powerful than any words we adults could have expressed. Students seemed to feel a particular closeness to this issue because it affected their peers.

Students discussed the impact of dropping out, the cycle of poverty it perpetuates, and its potential causes. Goodrich and I saw this as an opportunity to encourage a critical approach rather than allowing students to jump immediately to solutions. According to Cipolle (2004), Freire's problem-posing approach to learning "exposes and questions presuppositions, and allows students to see the injustices that must be overcome. By incorporating Freire's methodology, service-learning can participate in the unveiling and problematizing the current reality of inequity, oppression, and domination" (p. 22). We asked students to consider how they might gather more perspectives on the issue of dropouts. How might they figure out what assumptions they were making? How might they question their own interpretations of reality? Who might be the stakeholders and potential partners in this issue?

Through this reflective process, students decided to interview people, young and old, who had dropped out of school to learn why, and what might have changed their decision. One student wrote interview questions and shared them with the group. The students wanted the school administration to give them a list of recent dropouts, but for privacy reasons, the school would not release those names. However, students informally interviewed as many people as they knew and reported back what they had learned.

Students gained an understanding that there are as many reasons people drop out of school as there are people who drop out. Some of their assumptions: People were bored with classes, needed to raise money for a family, or take care of young children. But they gained new insights. Students who dropped out often felt a lack of connection with their classmates and teachers, a lack of support from the school community, and a sense of failure when their skills lagged behind those of other students. In discussing these reasons, several students expressed that they had never before thought about the way that they treat their classmates as having any impact on them. They expressed almost a sense of shame for not having done better in their interactions with peers and not having reached out to help students who were struggling. Lulu, a senior whose family is not wealthy, reflected on the connection that she saw developing between dropping out and poverty. She wrote, "PeaceJam has opened my eyes to the poverty that exists here in [our town]. I've lived here for most of my life, and I have never thought much about the poverty."

The learning during this part of the project was the closest we had come to helping students question the underlying social and political forces behind the community needs they were observing. For junior Shimdo, stories she heard during the interviews "opened my eyes to the fact that governments aren't always as fair as they appear to be."

It was gratifying to watch this critical consciousness develop. Although we could have continued exploring the root causes of the high dropout rate for another decade, we decided we knew at least enough to start working on an action plan.

The Graduation Pledge

The students decided that the dropout rate should be everyone's concern, not just those who were dropping out. Goodrich and an interested group of students wrote a graduation pledge (see Figure 8.1) with roles and responsibilities for each segment of the school community—students, teachers, parents, and community members.

Students circulated the pledge, explaining it to teachers, students, and administrators and urging them to sign. Then the group talked about how to reach a larger audience, in particular the community outside of the school. They reasoned that a community like ours, with plenty of wealth and a state university, should have the resources to radically increase high school graduation rates.

Students first went to the school board. Ashley Goodrich introduced Peace-Jam and spoke about the history and creation of the graduation pledge. Then one member of each segment represented by the pledge read that section aloud. The audience exploded into applause, and the board president thanked the group, offering encouragement for their efforts. Each of the school board members signed the pledge, as did many of the community members and parents present. Goodrich was contacted repeatedly by people who had heard about the pledge or had watched the board meeting on local television.

Figure 8.1. Graduation Pledge

- We pledge to help our community raise the graduation rate so that every child in Athens, Georgia, has the opportunity to live in a world without poverty.
- We recognize that raising the graduation rate demands a commitment from all of us.
- We understand for this to occur, we will need to reach out to one another, build relationships, and hold each other accountable.
- We believe that raising the graduation rate is one piece of the puzzle to ending the cycle of poverty.

Student:

- Encourage your friends to stay in school.
- Attend tutoring.
- Be a tutor.
- Open up to your peers, parents, teachers, counselors, and administrators to overcome difficulties in school.
- Become aware of the benefits of having a high school diploma.
- Get involved with school activities and clubs.
- Go to school every day.
- Look for opportunities that will help you be successful in school.
- Understand that you can be both successful in school and cool with your friends.
- Know that your teachers are there to help you, not to make your life harder.

Parent:

- Get involved in your child's education.
- Be aware of what the school and community has to offer for helping your child be successful in school (i.e., Parent Teacher Student Organizations, tutoring programs, school enrichment programs, parenting classes).
- Talk to your child about the importance of staying in school.
- Help your child overcome their academic struggles.
- Encourage your child to attend school every day.
- Volunteer in classrooms and at school functions.
- Help your child with homework.
- Know what your child is learning at school.
- Communicate with your child's teachers regularly.

(continued)

Figure 8.1. (continued)

Teacher:

- Foster an appreciation for learning.
- Partake in a poverty simulation.
- Offer students help before and after school.
- Create an engaging and culturally relevant curriculum.
- Help your students navigate the education system.
- Network with other teachers to target and assist struggling students.
- Be aware of emotional and social issues that students face.
- Be an advocate for your students.

Community Member:

- Mentor a child.
- Partner with a school.
- Volunteer with tutoring programs.
- Speak at local schools about your academic experiences, the importance of a high school diploma, and life after high school.

Everyone:

- Raise awareness about the effect of the graduation rate on poverty.
- Participate in community-wide efforts to raise the graduation rate.
- Contact your local representatives to put more funding toward education.

Energized by the experience, students wanted to do more. Our town hosts an annual Human Rights Festival. Goodrich convinced the festival organizers to give PeaceJam a 15-minute speaking slot on Saturday morning and then organized a march from our school to the downtown area where the festival was held. As mentioned previously, students had participated in a protest march during their first PeaceJam conference, and had learned how to make posters, chant slogans, and garner enthusiasm from passersby. Two of our usually reticent students had also attended the conference and volunteered to make flyers in Spanish so that all students at our school could participate. About 40 students marched downtown, chanting, "Beg, plead, scream, and shout . . . never let a friend drop out!" "Education is the key . . . to ending all this poverty!" and "We're aware and we can't wait . . . to raise the graduation rate!"

At the rally, three students gave speeches about the graduation rate, the cycle of poverty, and the graduation pledge. Then a group of current and future

PeaceJammers sang John Mayer's "Waiting for the World to Change." The crowd applauded wildly, and many people stopped by the PeaceJam booth that afternoon to sign the pledge and to express how impressed they were with the young activists. The organizers of the festival expressed the same sentiment and invited PeaceJam back the following year.

IMPACT ON INDIVIDUAL STUDENTS

One of the most rewarding aspects of PeaceJam has been watching the impact on individual students. For example, the students who attended the regional PeaceJam conference the third year worked with Iranian lawyer Shirin Ebadi and focused on the rights of women and children. More than any of the other laureates, her impact seemed to be specifically career-related, as two of the students who attended the conference returned with revised plans for their futures. Sophomore Marian told us, "I decided to become a lawyer. Because the thing about Shirin Ebadi is she was a really small lady that seemed really unassuming, but she was kind of, I guess like our emcee called her, this giant. I feel like I have the resources luckily to do whatever I want to do and there doesn't seem to be much of a more noble cause than helping other people who can't help themselves. . . . I kind of have thought about being a lawyer, but I got to high school and didn't even want to go to college, but now, I want to go to college." Junior Michael decided to drop his plans to be a corporate lawyer because of the money and instead work in the field of civil rights.

Many of the students who participated in PeaceJam were not involved in other school activities. They found in PeaceJam a sense of community and connection with their peers.

Edwin struggled academically his freshman year and showed little interest in doing better. He decided to join PeaceJam when he learned from Goodrich that the Nobel Peace laureate we would be meeting that year was Rigoberta Menchú Tum. As a native Guatemalan, he had met her previously. I think the idea of a club whose mission included respecting and studying the life of someone of his ethnic background made a difference to him. He attended meetings and shared his experiences, and I saw other PeaceJammers gain respect for him because of his life experiences. Edwin was generally quiet in his classes; PeaceJam was one of the only school contexts in which he interacted with other students. Tragically, Edwin was diagnosed with cancer later that year. The students organized a fundraiser to help his family financially. When Edwin was unable to attend the conference to meet Rigoberta Menchú Tum, the students took one of her biographies, told her Edwin's story, and gave Edwin the book signed with Tum's personal message hoping for his recovery.

Lulu joined PeaceJam during its first year, her sophomore year. I saw a generosity of spirit in her that I wanted to help foster. She worked so hard to ensure that all club activities were welcoming to our growing Latin@ student population. When she was close to graduation, she joked with me about coming back the following year to help lead the group and to chaperone during the conference trip, an idea I welcomed but did not take seriously; students seldom look back once they have graduated. However, at the beginning of the following school year, Lulu contacted me to ask if she and another student could come back and help lead the current PeaceJammers. I was thrilled.

Although the girls weren't able to lead sessions because of their class schedule, they did work with me every week during my planning period to develop the lessons on race for that year's students. Lulu was enrolled in a sociology class that required a community service project, and she convinced her instructor to allow her to serve as a PeaceJam curriculum planner. We communicated by email and in person every week, and Lulu's contributions became the basis for many of the readings and discussions about race that students experienced that year. We spent many hours discussing the lessons about race and class she was exploring through her coursework and the materials she gathered. She reflected, "When I became a part of PeaceJam I was a very quiet person. PeaceJam has taught me leadership skills and helped me feel more involved in the school and most importantly in the community. Those skills carried out through the rest of my high school years and now in my first year of college." Lulu continued,

> PeaceJam gave me an opportunity to feel like I could do something even though I was only a high school student. I was amazed at the infinite number of things I could do to make a change. As a Latina in this country it is not exactly easy to live while feeling as if you don't belong. But at our regular meetings we were able to voice our concerns and discuss with our peers. Not only that but we realized that no matter what our backgrounds were, we were similar and shared ideas.

Lulu's friend, Michelle, had been retained in 8th grade because of low state test scores, so she entered high school a year behind the students she had always known as her classmates. Michelle struggled her freshman year, including in my class, but it seemed to me that she just needed a focus for her energy, so I invited her to PeaceJam that first year. Michelle became a vocal advocate for our Latin@ students and translated many of our flyers and announcements into Spanish. She enthusiastically volunteered for jobs during meetings and yelled the loudest during protest marches. She was a lot of fun to be with, but perhaps more important, PeaceJam seemed to give her a reason for staying on track. Michelle graduated with her original class and told me before graduation that PeaceJam was largely responsible for her successful turnaround.

STUDENTS EVALUATE BECOMING PEACE AND JUSTICE ACTIVISTS

The academic, social, personal, and career benefits of service learning have been explored in depth elsewhere, but in studying the survey and interview responses of current and former PeaceJam participants, I identified three themes related to positive and lasting impact on students' lives: leadership, student voice, and preparation for adulthood.

The project leaders in particular seemed to gain leadership skills beyond what high school extracurricular activities often afford them. For example, when asked what she learned from Project Masada, senior Sanjana wrote,

> The most rewarding experience was the ability to be a group leader. Not only did this opportunity allow me to grow personally but also gain interpersonal skills. For as long as my project was underway, I was in full charge of what I wanted to do and when. This also allowed me to learn time and money management techniques. I used to think it was easy to coordinate programs, but I realized that putting a program into action is a lot harder than hypothetically thinking of one.

Many students expressed changes in their perceptions of their role within the world, no longer seeing their rights as being hindered by age or lack of power. Sophomore Avery wrote,

> I now see myself as more of a leader because I know I have a voice and that I can have an impact or make a difference. I now hold myself accountable for making a change for the better in the world.

Hand-in-hand with growth in leadership, many students' perceptions of themselves as being important voices of change grew. They no longer felt like powerless bystanders. Senior Shimdo wrote, "At first, I didn't see myself standing out in the community. Since I joined PeaceJam, I really see myself being an important aspect of my community." Many reticent students found in PeaceJam a safe space for exercising their voice and asserting their beliefs. Sophomore Avery wrote,

> Something as small as sitting around with a group of people in our club and talking about an issue and how we can help a situation was rewarding. Often times in classes we don't get the opportunity to really share our thoughts and opinions on things, and to be given free-rein to do so was very rewarding in so many ways.

As students put into action what they had discussed in meetings, they gained confidence as voices of change. Senior Sanjana explained, "In PeaceJam, I was treated like an adult. My ideas were heard, and I was encouraged to further pursue my plans."

Finally, several students identified their work through PeaceJam as practice for their adult roles in their communities. PeaceJam student founder Alice said, "Just making a difference on a small scale can give you an idea of how to make a difference on a larger scale." Senior Sally wrote, "PeaceJam informs high school students around the country of global issues and events that have an effect on people's rights and privileges as individuals. . . . It prepares students for how they wish to participate as adults in worldly matters." Junior Rebecca reflected on the importance of practicing handling conflict at her age so that those behaviors become ingrained as students move into adulthood. She said,

> It seems like however people respond to a violation of their rights now, that's how they will respond as adults. I think it is really important right now how someone goes about doing something like that.

As anyone who teaches knows, working with teenagers brings with it a natural ebb and flow. There were times that students found it difficult to sleep because their minds were racing with ideas and possibilities; there were also times when we seemed to lose our focus or get swallowed up in the demands of coursework and school responsibilities. My work with PeaceJam and the Rights of the Child inquiry group kept me afloat during times when it seemed as if the entire education world had gone mad. The sacred space created for and by PeaceJam students renewed me to face these challenges.

The discussion of rights through the Universal Declaration of Human Rights and the Rights of the Child gave us a foundation and anchor for discussions about local issues. This grounding in a concrete listing of rights helped prevent discussions from drifting (at least most of the time) too far away from the realities of life in our community. After all, for teenagers, as for most of us, our reality often appears as the only possible reality. It often takes interactions such as the ones we had in PeaceJam to start thinking about ways in which the world might be ordered differently.

Additionally, as a group we had to decide for ourselves if and how some of the rights on the list are rights in the first place. This was no easy task, as students often found their political and social beliefs being challenged by classmates. For example, during the development of the focus on education during the third year, some students were initially resistant to considering education a right for people who chose to drop out, regardless of potential external forces that may have contributed to this decision; after all, they argued, people who had dropped out had made that choice for themselves. However, once students felt comfortable enough with each other to voice their challenges, we were able to engage in some of the most transformative conversations of my teaching career. I grew personally alongside students through the discussions that unfolded.

Through our discussions at the beginning of each year and then our cycling back to the rights throughout the year, we addressed without explicitly invoking it Article 42, "Knowledge of Rights": "Governments [and I would add schools as government agencies] should make the Convention known to adults and children. Adults should help children learn about their rights, too." Despite our failings and the ways in which we would have worked differently given our current knowledge, the development of students' understanding of their rights and the responsibilities that accompany them has been cause for celebration.

I close with Alice, who inspired us to start PeaceJam and inspires me to continue. She seems to speak for PeaceJam students as well as for me as a teacher:

> I know PeaceJam had an impact on me because it made me want to go into education.... There are so many ways that the system is failing kids and teachers too and making it impossible for everyone to come together to reach this common goal.... I think it motivated me to do something bigger, to work towards being able to make a bigger difference.

9

Literature as a Springboard for Critical Inquiry

An Annotated Bibliography

Jaye Thiel, Jen McCreight, and Dawan Coombs

Invitation to Explore:
Children's Literature for Teaching the Rights of the Child

Initiating Experience:

It's a big deal to represent people, groups, and issues as authentically as possible, and we as teachers need help in selecting such texts. We briefly describe some of the ways we and other authors in this book employ children's literature in critical inquiries, including noticing charts, framing discussion with the 3 P's (power, position, and perspective; Jones, 2006), comparison charts, and invitations. The chapter includes a bibliography of books organized by the Rights of the Child that we taught, and that we feel are most likely to be addressed in K–12 classrooms.

Formal Invitation:

We invite you to explore the books in this annotated bibliography, and add to it as you tailor this resource for your own purposes. You may have information that challenges the authenticity of texts representing particular groups of people; this is an ongoing part of the inquiry for us.

Suggested Questions:

1. What ways can teachers at all grade levels use children's literature, especially picture books, to engage in critical inquiry?
2. What children's literature have you found that leads to in-depth discussion about social issues?

---

3. How can teachers introduce children's literature on social justice issues, including the Rights of the Child, in ways that allow for differing perspectives and critical inquiry?

Texts, Tools, and Resources:

We included an annotated bibliography, web resources, and professional references, plus strategies for using children's literature in critical inquiry. We address all the Rights of the Child Articles in this volume, with an overall commitment to Article 17, "Children have the right to get information that is important to their health and well-being. . . . Children should also have access to children's books."

As the participants in our workshop leafed through books displayed on tables around the room, the three of us chatted with teachers concerning their questions about the texts we selected. We had spent 30 minutes discussing the use of diverse pieces of children's literature to illustrate and develop a deeper understanding of social issues in the classroom and now participants were browsing the texts we had referenced. The conversations turned to American Indian representations in children's literature and why some were more appropriate than others. After our explanation about the importance of selecting texts that accurately depict American Indian culture, one woman asked, "Is it really that big of a deal? If this book portrays Native Americans in a beautiful way, how could it be a bad choice?"

As teachers, we've probably all asked that question in some form. Is it really that big a deal? In the scheme of classroom instruction and dialogue, does book choice really matter?

For us, the answer is a resounding yes.

The three of us work or have worked with students from different age groups and ability levels, Jen and Jaye in the southeast and Dawan in the southwest United States. Jen taught kindergarten in a school that was 70% Latin@, 25% African American, and 5% European American; 99% of the families qualified for free or reduced-price lunch (FRL). Jaye taught children across grade levels K–5 in a school that was 78% African American, 14% Latin@, 6% European American, and 2% Asian, with a similar FRL rate. Dawan taught struggling readers and writers in a high school with 35% Latin@ and 65% European American; 40% of the students qualified for FRL.

Despite our school differences, we all believe that the books we read to and with our student and the ways in which those books are read and discussed are integral to how students (and we) understand self, others, and the subjects we study through them. Stories offer ways for individuals to make sense of their experiences and transform their realities (Kearney, 2002). Therefore, it is vital that the stories we share and the conversations around them represent the lives of all our students, as well as the lives of children whom our students come to know only through literature.

As teachers who feel that part of our role is to advocate for all students, we have located children's literature that addresses the UN Rights of the Child *and* that represents children of diverse backgrounds. We employed the Articles of the Rights of the Child to organize this annotated bibliography, a critical literacy resource that represents a multitude of cultures and ideologies. It is important to emphasize that we know that one book cannot represent all cultures or all backgrounds and identities. Instead, we use this list as a starting place to engage students in critical conversations and dialogic practices that encourage going beyond self and preconceived ideas of who and what others are.

CHILDREN'S RIGHTS, CRITICAL LITERACY, AND STUDENT IDENTITIES

When faced with the demands of teaching, educators may find themselves turning to traditional texts and lectures to meet district, state, and federal standards and accountability mandates. Unfortunately, this type of teaching often mirrors the "banking concept" (Freire, 1970) where information is "deposited" instead of students actively seeking it based on their own interests, concerns, and backgrounds. Tired of timelines and "whitewashed" curriculum, we felt there had to be a better way to introduce students to academic concepts, a way in which student lives were valued and their rights as learners were honored. Instead of our students being spoken to, we wanted them to speak up (Wade, 2007). We wanted the "academic" to also reflect the social and political interests of the children in our classroom, the families we work with, and the communities in which they live.

The Rights of the Child lend themselves well to critical literacy and to addressing issues of social justice. We hoped that by inviting students to explore these topics, they would establish connections to social issues relevant to their own lives and develop deeper understandings of marginalized and underrepresented cultures and communities. We sought out children's literature as a trusted medium to help students investigate their own lives as well as the lives of those different from themselves.

However, our local bookstore carried few books by African American and Latin@ authors—this, in a town where the majority population in many public schools is African American and/or Latin@. Texts play a role in the shaping of students' identities, not just their reading skills. How will children who don't see themselves or their families in the books schools offer ever make connections to their individual and cultural identities? As Jones (2008) pointedly wondered, if "texts mediate understandings of ourselves and of the worlds around us . . . what if the mediator doesn't acknowledge our existence?" (p. 44).

New Literacies Studies frame literacy not as a neutral skill, but "a social practice . . . rooted in conceptions of knowledge, identity, and being" (Street, 2003, pp. 77–78). Literacy is heavily influenced by culture and social relations, demonstrating "how literacy practices are linked to people's lives, identities, and social affiliations" and the way literacy learning is about more than just the development of basic skills (Compton-Lilly, 2009, p. 88). It is no coincidence that "in many classrooms, students of color do reject literacy, for they feel that literate Discourses reject them" (Delpit, 1993, p. 290). Therefore, it is essential to provide students with literature that allows linguistically, ethnically, and socioeconomically diverse children to see themselves represented. It is our job as educators to provide these examples

Why, then, is it so difficult to find culturally authentic children's literature, books that are more than inaccurate portrayals of groups "in a beautiful way"? Joseph Bruchac (2011) pointed out that it's difficult for American Indian writers of children's literature to publish authentic stories that are not "cute" or commercial—stories that don't "fit the mold." American Indian authors like Bruchac are often told to "rewrite traditional tales or stories that are culturally accurate in ways that might make them more acceptable to a non-Indian editor but render them no longer authentic." He concluded that "we need to enlighten and educate not just the critics and the reading public, but also editors and presses" so that children can read "good books by a wide variety of writers accurately representing their own cultures" (p. 344).

In critical inquiry classrooms, children's literature serves as a catalyst, a springboard for discussion rather than stagnant statement of fact, reality, or "truth." Such a perspective allows us to open our classrooms to the complexities of the world through narratives. This idea continues to represent an essential part of what it means to implement a critical pedagogy in our classrooms by utilizing the Rights of the Child as a springboard for developing critical literacies.

CHILDREN'S LITERATURE AS A SPRINGBOARD:
INSTRUCTIONAL STRATEGIES

We understand that there is intense pressure on educators to prepare their students to pass reading and math standardized tests, which in turn, leaves little time left for social issues and topics that are important to students. However, we believe that by approaching literacy practices through the lens of the Rights of the Child, we can provide an excellent foundation for students to explore social interests by reading, writing, and discussing literature that is representative of a wide range of cultures and identities. Therefore, this bibliography is organized according to the Articles of the Rights of the Child.

We spent many hours poring over books in local and classroom libraries in order to find texts we felt appropriately represented race, class, gender, and other aspects of identity. We researched to the best of our ability and discussed at length the authenticity of each text and ways in which groups of people may have been misrepresented; we continue to reevaluate with every new reading of these texts. These books are meant to spark discussion, not to represent the experiences of all children from particular backgrounds, cultures, and identities, as we know that lives are complex, multiple, and varied. However, in sharing a variety of diverse experiences, we hope all children and teachers will benefit.

Every classroom is different, and these books will speak to each community of learners in different ways. With this in mind, we share the following teaching strategies in an effort to provide readers with possible starting points to engage readers and texts in meaningful ways.

Noticing Charts

Prior to reading books from any of the following groups, create a chart with space to write down what students notice about a specific group of text (see Figure 9.1). Post this chart in your room for the duration of your study and add to it as more texts are read. For a deeper understanding of noticing charts, visit Katie Wood Ray's work on reading like a writer in *Wondrous Words* (Ray, 1999).

The 3 P's: Perspective, Positioning, and Power

Stephanie Jones provides a critical literacy framework we have found highly useful in helping students examine assumptions as they read and discuss literature. Jones (2008) argued that

1. all texts are constructed by people informed by particular ideologies and therefore entrenched in perspective;
2. all texts make the experiences of some people seem more valuable than others, enabling some to exercise power more freely than others and therefore contribute to social and political positioning; and
3. all texts grow from language practices embedded in relations of social and political differentials that are inequitably distributed across society therefore both indicative—and generative—of power. (p. 49)

There are many books that lend themselves to discussion around each concept, and these may be used to introduce the 3 P's in the classroom. For instance, see these texts below: *Si, Se Puede! Yes We Can! Janitor Strikes in LA.* (Power), *Voices in the Park* (Position), and *Duck! Rabbit!* (Perspective). For further clarification on the 3 P's, see *Girls, Social Class, and Literacy* (Jones, 2006).

Anchor Charts

For visual learners, it may be useful to use Venn diagrams and t-charts to record comparisons between texts or to make connections between texts and student

Figure 9.1. Noticing Chart Example

Title:	What do you notice and why?	Name it:	Examples in other books:	Examples in historical and current events or our own experiences:
EX: *My Name is Yoon* by Helen Recorvitz	Yoon does not like writing her name in English.	I think this book represents culture and maybe power.	*The Name Jar* by Yangsook Choi	Sometimes I want to write in Spanish because I can say more than in English. But in school I have to use English. (Jose)
EX:				

experiences. During the thematic study, a class may compare one book's position with another book's position about a theme, providing the class with an opportunity to look at both texts with a critical eye. We also often begin a unit with a K-W-H-L chart in which the students provide what they *know* about a theme, what they *want* to know, *how* they could find out, and what they are *learning*.

Thematic Reader Response Forms

As students become familiar with the Rights of Child, our hope is that they will continue to build on the topics introduced in class. One way to ensure that students revisit themes previously discussed is through the use of reader response forms. One simple form we use provides an opportunity for students to share connections, disconnections, and discussion questions posed during independent and choice readings outside of a thematic study. Student record the title and author, and respond to two prompts: 1) My text fits into the _____ theme because _____; and 2) A question I have about this text/theme is _____.

Invitations and Critical Questions

Invitations are a way to invite learners to explore a topic of interest. They offer students opportunities to explore literature while thinking about specific questions related to the text. For example, a group of students may be invited to read books surrounding a particular theme, such as power, culture, or one of the Rights of the Child. There are many examples of invitations throughout this book.

Creating questions that foster critical inquiry can be a challenge in creating invitations. Mendoza and Reese (2001) argued that "teachers select books with strong positive images of people from groups that have been marginalized," and that they also help students interrogate all the literature they read with questions such as

- Are characters "outside the mainstream culture" depicted as individuals or as caricatures?
- Does their representation include significant specific cultural information? Or does it follow stereotypes?
- Who has the power in this story? What is the nature of their power, and how do they use it?
- Who has wisdom? What is the nature of their wisdom, and how do they use it?
- What are the consequences of certain behaviors? What behaviors or traits are rewarded, and how? What behaviors are punished, and how?
- How is language used to create images of people of a particular group? How are artistic elements used to create those images?
- Who has written this story? Who has illustrated it? Are they inside or outside the groups they are presenting? What are they in a position to know? What do they claim to know?
- Whose voices are heard? Whose are missing?
- What do this narrative and these pictures say about race? Class? Culture? Gender? Age? Resistance to the status quo?

Learning Walls

As you delve into critical inquiry, it is important to provide students with a way to reference the reading and the work they have done on each theme. Jen and Jaye used learning walls as a record of important texts, discussions, and student writing. Vivian Vasquez's (2008) *Negotiating Critical Literacies with Young Children* describes learning walls in her classroom of 3- to 5-year-olds as an "audit trail" that included book covers, transcripts of conversations about books, photographs, newspaper clippings, toys, ads, and other artifacts that represented "our theories of the world about things that mattered to us" (p. 3).

RIGHTS OF THE CHILD BIBLIOGRAPHY

The following annotated bibliography contains a list of children's literature that focuses on the issues specified in the Rights of the Child and a list of additional resources. It is important to note that we did not include each article but rather chose to focus on the rights we spent the most time with in our classrooms and that are most often referenced in this book. A brief overview of each right included precedes each list and is intended as background for instructional purposes. All books are in print, unless otherwise noted.

Article 1: Definition of the Child

Children are people below the age of 18, unless the laws of the country set the legal age of adulthood younger.

Arlon, Penelope (Ed.). (2003). *How people live.* New York: DK Publishing. [Informational; world literature.]

> *This book is organized into specific geographical regions and details the inhabitants of the regions. More of a reference text, the descriptions provide artifact and culturally relevant events via short text and vivid color photos. Teaching notes: This book could also be used as a discussion point for stereotypes and how generalizing people by regions could fuel stereotypical perceptions of the people who live there. (Also pair with Article 8: Preservation of identity.)*

Article 2: Non-discrimination

It doesn't matter where children live, what language they speak, what their parents do, whether they are boys or girls, what their culture is, whether they have a disability, or whether they are rich or poor. No child should be treated unfairly on any basis.

Bridges, Ruby. (1991). *Through my eyes.* New York: Scholastic Press. [Autobiography.]

> *An intriguing account of the events surrounding Ruby Bridges's life, this memoir not only tells the story of Ruby integrating schools but also follows her as she took the path of social activism throughout her life. The book is compiled with quotes, article clippings/headlines, sepia photographs, and firsthand accounts that examine power struggle within the racial context of our society. (Also pair with Article 28: Right to education and Article 29: Goals of education.)*

Krull, Kathleen. (2003). Harvesting hope: The story of César Chávez. Illus. Yuyi Morales. San Diego: Harcourt Publishers. [Biography]

> *Beautiful, flowing illustrations and glimpses of César Chávez's childhood draw readers into this biography. The text paints a picture of the difficulties migrant farm working families have historically faced, and the reasons behind Chávez's decision to do something about the poor treatment of farm workers. The book culminates in the vivid retelling of Chávez's nonviolent march protesting the working conditions of migrant farmers in California. (Also pair with Article 8: Preservation of identity and Article 30: Children of minorities/indigenous groups.)*

Lester, Julius. (2005). *Let's talk about race.* Illus. Karen Barbour. New York: Harper Collins Publishers. [Monologue.]

> *Written as a way to dispel prejudice associated with skin color, this book takes on the tough discussions associated with race. The narration examines the ways people are the same and questions the reader's perception of culture. Lester's book creates a text that explains race is just a piece of a person's identity, not the whole. (Also pair with Article 8: Preservation of identity and Article 30: Children of minorities/indigenous groups.)*

Mitchell, Margaree King. (1993). *Uncle Jed's barbershop.* New York: Simon and Schuster Books. [Realistic fiction.]

> *As a barber whose years of work take place within the years of the Great Depression and segregation, Uncle Jed's belief that he will one day own his own barbershop never wavers. Though the narrator, his niece Sarah Jean, explains again and again that her uncle has faced devastating setbacks, his perseverance toward this lifelong goal is undeterred. Uncle Jed finally realizes his dreams on his seventy-ninth birthday, and is able to stand proudly in the middle of a barbershop of which he is the owner. (Also pair with Article 27: Adequate standard of living.)*

Article 5: Parental Guidance

Governments should respect the rights and responsibilities of families to direct and guide their children so that, as they grow, they learn to use their rights properly.

Garza, Carmen Lomas. (1990). Illus. Carmen Lomas Garza. *Family pictures/Cuadros de familia.* San Francisco: Children's Book Press. [Personal narrative.]

> *Written in Spanish and English, Garza shares intimate details of her childhood, with each story providing vivid pictures of her young life within the spread of only one page. Brightly colored, detailed illustrations invite Garza's audience to immerse themselves in her world, and each brief narrative can easily be read again and again. (Also pair with Article 1: Definition of the child; Article 8: Preservation of identity; and Article 30: Children of minorities/indigenous groups.)*

Garza, Carmen Lomas. (1996). Illus. Carmen Lomas Garza. *In my family/en mi familia.* San Francisco: Children's Book Press. [Personal narrative.]

> *The follow up book to* Family Pictures, *this bilingual text invites readers into the lives of Garza and her family members. Made up entirely of short stories, the book is accessible to young children, while providing details that make each story come alive on the page. (Also pair with Article 1: Definition of the child; Article 8: Preservation of identity; and Article 30: Children of minorities/indigenous groups.)*

Kennedy, Fran. (2004). *The pickle patch bathtub.* Illus. Lisa Campbell Ernst. Berkely, CA: Tricycle Press. [Nonfiction.]

> *Set in the 1920s, this book tells the story of what happens when the children outgrow a washtub and the family is faced with raising money in order to purchase a real bathtub. Based on a true story, the text explores how a family works together in order to accomplish*

a goal. (Also pair with Article 24: Health and health services and Article 27: Adequate standard of living.)

Parnell, Peter. (2005). *And Tango makes three.* Illus. Justin Richardson. New York: Simon & Schuster Children's Publishing. [Nonfiction.]

> *A true story, this book details the life of two male penguins at the New York Central Park Zoo. Roy and Silo did not partner with penguins of the opposite sex but instead partnered together. Roy and Silo created a nest and tried to hatch rocks. They wanted to be a family. An observant zookeeper notices the couple and gives them an abandoned egg to hatch. Together, Roy and Silo hatch the egg to bring Tango into the world. (Also pair with Article 8: Preservation of identity.)*

Article 8: Preservation of identity

Children have the right to an identity. The government should respect children's right to a name, a nationality, and family ties.

Choi, Yangsook, (2001). *The name jar.* Illus. Yangsook Choi. New York: Libri. [Realistic fiction.]

> *As she begins her life in the United States, Unhei is unsure of how to bring parts of her Korean world to her new home. When classmates cannot pronounce her Korean name correctly, Unhei decides to ask for help in deciding on a new name. She soon finds that she is not the only one struggling to merge two different cultural backgrounds, and is strengthened by new relationships in her decision to keep her Korean name—and to teach her new friends about her family's history. (Also pair with Article 30: Children of minorities/indigenous groups.)*

hooks, bell. (1999). *Happy to be nappy.* Illus. Chris Raschka. New York: Jump at the Sun/ Hyperion Books. [Realistic fiction.]

> *This book is a celebration of hair! hooks provides a story that not only illuminates the beauty of African American hair but also details the bonding of "doing" hair with family in the home. This book not only provides the reader with a positive image of culture but also of self. (Also pair with Article 30: Children of minorities/indigenous groups.)*

Locker, Thomas. (2001). *Home: A journey through America.* Illus. Thomas Locker. Orlando, FL: Voyager Books. [Nonfiction.]

> *Through beautiful oil paintings and the words of celebrated authors, Locker depicts the varied landscapes that make up America. This is an excellent resource to use for teachers focusing on regionalism and a great way to make interdisciplinary connections.*

Park, Frances, & Park, Ginger. (2005). The Have a Good Day Café. Illus. Katherine Potter. New York: Lee & Low Books Inc. [Realistic fiction.]

> *This is a story of a Korean American family whose food cart is the primary source of income for this family and whose business is threatened by the movement of other food carts into the area. The grandmother and son decide to sell traditional Korean food out of the cart to make their cart unique and represent their culture, which in turn boosts their sales. (Also pair with Article 30: Children of minorities/indigenous groups.)*

Recorvitz, Helen. (2003). *My name is Yoon*. Illus. Gabi Swiatkowska. New York: Frances Foster Books. Realistic fiction. [Realistic fiction.]

> *Yoon struggles with the love for her family and the love of her Korean culture. Unhappy with her American written name, Yoon would rather write in Korean but her parents, teacher, and classmates want her to learn English. Renaming herself, in order to try to find a place of belonging in her American school, Yoon soon realizes that no matter how she writes her name, she will always be Yoon. (Also pair with Article 2: Non-discrimination and Article 30: Children of minorities/indigenous groups.)*

Woodson, Jacqueline. (2005). *Show way*. Illus. Hudson Talbott. New York: Putnam Juvenile. [Family history.]

> *Based on her own family history, Woodson shows the strengths of African American families through seven generations of girls and women through their quilts (made to "show the way" to slaves fleeing to freedom), art, and activism through freedom marches and the fight for literacy. Beautifully illustrated, inspiring, and lyrical, this book would be a good springboard to talk about family names, family beliefs, and family traditions as well as how countries have too often denied certain people (slaves, immigrants who are undocumented) the right to name themselves, speak their own language, claim their nationality, and keep their families together.*

Article 10: Family reunification

Families whose members live in different countries should be allowed to move between those countries so that parents and children can stay in contact, or get back together as a family.

Anzaldua, Gloria. (1997). *Friends from the other side/amigos del otro lado*. Illus. Consuelo Méndez. San Francisco, CA: Children's Book Press. [Realistic fiction.]

> *A powerful combination of text and drawings that present the realities of border crossing. A young Chicana girl living in Texas meets a boy who has crossed the border illegally with his mother. Through the young girl's eyes, the reader watches the way her new friend and his mother experience taunting, hiding from patrol officers, and the challenges of that kind of entry into the United States. Although families in this book are not separated, this book could easily serve as a catalyst of discussions about this issue. (Also pair with Article 2: Non-discrimination and Article 30: Children of minorities/indigenous groups.)*

Herrera, Juan Felipe. (2003). *Super cilantro girl: La superniña del cilantro*. Illus. Honorio Robledo Tapia. San Francisco, CA: Children's Book Press. [Modern fantasy.]

> *This is the story of a girl who rescues her mother, who is being detained at the border. Through a wish for her mother's safety, Esmeralda starts to turn bright green (the color of cilantro) and she obtains super powers. She then flies to her mother and brings her home. Bilingual: English and Spanish. (Also pair with Article 2: Non-discrimination and Article 30: Children of minorities/indigenous groups.)*

Article 12: Respect for the views of the child

When adults are making decisions that affect children, children have the right to say what they think should happen and have their opinions taken into account.

Browne, Anthony. (1998). *Voices in the park*. Illus. Anthony Browne. New York: DK Publishers. [Fiction.]

> *Through shifts in perspective, the experiences of four sets of eyes reveal very different experiences. The stories of four distinctly different individuals are reflected in both the words and pictures of the changing environment. A great book to use to teach point of view and perspective. (Also pair with Article 13: Freedom of expression and Article 31: Leisure, play, and culture.)*

Morrison, Toni & Morrison, Slade (1999). *The big box*. Illus. Giselle Potter. New York: Jump at the Sun. [Fiction.]

> *This book explores a world where students are placed inside a box if they "misbehave" or act "differently" from their peers and can't seem to "handle their freedom." The adults in this story take liberty away from these children by placing them in a box and controlling all aspects of their life. The box in this story serves as a powerful metaphor for resistance against individuality, freedom, and the rigid nature of the school environment. (Also pair with Article 13: Freedom of expression and Article 31: Leisure, play, and culture.)*

Rosenthal, Amy K. (2009). *Duck! Rabbit!* Illus. Tom Lichtenheld. San Francisco, CA: Chronicle Books. [Fiction.]

> *Is it a duck or a rabbit? That is the storyline behind this book. With simple, yet mesmerizing illustrations, this book goes back and forth between two narrators who see an outlined object in different ways. (Also pair with Article 13: Freedom of expression and Article 31: Leisure, play, and culture.)*

Skarmeta, Antonio. (1998). *The composition*. Illus. Alfonso Ruano. Berkeley, CA: Groundwood Books/House of Anansi Press. [Historical fiction.]

> The Composition *tells the story of a family living in a country under dictatorship. After seeing firsthand accounts of the pain brought to families who oppose the government, the young narrator in this story begins to form his own ideas and beliefs about those in power. Through the innocence of a child's thoughts and serious political turmoil, the author provides the reader with a realistic vision of political and social awareness in children. (Also pair with Article 13: Freedom of expression; Article 15: Freedom of association; and Article 19: Protection for all forms of violence.)*

Hopkinson, Deborah. (2005). *Saving Strawberry Farm*. Illus. Rachel Isadora. New York: Greenwillow Books. [Historical fiction.]

> *Set in the 1930s, this book tells the story of a farm that is being sold at a penny auction during the Great Depression. The book explains what happens when a child finds it in his heart to try to save the farm and how a community rallies around their neighbors. (Also pair with Article 27: Adequate standard of living.)*

Wyeth, Sharon Dennis. (1998). *Something beautiful*. Illus. Chris Soentpiet. New York: Bantam Doubleday. [Realistic fiction.]

> *In a community riddled by vandalism, one child searches to find beauty in spite of the vandals. During her quest, she realizes that the people who live in her community define beauty as the thing that makes them happy. Yearning for beauty that belongs to her, the child begins to clean her neighborhood, stating that she feels "powerful" by doing so. This book not only examines the many meanings of beauty but it also takes a look at how one act can empower a person. (Also pair with Article 13: Freedom of expression and Article 14: Freedom of thought, conscience and religion.)*

Article 13: Freedom of expression

The child has the right to express his or her views, including the right to share information in any way they choose, including by talking, drawing, or writing.

Carmi, Giora. (2003). *A circle of friends*. Illus. Giora Carmi. New York: Star Bright Books Inc. [Wordless picture book.]

> *Through powerful illustrations, Carmi tells the story of how a simple act of kindness can have a ripple effect across a people and communities. Starting with a young boy sharing a snack with a homeless man, the power of the gesture comes back to brighten the boy's life in a surprising way. (Also pair with Article 14: Freedom of thought, conscience and religion and Article 27: Adequate standard of living.)*

Giovanni, Nikki (2005). *Rosa*. Illus. Bryan Collier. New York: Henry Holt and Company. [Biography.]

> *This book takes a look at Rosa Parks and her famous stand against the injustice of the Montgomery bus system. This book does not pose Rosa as a victim, but as an activist in the movement for racial equality. (Also pair with Article 15: Freedom of association and Article 19: Protection from all forms of violence.)*

Rappaport, Doreen. (2002). *No more! Stories and songs of slave resistance*. Illus. Shane Evans. Cambridge, MA: Candlewick. [Nonfiction; lyrics.]

> *This book is a compilation of stories, songs, and poetry about slave resistance. Vignettes and traditional song lyrics are woven throughout the book, providing details about the lives of many African Americans. The text spans from the Middle Passage to the Underground Railroad to the Civil War. The book is an excellent resource to examine the resistance of slavery and the importance of rising up when power infringes on the rights of others. (Also pair with Article 15: Freedom of association and Article 19: Protection from all forms of violence.)*

Noble, Trinka. (2007). *The orange shoes*. Illus. Doris Ettlinger. Chelsea, MI: Sleeping Bear Press. [Realistic fiction.]

> *Delly Porter walks to her rural, one-room school without shoes only to be ridiculed by her classmates. However, she quickly learns that buying shoes doesn't change the perception her peers have of her. Frustrated, she decides to take action against the injustice in the one*

way she knows how: artistic expression. This is an excellent book to show that value can be found in things that do not cost money. (Also pair with Article 19: Protection from all forms of violence.)

Willems, Mo. (2009). *Naked mole rat gets dressed.* Illus. Mo Willems. New York: Hyperion. [Fiction.]

All mole rats are naked—all except one, that is. This humorous text tells the story of one mole rat that loves clothes and believes all mole rats should have the option to wear clothes. Firmly grounded in his belief, this mole rat stands up for himself and brings change to the community. (Also pair with Article 12: Respect for the views of the child; Article 14: Freedom of thought, consciousness, and religion; and Article 31: Leisure, play and culture.)

Article 14: Freedom of thought, conscience, and religion

Children have the right to think and believe what they want and to practice their religion, as long as they are not stopping other people from enjoying their rights.

Buller, Laura. (2005). *A faith like mine: A celebration of the world's religions—seen through the eyes of children.* New York: DK Publishers. [Nonfiction.]

This is an excellent reference material to explore several religions of the world. It details symbols and practices associated with the traditions surrounding each religion. In includes interviews with children describing what they like about their religion. (Also pair with Article 8: Preservation of identity and Article 15: Freedom of association.)

Diakite, Penda. (2006). *I lost my tooth in Africa.* Illus. Baba Wague Diakite. New York: Scholastic Press. [Personal narrative.]

Based on true events in the author's life, this book details an 8-year-old's journey to Africa to visit her family and the excitement surrounding her lost tooth. The book not only gives a glimpse at African culture but it also focuses on the culture built within a family. (Also pair with Article 5: Parental guidance; Article 30: Children of minorities/indigenous groups; and Article 31: Leisure, play, and culture.)

Article 15: Freedom of association

Children have the right to meet together and to join groups and organizations, as long as it does not stop other people from enjoying their rights.

Cohn, Diana. (2002). *Si, se puede! yes we can! janitor strikes in LA.* Illus. Francisco Delgado. El Paso, TX: Cinco Puntos Press. [Historical fiction.]

Told from the perspective of a janitor's son, this book was written in response to the April 2000 janitor strike in LA. The story, developed from primary source newspapers and interviews, recounts how a young son helps his mother by organizing his classmates to make signs for the strike. This book is an excellent way to encourage students to seek out and challenge social justice issues within their community. In addition, this book provides an excellent example of power structures and how people stand up against power that is distributed unequally. (Also pair with Article 13: Freedom of expression; Article 30: Children of minorities/indigenous groups; and Article 42: Knowledge of rights.)

DiSalvo, DyAnne. (2001). *A castle on Viola Street.* New York: Harper Children's. [Fiction.]

A young boy named Andy and his family find the house of their dreams through serving others and the help of Habitat for Humanity. As they work to transform old houses in need of repair into homes for other families, they, too, benefit as neighbors and the larger community come together. This is a great text to use to introduce service learning opportunities. (Also pair with Article 27: Adequate standard of living.)

Johnson, Angela. (2005). *A sweet smell of roses.* Illus. Eric Velasquez. New York: Simon and Schuster Books. [Historical fiction.]

This book is set during the civil rights movement of the 1960s and follows a young girl and her sister as they become engaged in a civil rights march in their hometown. The girls sneak past their mom in order to be a part of a march led by Martin Luther King Jr. Empowered by the speech and the chants for freedom, the girls return to tell their mother about the day's events. This story gives a simple example of how children were eager participants in the movement for equality during the 1960s and is an excellent introduction to social action at a young age. The text also challenges the distribution of power and racial divide. (Also pair with Article 13: Freedom of expression; Article 15: Freedom of association; and Article 42: Knowledge of rights.)

Article 16: Protection of privacy

The law should protect children from attacks against their way of life, their good name, their families, and their homes.

Williams, Vera B. (2004). *Amber was brave, Essie was smart.* Illus. Vera B. Williams. New York: HarperCollins. [Fiction in verse.]

Although neither Amber nor Essie might be described as typical heroines, through their stories told in verse the reader discovers that courage and triumph come through all kinds of experiences. Their ingenuity as they deal with the challenges of a father in jail and a mother who works long hours helps them rely on one another to make it through hard times. They experience the joys that come from true sisterhood as together they celebrate their own happy moments. (Also pair with Article 2: Non-discrimination and Article 8: Preservation of identity.)

Article 17: Access to information

Children have the right to get information that is important to their health and well-being. Mass media should particularly be encouraged to supply information in languages that minority and indigenous children can understand. Children should also have access to children's books.

Haskins, Jim (2005). *Delivering justice: W. W. Law and the fight for civil rights.* Illus. Benny Andrews. Cambridge, MA: Candlewick Press. [Biography.]

> *This book chronicles the life of Westley Law and his role in the civil rights movement. Angered by the discriminatory treatment of his family, Law becomes an activist for African American equality. He began by tutoring people in order to help them pass the voter's registration test and he led others in nonviolent protest. As a mailman, Law also tried to bridge the racial divide between White and Black residents in his community. (Also pair with Article 13: Freedom of expression; Article 14: Freedom of thought, conscience and religion; Article 28: Right to education; and Article 30: Children of minorities/indigenous groups.)*

Winter, Jeanette. (2005). *The librarian of Basra: A true story from Iraq.* San Diego, CA: Harcourt Children's Books. [Nonfiction.]

> *Based on true events, this book tells the story of librarian Aria Muhammad Baker and how she saved the books in the library from being destroyed by the ravages of war. Determined with her belief that books were of utmost importance, she moved the books to a new location only 9 days before the library was burned to the ground. (Also pair with Article 14: Freedom of thought, conscience, and religion and Article 28: Right to education.)*

Article 19: Protection from all forms of violence

Children have the right to be protected from being hurt and mistreated, physically or mentally.

Mochizuki, Ken. (1995). *Heroes.* Illus. Dom Lee. New York: Lee & Low Books Inc. [Historical fiction.]

> *It's the middle of the Vietnam War, and for Donnie, an Asian American kid, school can be tough. As the kids play war on the playground, he becomes the enemy, despite his American heritage and his highly decorated father and uncle, both veterans of World War II. Although they tell Donnie that "real heroes don't brag," they are faced with the choice of whether or not to come to Donnie's aid as the bullying continues.*

Article 23: Children with disabilities

Children who have any kind of disability have the right to special care and support, as well as all the rights in the Convention.

Elliott, R. (2011). *Just because.* UK: Lion. [Realistic fiction.]

> *This book is told from the perspective of a young brother who enjoys playing with his sister even though she can't move the way others do and is in a wheelchair. This is a beautiful story about siblings and the love they have for each other. (Also pair with Article 2: Non-discrimination; Article 8: Preservation of identity; Article 12: Respect for the views of a child; and Article 13: Freedom of expression.)*

Peete, H. R. (2010). *My brother Charlie*. New York: Scholastic Press. [Realistic fiction.]
   This book approaches autism through the eyes of a child as a sister, Callie, narrates the story of her relationship with her twin brother, Charlie, and how they are alike and different. (Also pair with Article 2: Non-discrimination; Article 8: Preservation of identity; Article 12: Respect for the views of a child; and Article 13: Freedom of expression.)

Article 24: Health and health services

Children have the right to good quality health care . . . to safe drinking water, nutritious food, a clean and safe environment, and information to help them stay healthy.

DiSalvo-Ryan, DyAnne. (1991). *Uncle Willie and the soup kitchen*. New York: Mulberry Books. [Realistic fiction.]
   A young boy experiences the daily comings and goings of adult and child patrons and workers at an urban soup kitchen. Through the stories and observations he shares, readers learn about homelessness and the people who experience it. Based on real-life experiences of the author, this text serves as an excellent catalyst for service learning possibilities, participation in community activities, as well as for discussions about human needs such as food, water, and shelter. (Also pair with Article 27: Adequate standard of living.)

Article 27: Adequate standard of living

Children have the right to a standard of living that is good enough to meet their physical and mental needs.

Bunting, Eve. (1993). *Fly away home*. Illus. Ronald Himler. San Anselmo, CA: Sandpiper. [Realistic fiction.]
   A family makes an airport terminal their temporary home. Told from the point of view of the child, this book explores what it means to be homeless, the inequalities of economic hardship, and the definition of what a home truly is. This book can be used to examine the distribution of power that creates homelessness as well as homeless culture. In addition, this story lends itself to the exploration of displacement that occurred to those that sought shelter in airports following the events of 9/11. (Also pair with Article 16: Right to privacy.)
Gunning, Monica. (2004). *A shelter in our car*. Illus. Elaine Pedlar. San Francisco, CA: Children's Book Press. [Realistic fiction.]
   Leaving their life in Jamaica, Zettie and her mom face an uncertain future. As Zettie's mom works to finish her degree at the community college, the two experience the realities of homelessness and unemployment in the United States. But the love and hope the Zettie and her mother share are as real as the struggles of their current situation. (Also pair with Article 5: Parental guidance and Article 16: Right of privacy.)
Locker, Thomas. (1988). *Family farm*. New York: Penguin Group. [Realistic fiction.]
   Owning a farm is not only hard work, but it can also be difficult to earn a living wage. This book details the struggles of one family to keep a farm going during economic hardship.

Napoli, Donna Jo. (2010). *Mama Miti.* Illus. Kadir Nelson. New York: Simon & Schuster Books for Young Readers. [Biography.]

> *Through the use of stunning fabric collage and painted illustrations, this biography expertly weaves the story of Wangari Maathai, also known as Mama Miti, with the lives of women across Kenya who were hungry for sustainable ways to care for their families. "Plant a tree," Mama Miti says to every woman who comes to ask for advice, and a countryside that was once desolate becomes bright with green leaves, each tree serving a purpose for the family that gave it life in Kenya's soil.*

Williams, Vera B. (1982). *A chair for my mother.* New York: Greenwillow Books. [Realistic fiction.]

> *A poignant story about a mother, grandmother, and young girl who have suffered through a house fire, this book speaks to one family's thankfulness for generous neighbors, who come to their aid in a time of need. Yet, they also long for the self-chosen comforts of their own home, and rejoice on the day they are finally able to purchase a plush chair for their living room.*

Article 28: Right to education

Young people should be encouraged to reach the highest level of education of which they are capable.

McBrier, Page. (2001). *Beatrice's goat.* Illus. Lori Lohstoeter. New York: Atheneum. [Biography.]

> *As a young girl in Uganda, Beatrice's family has never been able to send her to school, although she longs to go as she watches other children pass her by daily, clutching their textbooks. Self-sustainability is key to her family's ability to provide for themselves, and when goats are given to 12 families within her village, Beatrice realizes that this goat, and all that it provides for her family, has drastically changed her world. (Also pair with Article 5: Parental guidance and Article 29: Goals of education.)*

Perez, L. King. (2002). *First day in grapes/Primer dia en las uvas.* Illus. Robert Castilla. New York: Lee & Low Books. [Fiction.]

> *Working with his family as a migrant farmer has taken Chico all over California, but the constancy of the seasons always takes him back to the vineyards at the beginning of the school year. As he starts 3rd grade, he is pleasantly surprised with not only an understanding teacher, but also opportunities to flourish in his academic abilities, despite the taunts of some of his fellow students. (Also pair with Article 2: Non-discrimination; Article 5: Parental guidance; and Article 29: Goals of education.)*

Sis, Peter. (2007). *The wall: Growing up behind the iron curtain.* New York: Frances Foster Books. [Nonfiction.]

> *A graphic novel memoir, this book explains what it was like for Sis to grow up in a communist country and the problems he encountered once he began to actively seek out forbidden knowledge and eventually internally question the communist reign. The story outlines the power held by the Communist Party and how it dictated the lives of all living under its rule. The book also examines the power of a person's desire to learn as well as the power of artist talent. (Also pair with Article 13: Freedom of expression.)*

Article 29: Goals of education

Children's education should develop each child's personality, talents, and abilities to the fullest. It should encourage children to respect others' human rights and their own and other cultures. Education should aim to develop respect for the values and culture of their parents.

Blue, Rose, & Nadine, Corinne. (2009). *Ron's big mission.* Illus. Don Tate. New York: Dutton Children's Books. [Nonfiction.]

> *Based on the true, 1959 story of astronaut Ron McNair, this book illustrates the challenges a young African American boy faced one summer when trying to check out books about airplanes from his public library. Determined not to be denied literacy or his passion for flying, Ron takes action against the injustice. He stands up for his civil rights, resulting in his being allowed to own a library card and check out literature. (Also pair with Article 28: Right to education.)*

Sis, Peter. (1996). *Starry messenger.* New York: Farrar Straus Giroux. [Biography.]

> *Sis uses extraordinary illustrations to depict the life of Galileo Galilei in this book. The story details the insights Galileo had about the world and his pursuit to share his scientific discoveries with the world at large, despite condemnation and persecution. (Also pair with Article 13: Freedom of expression.)*

Article 30: Children of minorities/indigenous groups

Minority or indigenous children have the right to learn about and practice their own culture, language, and religion.

Cohn, Diana. (2009). *Namaste!* Illus. Amy Cordova. Great Barrington, MA: Steiner Books. [Fiction.]

> *This beautifully illustrated book joins a Sherpa's child, Nima, on her journey throughout town while her father is away, guiding visitors up the mountains of Nepal. The book includes a dictionary of culturally specific terms and an afterword about the mountains and mountain cultures within the region of Nepal. (Also pair with Article 8: Preservation of identity.)*

Martinson, David. (1975). *Real wild rice.* Illus. Vince Cody. Duluth, MN: Duluth Indian Education Advisory Committee. [Historical fiction.]

> *A poetic tribute to the Ojibway rice gatherers located around the Great Lakes, the text is simple and authentic. This book may be out of print. (Also pair with Article 8: Preservation of identity.)*

Santiago, Chiori. (2002). *Home to medicine mountain.* Illus. Judith Lowry. San Francisco, CA: Children's Book Press. [Nonfiction.]

> *Based on a true family story, this book details what it was like for two brothers of the Maidu and Pit-River Tribes of California during the 1930s. Forced to leave their home, the boys were sent to a boarding school that intended to "Americanize" the Indians by*

making them unlearn their tribal ways. Discouraged and homesick, the brothers decide to defy the rules set by the residential school and make the long journey home one summer on their own. This book takes a hard look at the power European Americans exerted over the Native American people. (Also pair with Article 8: Preservation of identity.)

Article 31: Leisure, play, and culture

Children have the right to relax and play, and to join in a wide range of cultural, artistic, and other recreational activities.

Bates, Artie Ann. (1995). *Ragsale.* Illus. Jeff Chapman-Crane. Boston: Houghton Mifflin Company. [Realistic fiction.]

> *This story narrates an Appalachian family and their exciting day looking for secondhand treasures at community rag sales. Told from the child's point of view, the story examines the simple pleasure of being a part of a family and the cultural significance of rituals within the family unit. (Also pair with Article 8: Preservation of identity.)*

Cooper, Melrose. (1998). *Gettin' through Thursday.* Illus. Nneka Bennett. New York: Lee & Low Books. [Realistic fiction.]

> *Thursdays are typically hard at André's home. Although there is a lot of love in the family, money is tight and mom doesn't get paid until Friday. So when he finds out he has earned a spot on the honor roll, André is sure that he is going to miss out on the grand celebration that his mom promised anyone who attained that lofty feat. However, he learns to never underestimate a resourceful family as together they show that creativity and caring can make all the difference. (Also pair with Article 27: Adequate standard of living.)*

Gilmore, Dorina K. Lazo. (2009) *Cora cooks pancit.* Illus. Kristi Vailant. Walnut Creek, CA: Shen's Books. [Realistic fiction]

> *Cora loves to cook with her family. Her favorite dish is pancit. But since she is the youngest, she is not able to do all of the steps alone. One day, all of her siblings go out and Cora is left alone with her mother and is allowed to do the jobs of the older family members. This story shows the beauty of family while highlighting a traditional Filipino dish. The recipe for pancit is even included in the back of the book. (Also pair with Article 8: Preservation of identity and Article 30: Children of minorities and indigenous groups.)*

Hazen, Barbara Shook. (1983). *Tight times.* Illus. Trina Hyman. London: Puffin Books. [Realistic fiction.]

> *This book tells the story of a family in which the father has recently lost his job. The young boy desperately wants a dog but his family is unable to give him one because of financial obligations. But when the boy finds a stray cat, his family is faced with the intersection of emotion and monetary constraint. (Also pair with Article 27: Adequate standard of living.)*

McKissack, Patricia. (2008). *Stitchin' and pullin': A gee's bend quilt.* Illus. Cozbi Cabrera. New York: Random House. [Historical fiction.]

> *Narrated by a young girl, this story details the making of a family quilt. The young quilter recites the important directions taught by generations before her and describes the*

importance of each cloth she stitches into her quilt. Based on the Gee's Bend Quilting Community, this book illuminates the importance of the quilting culture.

Mollel, Tololwa. (1999). *My rows and piles of coins.* Illus. E. B. Lewis. New York: Clarion. [Realistic fiction.]

A Tanzanian boy saves his coins to buy a bicycle so that he can help his parents carry goods to market. However, the boy learns that he still hasn't saved enough money when he goes to purchase the bike.

Sis, Peter. (2000). *Madlenka.* New York: Farrar Straus Giroux. [Realistic fiction.]

Eager to share the discovery of her new loose tooth, Madlenka travels the neighborhood to announce her exciting news. All of her neighbors represent different cultures within her community. Based on the author's daughter, this book explores how important diverse cultures are to building a community.

Article 35: Abduction, sale, and trafficking

The government should take all measures possible to make sure that children are not abducted, sold, or trafficked.

Levine, Ellen. (2007). *Henry's freedom box.* Illus. Kadir Nelson. New York: Scholastic Press. Biography. [Historical fiction.]

Based on the true story of Henry "Box" Brown, this book details the events following Henry's life as a slave and his extraordinary success of mailing himself to freedom. During his time as a slave, Henry is faced with a multitude of injustices. As a slave, he is required to work long hours of hard physical labor. In addition, his wife and children are sold to another plantation owner in the downtown square. Realizing that he would have to flee in order to find the freedom he deserved, Henry mails himself to the North. Henry reaches freedom after surviving the long, uncomfortable journey via the postal service. This text is a wonderful springboard for the discussion of how power held by some destroys lives. (Also pair with Article 8: Preservation of identity; Article 19: Protection from all forms of violence; and Article 30: Children of minorities and indigenous groups.)

Article 38: War and armed conflict

Governments must do everything they can to protect and care for children affected by war.

Bunting, Eve. (1998). *So far from the sea.* Illus. Chris Soentpiet. New York: Clarion Books. [Historical fiction.]

This book examines a family and the pain associated with the Japanese internment camps in the United States. Told from a 9-year-old's point of view, the story centers around a visit to the Manzanar War Relocation Camp in eastern California. The significance of the trip is compounded by the fact that the child is visiting her grandfather's gravesite at the memorial for the last time, as the family is moving to Boston. This story can open discussion to the maltreatment of Asian Americans during World War II and can be compared to the current treatment of Middle Eastern Americans. The story can also be used to examine what it means to be an American and how those of power can choose whom they consider an American. (Also pair with Article 8: Preservation of identity and Article 30: Children of minorities/indigenous groups.)

Yolen, Jane. (1992). *Encounter.* Illus. David Shannon. New York: Harcourt Brace. [Historical fiction.]

This book is told from the perspective of the Taino people. Seeing Columbus and his men as invaders, a young boy tries desperately to open the eyes of his tribe to the dangers of the newly arrived people. Yolen provides perspective on what it must have been like for the Taino to experience the encounter with the Spanish explorers and the shift of power that occurred as a result. However, the authenticity of the book has been challenged (see Jean Mendoza's essay about Encounter *in* A Broken Flute: The Native Experience in Books for Children, *Seale and Slapin, 2005), which would make for an excellent critical inquiry on both Columbus and the Taino people and on cultural authenticity. (Also pair with Article 8: Preservation of identity and Article 30: Children of minorities/ indigenous groups.)*

Winter, Jeanette. (2008). *Wangari's trees of peace: A true story from Africa.* San Diego, CA: Harcourt Children's Books. [Nonfiction.]

This book details the true story of environmental activist Wangari Maathai and her determination to replant the trees in her country that had been removed via deforestation. Wangari founded the Green Belt Movement in Kenya and significantly improved her country's economy by putting her environmental beliefs into action. (Also pair with Article 13: Freedom of expression and Article 15: Freedom of association.)

Article 42: Knowledge of rights

Governments should make the Convention known to adults and children. Adults should help children learn about their rights.

Amnesty International UK. (2008). *We are all born free: The Universal Declaration of Human Rights in Pictures.* London: Frances Lincoln Children's Books. [Nonfiction.]

This is a lovely translation of the UN Declaration of Human Rights into children's language with illustrations by 30 internationally renowned artists. One example of the wording: "If we are frightened of being badly treated in our own country, we all have the right to run away to another country to be safe."

Multiple authors. (1999). *Tikvah: Children's book creators reflect on human rights.* New York: SeaStar Books. [Nonfiction.]

Some of the most distinguished children's book authors and illustrators reflect on human rights, including child labor, religious freedom, freedom of expression, and hope. As Elie Wiesel writes in the Introduction, "Tikvah means hope and hope is represented by children."

ADDITIONAL RESOURCES

Reese, D. American Indians in Children's Literature blog. http://americanindiansinchild-rensliterature.blogspot.com/

Jain, M. (2009). Kahani: A South Asian literary magazine for children. Retrieved from http://kahani.com/

Learning to give: Curriculum division of the LEAGUE. Retrieved from www.learningtogive.org

Literacyhead. http://literacyhead.com/ Literacyhead uses picture books and visual art to teach reading and writing; many of the books touch on Rights of the Child themes.

Rethinking schools online. Retrieved from http://www.rethinkingschools.org/

Teaching tolerance: A project of the southern poverty law center. See book reviews in each issue. Retrieved from http://www.tolerance.org/

References

Abrams, J. (2009, February 25). Boxer seeks to ratify treaty to erode parental rights. Retrieved from http://www.foxnews.com/politics/2009/02/25/boxer-seeks-ratify-treaty-erode-rights/

Ada, A. F., & Campoy, F. I. (2004). *Authors in the classroom: A transformative education process*. Boston: Pearson Education.

Allen, J. (2000). Yellow brick roads: Shared and guided paths to independent reading. Portland, ME: Stenhouse.

Apple, M. (2009). Patriotism, pedagogy, and freedom: On the educational meaning of September 11. In A. Darder, M. Baltodano, & R. Torres (Eds.), *The critical pedagogy reader* (2nd ed., pp. 491–500). New York: Routledge.

Au, W., Bigelow, B., & Karp, S. (Eds.). (2007). *Rethinking our classrooms: Teaching for equity and justice*, Vol. 1, 2nd ed. Milwaukee, WI: Rethinking Schools.

Bakhtin, M. M. (1981). *The dialogic imagination*. Austin, TX: The University of Texas Press.

Bakhtin, M. M. (1993). *Toward a philosophy of the act*. Austin, TX: The University of Texas Press.

Barracca, D., & Barracca, S. (1990). *The adventures of taxi dog*. New York: Dial.

Berliner, D. C. (2006). Our impoverished view of educational reform. *Teachers College Record, 108*(6), 949–995.

Bethel, E. (2008). *Michael Recycle*. San Diego, CA: Worthwhile Books.

Billig, S. H. (2011). Making the most of your time: Implementing the K–12 service-learning standards for quality practice. *Prevention Researcher, 18*(1), 8–13.

Bomer, R., & Bomer, K. (2001). *For a better world: Reading and writing for social action*. Portsmouth, NH: Heinemann.

Brown, J. (1964). *Flat Stanley*. New York: HarperCollins Publishers.

Bruchac, J. (2011). Point of departure. Reading indigeneity: The ethics of interpretation and representation. In S. A. Wolf, K. Coats, P. Enciso, & C. Jenkins, C. (Eds.), *The handbook of research on children's and young adult literature* (pp. 342–344). New York: Routledge.

Bunting, E. (2004). *Fly away home*. Boston: Houghton Mifflin.

Carlson, N. (1989). *The family under the bridge*. New York; Harper Collins.

Castle, C. (2001). *For every child: The Rights of the Child in words and pictures*. New York: UNICEF.

Christensen, L. (2000). *Reading, writing, and rising up: Teaching about social justice and the power of the written word*. Milwaukee: Rethinking Schools.

Cipolle, S. (2004). Service-learning as a counter-hegemonic practice: Evidence pro and con. *Multicultural Education, 11*(3), 12–23.

Cole, A., & Knowles, J. (Eds.). (2001). *Lives in context: The art of life history research.* Walnut Creek, CA: AltaMira Press.

Coles, R. (2004). *The story of Ruby Bridges.* New York: Scholastic.

Compton-Lilly, C. (2004). *Confronting racism, poverty, and power: Classroom strategies to change the world.* Portsmouth, NH: Heinemann.

Compton-Lilly, C. (2009). What can new literacy studies offer to the teaching of struggling readers? *The Reading Teacher, 63*(1), 88–90.

Cowhey, M. (2006). *Black ants and Buddhists: Thinking critically and teaching differently in the primary grades.* Portland, ME: Stenhouse.

Cronin, D. (2000). *Click, clack, moo: Cows that type.* New York: Simon & Schuster.

Dalai Lama. (2009, August 10). *Human rights and culture.* Retrieved from http://newsletters.ahrchk.net/hrc/mainfile.php/hrcvol2/2510/

Delpit, L. D. (1993). The politics of teaching literate discourse. In T. Perry & J. W. Fraser (Eds.), *Freedom's plow* (pp. 285–295). New York: Routledge.

Ehrenreich, B. (2002). *Nickel and dimed: On (not) getting by in America.* New York: Owl Books.

Freire, P. (1994). *Pedagogy of hope.* New York: Continuum.

Freire, P. (1998). *Teachers as cultural workers: Letters to those who dare teach.* Boulder, CO: Westview Press.

Freire, P. (2000). *Pedagogy of the oppressed.* New York: Continuum. (Original Work published 1970)

Freire, P., & Macedo, D. (1987). *Literacy: Reading the word and the world.* New York: Routledge.

Gifford, D. (2004). *PeaceJam: How young people can make peace in their schools and communities.* San Francisco: Jossey-Bass.

Giroux, H. A. (2009). Critical theory and educational practice. In A. Darder, M. Baltodano, & R. Torres (Eds.), *The critical pedagogy reader* (2nd ed., pp. 27–51). New York: Routledge.

Gonzáles, N., Moll, L., & Amanti, C. (Eds.). (2005). *Funds of knowledge: Theorizing practices in households, communities, and classrooms.* Mahwah, NJ: Lawrence Erlbaum Associates.

Gorski, P. (2007). Savage unrealities: Classism and racism abound in Ruby Payne's framework. *Rethinking Schools, 21*(2), 16–19.

Gurian, M., & Stevens, K. (2007). *The minds of boys: Saving our sons from falling behind in school and life.* San Francisco: Jossey Bass.

Harris, V. (1993). African-American children's literature: The first one hundred years. In T. Perry & J. W. Fraser (Eds.), *Freedom's plow: Teaching in the multicultural classroom* (pp. 167–181). New York: Routledge.

Hart, S. (2006). Breaking literacy boundaries through critical service-learning: Education for the silenced and marginalized. *Mentoring & Tutoring: Partnership in Learning, 14*(1), 17–32.

Heath, S. (1983). *Ways with words: Language, life, and work in communities and classrooms.* Cambridge, MA: Cambridge University Press.

Hoffman, M. (1991). *Amazing grace.* New York: Dial Press.

hooks, b. (1994). *Teaching to transgress: Education as the practice of freedom.* London: Routledge.

hooks, b. (2000). *Where we stand: Class matters.* London: Routledge.

Iyengar, M. (2009). *Tan to Tamarind: Poems about the color brown.* San Francisco: Children's Book Press.

Jones, S. (2006). *Girls, social class, and literacy: What teachers can do to make a difference.* Portsmouth, NH: Heinemann.

Jones, S. (2008). Grass houses: Representations and reinventions of social class through children's literature. *Journal of Language and Literacy Education* [Online], 4(2), 40–58. Retrieved from http://www.coe.uga.edu/jolle/2008_2/representations.pdf

Jordan, J. (1980). Poem for South African women. In J. Jordan, *Passion: New Poems, 1977–1980.* Boston: Beacon Press.

Kearney, R. (2002). *On stories.* New York: Routledge.

Kotlowitz, A. (1992). *There are no children here: The story of two boys growing up in the other America.* Norwell, MA: Anchor.

Kozol, J. (1992). *Savage inequalities: Children in America's schools.* New York: Harper.

Kozol, J. (1996). *Amazing grace: The lives of children and the conscience of a nation.* New York: Harper.

Kozol, J. (2006). *The shame of the nation: The restoration of apartheid schooling in America.* New York: Three Rivers Press.

Lareau, A. (2000). *Home advantage: Social class and parental intervention in elementary education.* Lanham, MD: Rowman and Littlefield.

Lareau, A. (2003). *Unequal childhoods: Class, race, and family life.* Berkeley, CA: University of California Press.

Loewen, J. (1995). *Lies my teacher told me.* New York: Touchstone.

Longman, J. (2009, February 8). Punching back against despair on the high plains. *New York Times.* Retrieved from http://www.nytimes.com/2009/02/09/sports/othersports/09boxers.html

McLaren, P. (2009). *Critical pedagogy: A look at the major concepts.* In A. Darder, M. Baltodano, & R. D. Torres (Eds.), *The critical pedagogy reader* (pp. 61–83). New York: Routledge.

McLaughlin, L., & DeVoogd, G. (2004). *Critical literacy: enhancing students' comprehension of text.* New York: Scholastic.

MacNair, R. (2007, June 30). Forum: Anti-poverty plan needs "living wage." *Athens Banner Herald Newspaper.* Retrieved from http://onlineathens.com/stories/070107/opinion_20070701036.shtml

McBrier, P. (2001). *Beatrice's goat.* Riverside, NJ: Atheneum Books for Young Readers.

McPhail, D. (2002). *The teddy bear.* New York: Macmillan.

Mendoza, J., & Reese, D. (2001). Examining multicultural picture books for the early childhood classroom: Possibilities and pitfalls. *Early Childhood Research and Practice,* 3(2). Retrieved from http://ecrp.uiuc.edu/v3n2/mendoza.html

Morrell, E. (2004). *Becoming critical researchers: Literacy and empowerment for urban youth.* New York: Peter Lang.

Morrison, T., & S. Morrison. (1999). *The big box.* New York: Hyperion.

Mortenson, G., & Roth, S. (2009). *Listen to the wind: The story of Dr. Greg and three cups of tea.* New York: Dial.

National Writing Project. (2006). *Writing for a change: Boosting literacy and learning through social action.* San Francisco: Jossey-Bass.

Ng, J., & Rury, J. (2006). Poverty and education: A critical analysis of the Ruby Payne phenomenon. *Teachers College Record.* Retrieved from http://www.tcrecord.org/content.asp?contentid=12596

Nieto, S. (1999). *The light in their eyes: Creating multicultural learning communities.* New York: Teachers College Press.

Nieto, S. (2002). *Language, culture, and teaching: Critical perspectives for a new century.* Mahwah, NJ: Lawrence Erlbaum Associates.

Orenstein, P. (1995). *Schoolgirls: Young women, self esteem, and the confidence gap.* Norwell, MA: Anchor.

Payne, L. M. (1997). *We can get along: A child's book of choices.* Minneapolis, MN: Free Spirit Publishing.

Payne, R. K. (1998). *A framework for understanding poverty.* Highlands, TX: RFT Publishing.

Perez, A. (2002). *My diary from here to there/Mi diario de aqui hasta alla.* San Francisco: Children's Book Press.

Peterson, B. (2007). Teaching for social justice. In W. Au, B. Bigelow, & S. Karp (Eds.), *Rethinking our classrooms: Teaching for equity and justice,* Vol. 1, 2nd ed. (pp. 28–34). Milwaukee, WI: Rethinking Schools.

Pew Hispanic Center. (2009). *Between two worlds: How young Latinos come of age in America.* Washington, DC: Pew Hispanic Center.

Rappaport, D. (2002). *Martin's big words: The life of Dr. Martin Luther King Jr.* Norwalk, CT: Weston Woods.

Ray, K. (1999). *Wondrous words.* Urbana, IL: National Council of Teachers of English.

Ringgold, F. (2005). *If this bus could talk.* New York: Scholastic.

Rocha, R., & Roth, O. (2000). *Universal declaration of human rights: An adaptation for children.* Blue Ridge Summit, PA: United Nations Publications.

Rodriguez, L. (1998). *America is her name.* Willimantic, CT: Curbstone.

Seale, D., & Slapin, B. (2005). *A broken flute: The Native experience in books for children.* New York: Altamira Press.

Shamblin, A., & Seskin, S. (1999). *Don't laugh at me* [Recorded by M. Wills]. On *Wish you were here* [CD]. Nashville: Mercury.

Shipler, D. (2005). *The working poor: Invisible in America.* Norwell, MA: Vintage.

Shor, I. (2009). What is critical literacy? In A. Darder, M. Baltodano, & R. Torres (Eds.), *The critical pedagogy reader* (2nd ed., pp. 282–304). New York: Routledge.

Smith, M. (2009, January). UN treaty might weaken families. Retrieved from http://www.washingtontimes.com/news/2009/jan/11/un-treaty-might-weaken-families/

Street, B. (2003). What's "new" in new literacy studies? Critical approaches to literacy in theory and practice. *Current Issues in Comparative Education* 5(2), 77–91.

Sweeney, M. (1999). Critical literacy in a fourth-grade classroom. In C. Edelsky (Ed.), *Making justice our project: Teachers working toward critical whole language practice* (pp. 96–114). Urbana, IL: National Council of Teachers of English.

Tafolla, C. (2009). *¿Qué puedes hacer con una paleta? (What can you do with a paleta?)*. New York: Tricycle Press.

Thurmond, M. (2001). *A story untold: Black men and women in Athens history*. Athens, GA: McNaughton & Gunn. UNICEF. (2001). *For every child: The Rights of the Child in words and pictures*. New York: Phyllis Fogelman Books/Penguin Putnam.

UNICEF. (2007, November 29). UNICEF: Protecting children's rights in Somalia. Retrieved from http://sclipo.com/videos/view/unicef-protecting-children-s-rights-in-somalia

UNICEF. *Rights of the child*. Retrieved from http://www.unicef.org/photoessays/30048.html

UNICEF (n.d.). Voices of youth. Retrieved from http://www.unicef.org/voy/explore/rights/explore_rights.php

UNICEF. (n.d.). Voices of youth: Disabilities and children. Retrieved from http://www.unicef.org/explore_3888.html

UNICEF. (n.d.). Voices of youth: Photo journal. Retrieved from http://www.unicef.org/explore_3890.html

UNICEF Fact Sheet. A summary of the rights under the Convention on the Rights of the Child,   Retrieved from http://www.unicef.org/crc/files/Rights_overview.pdf July 22, 2012

United Nations Convention on the Rights of the Child. (2009). Parental Rights. Retrieved from http://www.parentalrights.org/index.asp?Type=B_BASIC&SEC=%7B53D4DCA7-5899-4242-B244-54A253AFC137%7D

U.S. Census Bureau (2010). Retrieved from http://www.census.gov/hhes/www/poverty/

Van Sluys, K. (2005). *What if and why? Literacy invitations for multilingual classrooms*. Portsmouth, NH: Heinemann.

Vasquez, V. M. (2008). *Negotiating critical literacies with young children*. New York: Routledge, Taylor, & Francis.

Vygotsky, L. (1986). *Thought and language*. Cambridge, MA: The MIT Press.

Wade, R. (2007). *Social studies for social justice; teaching strategies for the elementary classroom*. New York: Teachers College Press.

White, C. L. (2001). Examining poverty and literacy in our schools: Janice's story. In S. Boran & B. Comber (Eds.), *Critiquing whole language and classroom inquiry* (pp. 169–199). Urbana, IL: National Council of Teachers of English.

Wilson, A. (1986). *Fences*. New York: Penguins Books.

Wiggins, G., & McTighe, J. (1998). *Understanding by design*. New York: Prentice Hall.

Wyeth, S. (1998). *Something beautiful*. New York: Doubleday Books for Young Readers.

Zou, Y., & Trueba, E. (Eds.). (2002). *Ethnography and schools: Qualitative approaches to the study of education*. Lanham, MD:: Rowman and Littlefield.

About the Editors and Contributors

Lois Alexander is a high school English teacher and a former co-director of the Red Clay Writing Project at the University of Georgia. Her graduate research includes literacy in poverty-stricken neighborhoods and culturally relevant teaching. She is a playwright, who has written ten plays.

JoBeth Allen is co-director of the Red Clay Writing Project, where she works with incredibly creative and dedicated teachers, including the authors of this volume. She teaches writing, critical pedagogy, poetry, and family-school partnerships in the Language and Literacy Education Department at the University of Georgia. Her previous books include *Class Actions* (1999), *Creating Welcoming Schools* (2007), and *Literacy in the Welcoming Classroom* (2010).

Kelli Bivins has proudly served families of Athens, Georgia, as a middle-school ESOL teacher and friend for 12 years. Bivins family consists of five generations, four of who work or have worked in poultry plants. This personal knowledge of poultry work helps her form deeper relationships with the families she serves, most poultry laborers. Bivins enjoys laughing and living with her husband and two sons, lizard, three turtles, chicken, two pigeons, one dog, and three-legged toad.

Paige Cole is a high school social studies teacher working on a Ph.D. in language and literacy at the University of Georgia. Her research interests include religious discourses in public schools and in the lives of adolescents. Paige has presented at conferences for the National Writing Project, the National Council of Teachers of English, and the College Board. She is grateful to be a teacher consultant for the Red Clay Writing Project.

Dawan Coombs, a former high school teacher and current teacher educator, completed her Ph.D. in language and literacy education at the University of Georgia. She is an assistant professor at Brigham Young University, where she teaches in the English education program. Her research interests include struggling reader identity issues, adolescent literacy, and teacher education. Dawan also serves on the committee for the International Reading Association Children's and Young Adults' Book Awards.

Lindy Crace is a high school English teacher in Greenville, South Carolina. She continues to learn more about language, literacy, and critical pedagogy through raising her two children. She completed an education specialist degree in learning, design, and technology at the University of Georgia and is putting that knowledge to work through online teaching. Lindy also teaches conflict management skills at the Georgia Conflict Center to help each of us find peace in all areas of our lives.

Lindsey Lush is teaching a multi-age class of 2nd and 3rd graders. She earned her master's degree in language and literacy education at the University of Georgia. In her eighth year of teaching, Lindsey can most often be found sitting on her classroom floor with a student and a book. She serves the students and families of her school with LIFE meetings, Fit Girls, and the Farm to School initiative with Stephen Lush.

Stephen Lush has been a special education teacher and is now in his 5th year as a 4th-grade teacher. He received his master's degree in early childhood education from the University of Georgia. In addition to creating and facilitating the LIFE group, Stephen initiated the Social Justice League for upper elementary students and is involved in the Farm to School initiative, which encourages schools, students, and families to grow, eat, and learn about where their food comes from. Stephen also likes to build, advocate for, and ride on mountain bike trails.

Jen McCreight, a former kindergarten and 1st-grade teacher, is an assistant professor in early childhood education at Hiram College in Hiram, Ohio. As a doctoral candidate in language and literacy education at the University of Georgia, her research interests include building family-school partnerships in diverse school contexts and engaging with students and families around the way we use words in our world.

Andrea Neher is a former primary grades teacher, who is now serving two elementary schools as an instructional coach. As a doctoral candidate in the department of language and literacy education at the University of Georgia, her research interests include critical perspectives on education policy implementation, educational equity, and literacy teaching and learning.

Tonia Paramore is an elementary instructional coach in Barrow County, Georgia. She has a master's and a specialist degree in children's literature and language arts from the University of Georgia and has had the opportunity to present for the National Writing Project and the National Council of Teachers of Education. She finds joy in reading and writing, especially with her family.

Stephanie Smith is an elementary school teacher working in collaborative inclusion classrooms. She recently completed her master's degree in language and literacy education from the University of Georgia. Stephanie has presented on critical literacy in primary grades at the Georgia Children's Literature Conference and at the International Reading Association Conference.

Jaye Thiel is a former elementary school teacher, who is pursuing her doctorate in language and literacy education at the University of Georgia, where she is the Red Clay Scholar. Her research interests are grounded in a strong commitment to educational equity and include exploring how social class, gender, race, and locale intersect in language and literacies, particularly the literacies of children.

Index

Abduction, sale, and trafficking.
   See Article 35
Abrams, Joseph, 14
Access to information. *See* Article 17
Accountability of educators, 6
Ada, Alma Flor, 20, 25, 64
Adulthood: PeaceJam as fostering, 147,
   148
Allen, Janet, 122
Alvarez, Mary, 74, 78, 79, 80
Amanti, C., 10
Anchor chart, 154–55
Apple, M., 4
Article 1 (equal rights for everyone),
   12, 157
Article 2 (non-discrimination), 1, 78
   annotated bibliography about,
      157–58
   PeaceJam and, 19, 127–49
Article 5 (parental guidance), 158–59
Article 8 (identity rights)
   annotated bibliography about,
      159–60
   culture, identity, freedom of thought
      inquiry about, 18, 109–26
   teachers as protected by, 126
Article 10 (family reunification)
   annotated bibliography about, 160
   immigrants/minorities protections
      inquiry and, 18, 72–89
Article 12 (respect for views of
   children)
   annotated bibliography about,
      161–62

culture, identity, freedom of thought
   inquiry and, 110, 111, 126
health and well-being inquiry and,
   17, 21, 31, 34
immigrants/minorities protections
   inquiry and, 78
teachers as protected by, 126
Article 13 (freedom of expression)
   annotated bibliography about,
      162–63
   critical content framework and, 4
   culture, identity, freedom of thought
      inquiry about, 18, 109–26
   health and well-being inquiry and, 34
   invitation about right to, 109–10
   study group inquiry about, 13
   teachers as protected by, 126
   tenth-grade history students inquiry
      about, 18, 109–26
   texts, tools, and resources about,
      110, 119–23
   thrice-born concept and, 18, 109–26
Article 14 (freedom of thought,
   conscience, and religion)
   annotated bibliography about, 163
   culture, identity, freedom of thought
      inquiry about, 18, 109–26
   invitation about, 109–10
   teachers as protected by, 126
   tenth-grade history students inquiry
      about, 18, 109–26
   texts, tools, and resources about,
      110, 119–23
   thrice-born concept and, 18, 109–26

Article 15 (freedom of association), 78,
    163–64
Article 16 (privacy rights), 78, 164
Article 17 (access to information)
    annotated bibliography about,
        164–65
    health and well-being inquiry and,
        17, 20, 21, 22, 27, 33
    LIFE and, 18, 54–71
    literature for teaching the rights of
        children and, 151
Article 19 (violence protection)
    annotated bibliography about, 165
    children with disabilities inquiry
        and, 36
    immigrants/minorities protections
        inquiry and, 78
    PeaceJam and, 19, 127–49
Article 23 (children with disabilities
        inquiry)
    annotated bibliography about,
        165–66
    study group inquiry about, 13
    third-grade students inquiry about,
        17, 35–53
Article 24 (health and well-being)
    annotated bibliography about, 166
    children with disabilities inquiry
        and, 36
    1st and 2nd graders inquiry about,
        17, 20–34
    immigrants/minorities protections
        inquiry and, 76
    LIFE and, 61
    PeaceJam and, 19, 127–49
Article 26 (funding for families in
        need), 43
Article 27 (standard of living)
    annotated bibliography about,
        166–67
    children with disabilities inquiry
        and, 43

health and well-being inquiry and,
    17, 21, 27, 34
poverty inquiry concerning, 18, 91,
    93, 97–98
Article 28 (right to education)
    annotated bibliography about,
        167
    children with disabilities inquiry
        and, 36, 43
    PeaceJam and, 19, 127–49
    poverty inquiry concerning, 18, 91,
        93, 95–96, 107
    study groups inquiry about, 13
    suggested questions about, 91
    texts, tools, and resources about, 91
Article 29 (aims/goals of education
        and respect for values and culture
        of parents)
    annotated bibliography about, 168
    immigrants/minorities protections
        inquiry and, 81
    LIFE and, 18, 54–71
    study group's inquiry about, 13
Article 30 (minorities/indigenous
        groups)
    annotated bibliography about,
        168–69
    immigrants/minorities protections
        inquiry and, 18, 72–89
    PeaceJam and, 19, 127–49
Article 31 (leisure, play, and culture),
    78, 169–70
Article 33 (protection from harmful
        drugs and drug trade), 78
Article 34 (sexual abuse protections),
    78
Article 35 (abduction, sale, and
        trafficking), 78, 80, 170
Article 38 (war and armed conflict),
    13, 78, 80, 170–71
Article 42 (knowledge of rights), 149,
    171

Association, freedom of (Article 15),
    78, 163–64
Au, W., 11

Bakhtin, M. M., 115, 117
Banking concept, 75, 152
Barracca, D., 24
Barracca, S., 24
Beegle, Donna M., 94
Being a Good Friend (invitation), 35,
    46, 47, 52
Bethel, E., 24
Bigelow, Bill, 11
Billig, S. H., 129
Bivins, Kelli, Freire's influence on,
    74–75
Black on Black crime issue, 105, 107
Black history celebration, 107–8
Bomer, Katherine, 7
Bomer, Randy, 7
Brown, Dee, 119
Brown, J., 1, 43
Brown–Rihanna case, Chris, 137
Bruchac, Joseph, 153
Bunting, E., 24, 43

Campoy, F. I., 25
Caputo, Philip, 122, 124–25
Carlson, N., 24
Carver, George Washington, 31
Castle, C., 13
Change agents. See Social action/
    change
Charts
    anchor, 154–55
    noticing, 154, 155
Chavez, Cesar, 27
Children with disabilities inquiry
    (Article 23)
    annotated bibliography about,
        165–66
    Article 19 and, 36

Article 24 and, 36
Article 26 and, 43
Article 27 and, 43
Article 28 and, 36, 43
classroom culture and, 38–39
critical literacy and, 35–37, 40, 44, 45
Flat Stanley and, 1–2, 35, 43–45,
    46–51, 53
history and, 53
human rights study and, 38–42
immigrants/minorities protections
    inquiry and, 79
initiating experience for, 35
invitations about, 35–36, 46–51, 52
and lack of information/awareness
    about rights, 38–40
reflections about, 51
Rights of the Child and, 35, 36, 37,
    40–42, 44–45, 50, 53
sharing work about, 52–53
standardized curriculum and, 36, 37
suggested questions about, 35–36
texts, tools, and resources for, 36, 46,
    47, 48, 49, 50
third-grade students inquiry about,
    17, 35–53
Children's literature
    children with disabilities inquiry
        and, 36, 42–43
    health and well-being inquiry and,
        21, 24
    rights of the child in, 42–43
    as springboard for teaching about
        the rights of children, 153–54
    study of literacy and social class and,
        10–11
    See also specific book or author
Christensen, L., 3, 11
Cipolle, S., 135, 141
Citizenship, 2, 14, 89, 94
Classroom: culture/environment of, 7,
    38–39

Cole, A., 81
Cole, Paige, interview of mother of,
    120
Coles, R., 26
Columbus, Christopher: discussion
    about, 36–37, 53
Comics, 119, 120–21, 122
Community
    critical literacy and, 7
    health and well-being inquiry and,
        21, 31–33
    PeaceJam and, 132–33, 142, 144
    poverty inquiry and, 90, 93–95,
        96–97, 98
    school relations with, 31–33
    standard of living rights inquiry
        and, 90, 93–95, 96–97, 98
    violence in, 132–33
Community reflection forums, 123–25
Community service: service learning
    distinguished from, 129
Compton-Lilly, Cathy, 10, 153
Consumer identity: Lori's project
    about, 116–17
Conversations
    critical literacy and, 7
    interviews and, 120
Cowhey, M., 3, 11, 20, 21, 29, 30, 45
Criterion Referenced Competency Test
    (CRCT), 59, 60
Critical action research, 75
Critical educators: characteristics of, 5
Critical inquiry
    benefits of, 75
    challenge of, 16
    change agents and, 75
    characteristics of, 4–5
    commitment of educators and, 2
    critical thinking connection to, 91
    health and well-being inquiry and,
        27
    invitation format and, 16

invitations for, 15–16
meaning of, 4–5
Rights of the Child as framework
    for, 1–19
teachers as creating options
    concerning, 91
as way of life, 108
See also Critical literacy; Critical
    questions; Critical stance;
    specific inquiry
Critical literacy
    as central to critical pedagogy, 7
    children with disabilities inquiry
        and, 35–37, 40, 44, 45
    critical content framework and, 7, 9
    critical inquiry and, 4, 9–11
    definition of, 7, 37
    health and well-being inquiry and,
        21, 23–27, 30–31
    invitations for, 2, 15
    literature for teaching the rights of
        children and, 152–56
    meaning of, 4, 40
    Peace, Power, and Action and, 21,
        23–27, 30–31
    social action and, 30–31
    study group's inquiry about, 10
    teacher's role in, 7, 26
Critical pedagogy
    benefits of, 75
    critical content framework and, 2–4
    critical literacy as central to, 7
    Cultural Notebooks and, 80–88
    as humanizing teaching philosophy,
        75
    literature for teaching the rights of
        children and, 153
    motivations of educators and, 2–3
    PeaceJam and, 135
    publications about, 2, 9
    study group's concerns about, 2
    See also specific topic

Critical questions, 4, 8–9, 11, 16,
    155–56
Critical social theory, 10
Critical stance, 4, 5–6, 8–9
Critical teaching: definition of, 45
Critical thinking, 76, 77, 91, 93–95,
    107
Cronin, D., 24
Cultural Notebooks: immigrants/
    minorities protections, inquiry
    and, 72, 80–88
Culturally conscious learning: about
    poverty, 95–99, 100–101, 107
Culture Pie, 109, 114
Culture Projects: culture, identity,
    freedom of thought inquiry and,
    18, 109–26
Culture(s)
    classroom, 7, 38–39
    critical content framework and, 3
    definition of, 113
    exploring other (second birth),
        118–23
    first birth (own culture) and, 112–18
    immigrants/minorities protections
        inquiry and, 76
    invitation about right to, 109–10
    Nazi, 109, 119–22
    outdated/backward practices of, 123
    parenting and, 102
    poverty and, 90, 93–95, 96
    right to, 18, 109–26
    second birth (connecting) and,
        123–25
    standard of living rights inquiry
        and, 90, 93, 96
    suggested questions about, 109–10
    teachers as protected by rights to,
        126
    texts, tools, and resources about,
        110, 119–23
    thrice-born concept and, 18, 109–26

    See also Article 29; Cultural
        Notebooks; Culturally
        conscious learning
Curriculum
    critical content framework and, 3, 4
    critical literacy and, 7
    See also Standardized requirements/
        tests

Dalia Lama, 38
Deficit myth, 10
Delpit, L., 153
Democracy, 8, 14, 136
DeVoogd, Glenn L., 7, 37
Disabilities, children with. See
    Children with disabilities inquiry
    (Article 23)
Discovering Types of Disabilities
    (invitation), 35, 46, 49, 52
Douglass, Frederick, 38
Drinking water, right to (Article 24),
    76
Dropouts
    Latin@ students as, 73
    PeaceJam project about, 142–45, 148

E-portfolios, 104–5, 107
Ebadi, Shirin, 130, 145
Economic Justice Coalition, 128
Education, goals of. See Article 29
Education, right to. See Article 28
Educators: accountability of, 6
Ehrenreich, Barbara, 9
Elections: students interest in, 29
Evaluation
    definition of, 105
    form for, 106
    poverty inquiry and, 104–7
    of Tic-Tac-Toe projects, 104–7

Fall Festival: LIFE and, 55, 64–65, 71
Fences (Wilson play), 91, 101–4, 105

First birth (own culture): thrice-born
  concept and, 112–18
First and second graders: health and
  well-being inquiry of, 17, 20–34
Flat Stanley: children with disabilities
  inquiry and, 1–2, 35, 43–45,
  46–51, 53
Flat Stanley (Brown), 43, 44, 45, 46
Fleishman, Paul, 83
Fleming, Virginia, 47
Food drive, 11
Forest Hills Elementary School (FHES)
  (Georgia) *See* Health and well-
  being
Freedom of association (Article 15),
  78, 163–64
Freedom of expression. *See* Article 13
Freedom of thought. *See* Article 14
Freire, Paulo
  banking concept of, 75, 152
  critical inquiry and, 2, 16, 75
  critical literacy and, 7, 37
  Cultural Notebook process of, 72, 81
  on goals of teachers, 92
  historical awareness comment of, 126
  on identity, 119
  influence on study group members
    of, 10, 74–75, 112
  questioning/problem-posing
    approach of, 5, 141
  on respect for others, 112
  social action and, 30
  student stories and, 74, 89
  on tasks of dialogical teachers, 117
  on teacher-student relations, 5–6,
    74–75
  teachers as co-learners and, 21
  on teachers as role models, 8
Funds of knowledge, 10

Gandhi, Mahatma, 38
Garden (Plants for Peace): school-
  community relations and, 31–33

Garza, Carmen Lomas, 64
Gay rights: PeaceJam and, 130, 136
Georgia Performance Standards. *See*
  Standardized requirements/tests
Gifford, D., 129
Giroux, H. A., 75
Global Call to Action (PeaceJam), 130,
  140
Gonzales, N., 10
Goodrich, Ashley, 129, 130–31, 141,
  142, 144, 145
Gorski, P., 10, 94, 107
Graduation Pledge (PeaceJam), 142–45
Graphic novel format, 119, 121
Groves, Steven, 14
Gurian, Michael, 94

Haiti, 108
Harman, Ruth, 74, 79
Harris, V., 22, 97
Hart, S., 28, 33, 133, 135–40
Head Start program, 120
Health and well-being (Article 24)
  annotated bibliography about, 166
  Article 12 and, 17, 21, 31, 34
  Article 13 and, 34
  Article 17 and, 17, 20, 21, 22, 27, 33
  Article 27 and, 17, 21, 27, 34
  critical inquiry and, 27
  critical literacy and, 21, 23–27,
    30–31
  first and second graders' inquiry
    about, 17, 20–34
  first steps of inquiry about, 22–23
  history and, 28–29
  initiating experience for, 20
  invitation about, 20–21, 33–34
  LIFE and, 61
  life experiences and, 25, 26–27, 28
  mapping the course for, 27–30
  PeaceJam and, 19, 127–49
  Plants for Peace garden and, 31–33
  poverty and, 17, 20–34

power and, 17, 20–34
reflections about, 33–34
Rights of the Child and, 34
social justice, 28–29, 31
social studies and, 27–30
suggested questions for, 21
texts, tools, and resources about,
    21
Heath, S., 9
Heritage Foundation, 14
High school: critical pedagogy in, 11
High school English students (10th
    grade): standard of living/poverty
    inquiry of, 18, 90–108
High school students: as social
    activists, 19, 127–49
History
    children with disabilities inquiry
        and, 53
    health and well-being inquiry and,
        28–29
History students, 10th grade: culture,
    identity, freedom of thought
    inquiry by, 18, 109–26
Hoffman, M., 28
Home-schooling, 14–15
hooks, bell, 5, 9, 25, 75
Human rights
    children with disabilities inquiry
        and, 38–42
    difficulty of teaching about, 76
    invitation about working for, 127–28
    PeaceJam and, 19, 127–49
    responsibility and, 41–42
    U.S. debate about, 89
    See also Universal Declaration of
        Human Rights
Human Rights Festival: PeaceJam and,
    144–45
Human Rights Resource Center,
    Minnesota, 12

"I Am" poems, 91–92

Identity (Article 8)
    Alex's project about religious,
        115–16
    annotated bibliography about, 159–60
    Freire comment about, 119
    of Haiti, 108
    invitation about right to, 109–10
    literature for teaching the rights of
        children and, 152–56
    Lori's project about consumer,
        116–17
    poverty inquiry and, 90, 93–95
    standard of living inquiry and, 90,
        93–95
    teachers as protected by, 126
    tenth-grade history students inquiry
        about, 18, 109–26
    texts, tools, and resources about,
        110, 119–23
    thrice-born concept and, 18, 109–26
    Tyrell's project about racial, 117–18
Immigrants/minorities inquiry
    (Article 30)
    annotated bibliography about,
        168–69
    Cultural Notebooks and, 72, 80–88
    deportation and family separation
        protections (Article 10) and, 18,
        72–89
    initiating experience about, 72
    invitation for, 72–73
    of middle school students, 18, 72–89
    PeaceJam and, 19, 127–49
    Rights of the Child as framework
        for, 72, 74, 75, 76, 77–80, 88–89
    standardized requirements/tests
        (Georgia) and, 72, 75–76, 77,
        79–80, 82–88
    suggested questions for, 73
    texts, tools, and resources for, 73
    writing stories for, 74, 80–88
Independent Literacy Exploration
    (ILE), 122–23

India
  Masada Project in, 137–39, 147
  poverty in, 30–31
  social action and, 30–31
Information, access to. *See* Article 17
Initiating experience, 16. *See also*
  specific inquiry
Institutional Review Board, 74
Instructional strategies, 153–54
International Covenant on Economic,
  Social, and Cultural Rights, 3–4
Invitation(s)
  for children with disabilities inquiry,
    35–36, 46–51, 52
  for critical inquiry, 15–16
  for critical literacy, 2, 15
  definition of, 15
  format for, 15–16
  and inquiries as addictive, 101
  literature about, 155
  properties of, 15
  purpose of, 26, 46
  See also specific inquiry
Isadora, Rachel, 13
Iyengar, Malathi Michelle, 64

Jefferson Road Elementary School
  (Georgia). *See* LIFE
Johnson, Lyndon B., 38
Jones, Stephanie, 10, 150, 152, 154
Jordan, June, 16
Journaling, 7
Jubilee Partners, 128

Karp, S., 11
Kearney, R., 152
King, Coretta Scott, 21, 29
King, Martin Luther Jr., 28–29, 38, 95,
  107, 108, 120
King, Rodney, 121
Kingsolver, Barbara, 110
Knowledge of rights (Article 42),
  149, 171

Knowles, J., 81
Kotlowitz, Alex, 9, 94
Kozol, Jonathan, 9, 94, 95, 99, 108

Language
  critical content framework and, 4
  critical stance and, 6
  immigrants/minorities protections
    inquiry and, 81
  power and, 66–70
  study group inquiry about, 9
Lareau, A., 9
Latin@, 6, 73. *See also* LIFE
Leadership: PeaceJam as fostering, 147
Learning walls, 156
Leisure, play, and culture (Article 31),
  78, 169–70
Life experiences
  health and well-being inquiry and,
    25, 26–27, 28
  immigrants/minorities protections
    inquiry and, 73, 78
  PeaceJam and, 145
  poverty inquiry and, 97–101, 103–4,
    105, 107
  teacher-student relations and, 73
LIFE (Latinos for Involvement in
    Family Education)
  access to information (Article 17)
    and, 18, 54–71
  benefits of, 61
  creation of, 4, 54, 55–56, 57
  early activities of, 57–60
  fairs/festivals and, 55, 64–66, 71
  as family within school, 61
  first meeting of, 59–60
  function of, 55–56
  funding/fundraising for, 58, 64–66,
    71
  future of, 70–71
  goals of education (Article 29) and,
    18, 54–71
  Latin@ term and, 6

library for, 61–64, 71
Lush (Stephen and Lindsey),
    descriptions of experiences
    with, 66–70
need for, 55–57
PTO photo with members of, 70–71
as service learning project, 57, 59
state requirements/tests and, 59, 60,
    67
students and families role in,
    60–61, 62, 63–64, 66
suggested questions about, 55
support for, 66
texts, tools, and resources concerned
    with, 55
Literacy
    immigrants/minorities protections
        inquiry and, 82
    study group concerns about, 2, 9–11
    See also Critical literacy
Literature students, high school:
    standard of living inquiry of, 18,
    90–109
Literature for teaching the rights of
    children
    annotated bibliography of, 156–72
    critical literacy and, 152–56
    identity and, 152–56
    initiating experience for, 150
    invitation for, 150–51
    selection of, 151–56
    suggested questions about, 150–51
    texts, tools, and resources about,
        151–56
Loewen, James, 8
Longman, J., 119

Macedo, D., 21, 75, 81
MacNair, Ray, 94
Maus Project, 109, 119–22, 123,
    124, 126
Maus (Spiegelman), 110, 119
Mayer, John, 145

McBrier, P., 24
McLaren, P., 28, 33, 75
McLaughlin, Maureen,
    7, 37
McPhail, D., 24
McTighe, J., 3, 76
Meadow Brook High School
    (Georgia). See High School
    English students: standard of
    living/poverty inquiries by
Memoirs: reading historical, 122–23,
    126
Mendoza, J., 156
Mentors, 7
Mini-lessons: immigrants/minorities
    protections inquiry and, 72, 77,
    78, 79, 84
Minorities/indigenous groups. See
    Article 30
Moll, L., 10
Moody, Anne, 122
Morales, Yuyi, 64
Morrell, E., 3, 11
Morrison, S., 24
Morrison, T., 24
Mortenson, G., 30–31, 43
Multicultural Fair: LIFE and,
    65–66
Muñoz, Claudio, 13

Natal culture. See First birth
National Honor Society (NHS), 128
National Writing Project (NWP),
    9, 10
Nazi culture, 109, 119–22
Neher, Andrea
    goals of, 24
Ng, J., 10
Nieto, Sonia, 80–81, 96
No Child Left Behind Act, 37, 79
Nobel peace laureates: PeaceJam and,
    127, 128, 129, 130, 131, 138,
    139, 145

Non-discrimination (Article 2), 1, 78
  annotated bibliography about,
    157–58
  PeaceJam and, 19, 127–49
Noticing chart, 154, 155

Obama, Barack, 29
O'Brien, Tim, 122
Oral history research, 81–88
Orenstein, Peggy, 94
Overcoming Obstacles (invitation), 35,
    46, 48

Paramore, Tonia, 1–2
Parental Rights group, 14
Parents/families
  annotated bibliography about,
    158–59, 160
  Article 5 (parental guidance) and,
    158–59
  Article 10 (family reunification) and,
    18, 72–89, 160
  Article 26 (funding for families in
    need) and, 43
  Article 29 (respect for values and
    culture of parents) and, 18,
    54–71
  complexity of parenting and, 102–3
  controversy about U.N. Convention
    on the Rights of the Child and,
    14–15
  critical literacy and, 7
  culture, identity, freedom of thought
    inquiry and, 120
  Fences discussion and, 101–4
  health and well-being inquiry and,
    32
  immigrant/minority rights inquiry
    and, 18, 72–89
  interviews of, 83–88, 120
  PeaceJam and, 131, 133, 142, 143
  poverty and, 90, 101–4
  as resource, 110

  rights of, 14–15
  stories of, 80–88
  study group's literacy and social class
    inquiry and, 9, 11
  teachers' communications/
    interactions with, 56–71
  See also LIFE
Parker, Toni Trent, 94
Partnerships: invitations and, 25–26
Payne, Ruby, 9–10, 28
Peace, Power, and Action
  critical literacy and, 23–27, 30–31
  invitation about, 20–21, 23–24
  mapping the course and, 27–30
  reflections about, 33–34
  school-community relations and,
    31–33
  See also Health and well-being
    inquiry
PeaceJam
  curriculum for, 130
  dropping out/graduation pledge
    project of, 142–45, 148
  expanding projects of, 135–40
  "family groups" of, 139
  fear of failure and, 134
  formation of chapter of, 128–29
  fundraising by, 138–39, 145
  Global Call to Action and, 130, 140
  high school students working for
    human rights and, 19, 127–49
  impact on individual students of,
    145–46
  invitation to participate in, 127–28,
    131
  mission of, 129, 131, 132, 145
  Nobel peace laureates and, 127, 128,
    129, 130, 131, 138, 139, 145
  Peacemaker Recognition Program
    of, 131
  reflection and, 133, 134–35
  regional conference of, 139–40, 145
  resistance to, 134

Rights of the Child as framework
for, 128, 129–30, 135, 148
service learning and, 127, 129–30
and students' views of social action,
147–49
suggested questions about, 128
texts, tools, and resources about, 128
turning point for, 132–33
Tutoring Project of, 131–32, 134,
135, 136, 143
Universal Declaration of Human
Rights as focus of, 130, 136,
139, 148
Year 1 of, 130–35
Year 2 of, 135–40
Years 3 and 4 of, 140–45
Peacemaker Recognition Program
(PeaceJam), 131
People for a Prosperous Athens, 93
Perez, Amada Irma, 64
Perspective (3 P's), 150, 154–55
Peterson, Bob, 5, 11
Pew Hispanic Center, 73
Pinkney, Jerry, 13
Plants for Peace (health and well-being
inquiry project), 31–33
Poems: poverty inquiry and, 99–100,
105
Polacco, Patricia, 43
Positioning (3 P's), 150, 154–55
Poverty
Black on Black crime and, 105, 107
change agents and, 94, 107–8
children with disabilities inquiry
and, 39–40
community and, 90, 93–95,
96–97, 98
critical content framework and, 6
critical stance and, 6
critical thinking about, 93–95
culturally conscious learning about,
95–99, 100–101, 107
culture and, 90, 93–95, 96

definition/meaning of, 93, 97–98
dropouts and, 143–44
evaluation of inquiry about, 104–7
Fences decussion about, 101–4
framework for understanding, 10
generational, 99
as global issue, 99
health and well-being inquiry and,
17, 20–34
"I Am" poem about, 91–92
identity and, 90, 93–95
invitations about, 20–21, 23–24, 93,
94, 95
lack of information/awareness of,
39–40
life experiences of students and,
97–101, 103–4, 105, 107
as multifaceted, 96
parenting and, 101–4
PeaceJam discussions about, 131–32,
133, 141, 143, 144
questions about, 94, 99–101
right to education (Article 28)
inquiry and, 18, 91, 93, 95–96,
107
Rights of the Child framework and,
91, 93, 95, 96, 107
schools-within-schools and, 131–32
sharing during inquiry about, 100–
101, 105, 107
social action and, 30–31
standard of living inquiry (Article
27) and, 90–104
study groups's inquiry about, 9–11
text, tools, and resources concerning,
94, 95, 96–97, 100–101
Tic-Tac-Toe projects about,
104–7
Power
critical literacy and, 7
critical questions and, 8
culture, identity, freedom of thought
inquiries and, 111

Power *(continued)*
  health and well-being inquiry and,
    17, 20–34
  immigrants/minorities protections
    inquiry and, 76
  language and, 66–70
  Rights of the Child as framework for
    discussion of, 3
  study group's inquiry about, 10
  teacher-student relations and, 21,
    132
  teachers as co-learners and, 21
  3 P's and, 150, 154–55
Prior knowledge
  immigrants/minorities protections
    inquiry and, 76, 77
  See also Life experiences
Privacy rights (Article 16), 78, 164
Progressive education, 4, 5
Project Masada (PeaceJam), 137–39,
  147
Project Outreach, 9
Project Safe, 128

Questions. *See* Critical questions;
  specific inquiry

Race
  culture, identity, freedom of thought
    inquiry and, 122, 125
  hatred, 125
  as identity, 117–18
  immigrants/minorities inquiry and,
    74
  PeaceJam and, 131–32, 140–41,
    146
  schools-within-schools and, 131–32
  standard of living rights and, 90
  Tyrell's project about racial identity,
    117–18
Rappaport, D., 28
Ray, Katie Wood, 154

Reading
  buddy, 28
  clubs for, 7
  critical literacy and, 7
  culturally conscious learning and, 97
  health and well-being inquiry and,
    28
  of historical memoirs, 122–23, 126
  importance of student's connection
    to, 97
  independent, 7, 28
  strategies for, 122–23
Red Clay Project Outreach (study
  group), 93
Red Clay Right of the Child Project,
  111
Red Clay Writing Project, 4, 37
Reese, D., 156
Reflections
  Alexander's goal concerning, 92
  children with disabilities inquiry
    and, 51
  community forums for, 123–25
  culture, identity, freedom of thought
    inquiry and, 119–22, 123–25
  on LIFE meeting, 60
  PeaceJam and, 133, 134–35
  service learning and, 129
  sheets for recording, 25
Religion: Alex's project about, 115–16
Resilience of children: standard of
  living rights inquiry and, 92–93,
  95–104
Resources. *See* Texts, tools, and
  resources
Respect for children's views.
  See Article 12
Respect for parents/families values
  and culture. *See* Article 29
Responsibilities
  human rights and, 41–42
  of teachers, 28, 33

Rethinking Schools journal, 2, 5, 10, 11
Rights
    definition of, 11–12
    lack of information/awareness of,
        38–40
    PeaceJam debate about, 148
Rights of the Child (ROC), U.N.
        Convention on the
    children with disabilities inquiry
        and, 35, 36, 37, 40–42, 44–45,
        50, 53
    controversy about, 14–15
    core principles of, 14
    creation of, 3–4
    as critical content framework, 9
    critical content inquiries and, 3–4,
        13–14
    as critical inquiry framework, 1–19
    critical literacy and, 7
    critical questions and, 8
    culture, identity, freedom of thought
        inquiries and, 111, 112, 118, 126
    format for invitations and, 16
    in Haiti, 108
    health and well-being inquiry and,
        34
    immigrants/minorities protections
        inquiry and, 72, 74, 75, 76,
        77–80, 88–89
    importance of teaching about, 37
    LIFE and, 71
    party to celebrate, 79
    PeaceJam and, 128, 129–30, 135, 148
    photo essay about, 77, 96
    poverty inquiry and, 91, 93, 95,
        96, 107
    rights, definition of, and, 11–12
    Somalia and, 96
    standard of living inquiry and, 91,
        93, 95, 96, 107
    study group's inquiry about, 4, 43,
        135, 148
    teachers as protected by, 126
    thrice-born concept and, 109, 112,
        118, 126
    Wall's students' study of, 4, 11–14
    See also specific article
Rights for Everyone (invitation),
    35, 46, 50, 52
Ringgold, F., 24
Rocha, Ruth, 11–12
Rodriguez, L., 28
Roe v. Wade, 110
Roosevelt, Eleanor, 3, 38, 41
Roosevelt, Franklin D., 38
Roth, Otavio, 11–12
Roth, S., 30–31
A Rumor of War (Caputo), 122, 124–25
Rury, J., 10
Ryan, Pam Munoz, 64

Schooling practices: study of literacy
    and social class and, 10
Schools
    community relations with, 31–33
    parents/families relations with,
        56–71
    as schools-within-schools, 131–32
Second birth (exploring other
    cultures): thrice-born concept
    and, 118–23
Second grade
    health and well-being inquiry of, 17,
        20–34
    See also Wall, Rebeccah Williams
Service learning
    community service distinguished
        from, 129
    definition of, 129
    Freire's methodology and, 141
    LIFE as project for, 57, 59
    PeaceJam and, 127, 129–30, 141
    reflection and, 129
Seskin, S., 52

Seventh and eighth grade: immigrant/
    minority rights inquiry of, 18,
    72–89
Sharing
    about children with disabilities
        inquiry, 52–53
    of family stories, 83–88
    health and well-being inquiry and,
        29–30
    immigrants/minorities inquiry and,
        79
    poverty inquiry and, 100–101, 105,
        107
    of Tic-Tac-Toe projects, 105, 107
Shipler, David, 9, 95
Shor, I., 3, 16
Smith, Michael, 14–15
Social action/change
    critical content framework and, 2
    critical inquiry and, 75, 92
    critical literacy and, 7, 30–31
    critical theory and, 136
    failed attempts at, 21
    Gorsky comment about, 94
    health and well-being inquiry and,
        20, 21, 28–29, 30–31
    and high school students as activists,
        19, 127–49
    Kozol views about, 94
    PeaceJam and, 19, 127–49
    poverty and, 30–31, 94, 107–8
    Rights of the Child as framework
        for, 37
    from school projects to, 107–8
    study group's inquiry about, 10
Social criticism: critical content
    framework and, 2, 4
Social justice
    and causes of injustice, 135
    health and well-being inquiry and,
        21, 22, 28–29, 31
    literature for teaching the rights of
        children and, 152

PeaceJam and, 135, 141, 147–49
    Rights of the Child as framework for
        discussion of, 3
    study group's inquiry about, 11
Social studies
    critical content framework and, 4
    health and well-being inquiry and,
        27–30
    immigrants/minorities protections
        inquiry and, 72–89
Socioeconomic class, 2, 3, 6, 9–11, 25,
    131–32. *See also* Poverty
Somalia: Rights of the Child in, 96
Special education
    teacher-student relations and, 91
    See also Children with disabilities
        inquiry
Spiegelman, Art, 119
Srinivas, M. N., 109, 111, 112
Standard of living, right to adequate
    (Article 27)
    annotated bibliography about,
        166–67
    high school English students inquiry
        about, 18, 90–108
    identity and, 90, 93–95
    initiating experience about, 90
    invitation concerning, 90–91
    meaning of, 97–98
    poverty inquiry and, 92–93, 95–104
    resilience of children and, 92–93,
        95–104
    suggested questions about, 91
    texts, tools, and resources about, 91
    See also Article 27
Standardized requirements/tests
    (Georgia)
    children with disabilities inquiry
        and, 36, 37, 38, 41
    critical content framework and,
        3, 4, 9
    health and well-being inquiry and,
        23

immigrants/minorities protections
  inquiry and, 72, 75–76, 77,
  79–80, 82–88
LIFE and, 59, 60, 67
ROC as framework for critical
  content inquiries and, 14
Stevens, Kathy, 94
The Story of Ruby Bridges (Coles),
  26
Street, B., 153
Student voice: PeaceJam as fostering,
  147–48
Study group
  critical pedagogy concerns of, 2
  Freire influence on, 10
  Rights of the Child (ROC) concerns
    of, 4, 43, 135, 148
  study of literacy and social class by,
    9–11
  See also Red Clay Project Outreach
Suggested questions. *See* Critical
  questions; *specific inquiry*
Sustained Silent Reading (SSR),
  122–23
Sweeney, Maria, 7, 8

Tafolla, Carmen, 64
Taking Human Rights Temperature of
  Your Classroom (survey),
  12–13
Teacher education program, 2
Teacher-student relations, 5–6, 21, 73,
  74–75, 91, 132
Teachers
  as co-learners, 21
  critical inquiry role of, 4–5
  critical literacy role of, 7
  parents' communications/
    interactions with, 56–71
  protections for, 126
  responsibilities of, 2, 28, 33
  role in critical literacy of, 26
  as role models, 8

Teaching
  authoritarian model of, 126
  and difficulty of teaching about
    human rights, 76
Tenth-grade history students
  Cole's goal for, 110–11
  culture, identity, and freedom of
    thought inquiry and, 18,
    109–26
  history as controversial and, 110
  thrice-born concept of, 18, 109–26
Texts, tools, and resources
  format for invitations and, 16
  selection of, 151–56
  See also specific inquiry
Thematic Reader Response Forms,
  155
Third graders: children with
  disabilities inquiry of, 17, 35–53
3 P's (Perspective, Positioning, and
  Power), 150, 154–55
Thrice-born concept
  culture, identity, and freedom of
    thought inquiry and, 18, 109–26
  first birth (own culture), 112–18
  floating between births and, 126
  meaning of, 109
  overview about, 111–12
  second birth (exploring other
    cultures), 118–23
  tenth-grade history students inquiry
    and, 18, 109–26
  third birth (connecting cultures)
    and, 123–25
Thurmond, Michael, 94, 97
Tic-Tac-Toe projects, 104–7
Tolstoy, Leo, 112
Trueba, E., 75
Tubman, Harriet, 38, 108
Tum, Rigoberta Menchú, 130, 145
Tutoring Project (PeaceJam), 131–32,
  134, 135, 136, 143
Tutu, Desmond, 11, 13, 111–12

U.N. Convention on the Rights of the Child. *See* Rights of the Child (ROC), U.N. Convention on the
U.N. International Year of the Child (1979), 4
UNICEF, 11, 77, 89, 96
United Nations (U.N.), 3, 39, 41
Universal Declaration of Human Rights (UDHR), U.N., 3, 11–12, 128, 130, 136, 139, 148
Urban Food Collaborative, 21

Van Sluys, K., 2, 15, 21, 23, 26, 27, 46, 93
Vasquez, Vivian, 3, 10–11, 40, 156
Vietnam War: reflections about, 121–22, 124–25
Violence. *See* Article 19
Vygotsky, L., 112, 113

Wade, R., 3, 151
Wall, Rebeccah Williams, 4, 11–14

War and armed conflict (Article 38), 13, 78, 80, 170–71
Wetherington, Luciane, 66
White, C. L., 22, 26, 27
Wiggins, G., 3, 76
Williams, Betty, 130, 140
Wilson, August, 91, 101
Writings, student
    health and well-being inquiry and, 26–27
    immigrants/minorities protections inquiry and, 77, 78–79
    informational, 82, 83
    narrative, 26–27, 78, 82–88
    persuasive, 104, 105
    See also Cultural Notebooks
Wyeth, S., 24

Yolen, Jane, 36

Zou, Y., 75